D0801856

# POWER CYCLES

## ACKNOWLEDGEMENTS

Dedicated to: William and Frances Kirkland, whose constant attention and positive reinforcement has provided the emotional strength upon which our ability to operate successfully in the market rests.

Peggy and Karla Kirkland whose love and dedication has given us the peace of mind necessary to proceed unhindered with our research.

John Stephens, Paul Frederickson, Jesse Livermore, Hamilton Bolton, Joseph Granville, Gerald Appel, Charles Patel, Robert Prechter, Martin Schwartz, Richard Dennis, and all the other authors, market letter writers and traders who have provided pieces of information necessary for our trading program and market philosophy.

*WILLIAM and DOUGLAS KIRKLAND*

# POWER CYCLES
## A STRATEGY FOR BUSINESS AND INVESTMENT EXCELLENCE, IN THE EIGHTIES...AND BEYOND

*Published by PROFESSIONAL COMMUNICATIONS*

# POWER CYCLES

# Table Of Contents

# Preface

After having written this book, we found, in our last reading of it, that the goals we had set out to accomplish were achieved remarkably well.

Our main goal was to produce a book that dealt with the complex forces of the market in a way that was understandable by the layman.

We have tried, throughout the creation of this work, to communicate. This is especially important in light of the difficult period that we see lying ahead.

It must be understood also, that although the presented information has been carefully researched, there may be inadvertent errors. We would appreciate correspondence to this regard so that they can be corrected in later editions.

It must also be understood that the views expressed are personal ones, produced from years of research and reflection. They cover what we believe is a "most likely" scenario. However, it is not the only possible scenario for the future economy. In later publications we will cover, more fully, ways to recognize potential changes in the POWER CYCLE scenario.

The best use of POWER CYCLES is a long-term market philosophy, a way to produce the correct state of mind to act aggressively on a trading basis. Theories of actually making trading decisions are a complex subject unto themselves.

It is our strong hope that you will find the book useful. If so, we will have partially repaid the debt we owe to individuals who have freely given their advice throughout market history, and we will have added our small amount to the burgeoning store of market knowledge that is and will be so useful to ourselves and future generations.

*"Timing is strategy. There is timing in everything."*
—Miyamoto Mushashi
(Considered the greatest
swordsman in Japanese history.)

# Chapter I
# Cycles in the Affairs of Man

## EARLY DISCOVERY OF THE "WAVE" PRINCIPLE

From man's beginning, his survival and advancement have often depended upon an understanding of the nature and effects of such natural phenomena as the rising and setting of the sun and moon, the change in seasons, and the cycles of birth and death. In many of the earliest recorded civilizations, such as the Chinese, Greek, Egyptian, and Aztec, so much importance was placed on cyclical phenomena that entire cultures were built around them.

As the world's population increased, society assumed more complex economic structures. With this complexity came an even greater necessity to understand natural cycles. Eventually, research was begun by early scholars into the inter-relationships between business, commerce, and politics in an attempt to discover and better utilize these basic social and economic building blocks.

In ancient China, the concept of yin and yang was first introduced by theologians in an attempt to explain the ongoing cycles of birth, growth, decline, and rebirth of many natural phenomena. Its fundamental maxim is that life is a sequence of overextensions and underextensions from a common point of stability. *Whenever an aspect of life deviates from a position of stability, natural forces act to return it to equilibrium. The simple conceptualizations of this theory laid the philosophical groundwork for explaining the interaction of social and economic phenomena for thousands of years.*

Later scholars and theologians from Egypt and Persia refined astrology and mathematics to improve their understanding of the cycles of nature. In other parts of the Mideast, Hebrew scholars also acknowledged the power of cycles in expounding "the tides in the affairs of men" (*Ecclesiastes* 3:1-8), in which they recognized the significance of the rise and fall of various social and economic phenomena. For exactly the same reasons as the Chinese, these Middle Eastern civilizations recognized the advantages of being in harmony with their environment.

With the increasing complexity of world civilizations, as demonstrated by the progression from agrarian societies to cultures dominated by commerce and trade, the need became apparent for a better understanding of the basic nature of money and markets.

Beginning with the emergence from the Dark Ages and progressing through the Industrial Revolution, a wide variety of domestic and international markets began to shape the social and economic structures of society. Due to the fierce competition necessary to maximize the production of goods and minimize costs in each of these markets, a new breed of philosophers emerged. These individuals, the predecessors of today's economists, sought to understand the increasingly complex social and economic problems faced by the rapidly integrating world. After researching the history of prior periods of economic growth and decline, many of them came to the conclusion that markets tended to rise and fall around a natural level of equilibrium in a relatively precise and periodic manner. This reinforced the observations made by Chinese and Middle Eastern philosophers centuries earlier. These philosopher-economists had discovered the repetitive boom-and-bust phenomenon we now call the business cycle.

In the early 1900s, Joseph Schumpeter, one of the most famous of the early analysts of the business cycle, published the first of his many great works on the cyclical nature of European financial and commodity markets. He centered his early research on the price histories of commodities, such as wheat, cattle, copper, and real estate, dating back more than 500 years. From his research, he found that various commodities tended to have differing, yet precise, periods of rising and falling prices. For example, he noted that the price of commercial and agricultural real estate tended to fluctuate in a cycle approximately 18 years in length, while wheat moved in a seven-year cycle, and cattle around four.


## THE 50- TO 60-YEAR CYCLE

In later works, after carefully analyzing an even broader range of commodity price histories and business activity over longer time frames, *Schumpeter concluded that the prices of most commodities used in business and international trade, as well as interest rates, stock prices, and wages, seemed to move collectively in larger cycles of between 50 to 60 years.*

Other economists soon began to substantiate Schumpeter's long-term economic theories. In 1927, the famed English statistical economist Rogers, in his *History of Agricultural Prices in England*, quantified the periodicity of the price of wheat in England from 1269 through 1926 as having 13½ complete, long-term cycles averaging a little over 50 years in duration (Figure 1).

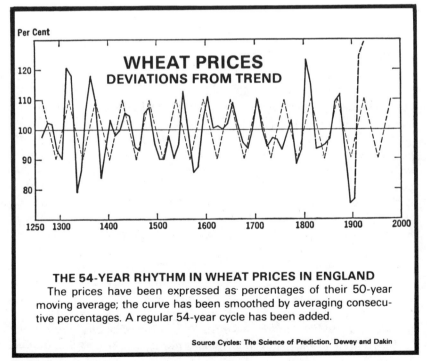

**THE 54-YEAR RHYTHM IN WHEAT PRICES IN ENGLAND**
The prices have been expressed as percentages of their 50-year moving average; the curve has been smoothed by averaging consecutive percentages. A regular 54-year cycle has been added.

Source Cycles: The Science of Prediction, Dewey and Dakin

Figure 1.

Other statisticians supplemented Schumpeter's business cycle theory
to include various social, political, and theological aspects of society
interacting within the framework of long-term business cycles. In one
study, conclusive evidence of a cycle of war and inflation approximately
50 years in length was found in both the Greek and the Roman civilizations from the Peloponnesian War period (circa 430 B.C.) through
the fall of the Roman Empire.

In a similar study encompassing the same approximate Greco-Roman
time frame, another 50-year cycle relating to poverty and depressions
was found halfway around the world in the isolated pre-Columbian
civilizations of Central and South America.

One of the best-documented attempts to recognize and control the
destructive nature of the depression phase of the 50-year cycle was
implemented by Jewish tribal leaders in the pre-Christian era. In the
Old Testament, the important festival of the Jubilee was celebrated
every 50 years to absolve debtors of their financial obligations by
reinstating the rights of all possessions and landholdings to their original
owners. The tribal leaders learned from experience the threshold level
of accumulated debt that a society can tolerate before significant civil
disruptions begin to occur.

## THE KONDRATIEFF WAVE

Near the beginning of the 20th century, an obscure Russian economist
named Nicholai Kondratieff became intrigued by the potential implications of this research. *Kondratieff set out to prove that capitalistic
economic systems tend to ebb and flow from prosperity to depression
in a predictable and periodic manner that cannot be effectively ma-
nipulated and controlled by governments and other powerful financial
institutions.* Up until the time Kondratieff was sent to Siberia by the
newly instituted Communist regime for allegedly anti-Soviet economic
thought, he directed his entire research effort toward understanding
the nature and future implications of the 50- to 60-year trend of social
and business activity.

In the mid 1920s, Kondratieff first published the results of his ex-
haustive research. He focused on the long-term trends of interest rates
and commodity prices in Germany, France, and England. In his publi-
cation, Kondratieff proved to his own satisfaction *the existence of a
definite and predictable long-term cycle of prosperity and depression
in the world's capitalist economic systems averaging 54 years in duration*
(Figure 2).

| PHENOMENA | | Period in Years |
|---|---|---|
| Shipbuilding, U.S.A. | From 1800 | 54 |
| Wheat Prices, Europe | From 1545 | 54 |
| International War Battles | From 1700 | 53.5 |
| Coal Consumption, France | From 1831 | 54 |
| Coal Production, England | From 1859 | 54 |
| Coal Production, Worldwide | From 1873 | 54 |
| Exports, France | From 1810 | 54 |
| Foreign Trade, England | From 1810 | 54 |
| Foreign Trade, Total, France | From 1831 | 54 |
| Imports, France | From 1848 | 54 |
| Lead Production, England | From 1859 | 54 |
| Pig Iron Production, England | From 1844 | 54 |
| Pig Iron Production, Worldwide | From 1873 | 54 |
| Portfolio of Bank of France | From 1810 | 54 |
| Rainfall, England | From 1727 | 52 |
| Thickness and Thinness of Arizona Tree Rings, | 1000 A.D. | 54 |
| Coal Production, Germany | From 1893 | 54 |
| Cotton Acreage, U.S.A. | From 1874 | 54 |
| Oat Acreage, France | From 1830 | 54 |
| Wheat Prices, England | From 1545 | 54 |
| Copper Prices, U.S.A. | From 1840 | 54 |
| Coal Production, U.S.A. | From 1893 | 54 |
| Pig Iron Production, U.S.A. | From 1875 | 54 |
| Prices, England | From 1700 | 54 |
| Prices, France | From 1858 | 54 |
| Prices, U.S.A. | From 1790 | 54 |
| Interest Rates, England | From 1830 | 54 |
| Interest Rates, France | From 1830 | 54 |
| Wages of Agricultural Workers, England | From 1790 | 54 |
| Bond Yields, Domestic, Corporate, All Grades | From 1820 | 54 |
| Wholesale Commodity Prices, U.S.A. | From 1761 | 54 |
| Deposits, Savings Bank, France | From 1800 | 54 |
| Sunspots, | From 1700 | 54.3 |

**THE 54 YEAR CYCLE**

Cycles from 52 to 56 years as variously indicated, the spans of time over which they were observed and the periods determined.

Figure 2.

From the results of his study, Kondratieff hypothesized that the now popularly termed 54-year Kondratieff Wave was primarily a function of the complicated interactions of social, military, political, and monetary events that melded into a logical and repetitive boom-and-bust economic cycle. He concluded that *the fundamental cause behind the periodicity of depression and prosperity relates to natural phenomena, and is therefore not affected by human action.* He hypothesized that these cycles are caused to a great extent by mass social interactions that overextend or underextend themselves in a way similar to many other natural phenomena.

From his studies, it can be rationalized that *if an individual equipped with an understanding of the general nature of the various long-term social and economic factors that interact to form the basis of the Kondratieff Wave could, at any given time, pinpoint with acceptable accuracy his current position in the cycle, he could then place investment capital in the area that demonstrated minimum risk and maximum profit potential.*

It is the purpose of this book to delineate the authors' interpretation of the basic concept of Kondratieff Wave Theory, to evaluate our economy's current position in the cycle, and to suggest a logical investment game plan that can be used to protect and even increase investment capital during this and future long-term cycles.

*"When business embarks on a rampage which does not help humanity to live and grow—when it pushes beyond this range of usefulness and overproduces human needs—or when it falls behind and outlives its usefulness—it runs into trouble of some kind. And when the business tree is crowded with these dead or dying branches, the tree as a whole begins to suffer. We run into a business depression or plunge into industrial war to shake the rotten branches down."*

—V.C. Kitchen

# Chapter II
# How the Boom-to-Bust Cycle Works

## THE KEY TO THE KONDRATIEFF WAVE

Almost from the very day Kondratieff presented his controversial theory, economic historians and statisticians have subjected it to rigorous scrutiny. Most detractors suggest his statistical analysis was not performed on a broad enough range of economic variables. Others suggest that Kondratieff did not delve deeply enough into history to satisfactorily prove that the 54-year wave theory is any more than a short-term statistical fluke. However, after extensive analysis of his statistics and careful consideration of his theories, many eminent economists and social scientists have concluded that Kondratieff's ideas have validity.

In a recent study published in the *Financial Analysis Journal*, Dr. Jay Forrester, Professor of Economics at the Massachusetts Institute of Technology, suggested that the underlying rationale for the boom-and-bust nature of the Kondratieff Wave can most adequately be accounted for by the rise and fall of capital investment. According to Forrester, during the expansion phase of the Kondratieff Cycle, an ever-increasing economic demand exists for the production of capital goods, such as plants and equipment, and durable goods, such as automobiles and television sets. Because of this demand, raw material and labor shortages occur. This sharply increases the rate of inflation to unreasonable levels, which eventually reduces demand for these goods. Widespread unemployment and bankruptcy eventually ensue followed by a long period of economic stagnation or depression. Other well-known economists, including Schumpeter, feel the growth phase of the Kondratieff Wave is primarily the result of the introduction of new and innovative production technologies, while the depression phase is caused by the obsolescence of such technologies. To illustrate, Schumpeter suggests the failure of the railroad industry to respond to competition from the auto industry contributed significantly to the debt crisis of the Great Depression in the 1930s. By analogy, one might surmise that debt defaults caused by the replacement of the present telephone and mail industries by telecommunications via satellite may contribute to the next depression.

In our opinion, these theories touch only the essence of what Kondratieff was attempting to explain. They leave unanswered many of the subtle economic interactions found in the authors' historical analysis of prior waves. *After careful analysis of all the primary economic variables constituting the Kondratieff Wave, we have concluded that its underlying cause evolves primarily from the manner in which human beings react to their ongoing economic situation on a worldwide basis.*

Using this concept as a basis for our research, we have constructed a hypothetical scenario of one complete Kondratieff Cycle from our analysis of past and present long-term Kondratieff Cycles in the United States. As shown in Figure 3, the complete idealized Kondratieff Cycle is divided into four separate and distinct phases. The first phase is called the growth phase and is characterized by a long period of economic growth and prosperity. It usually lasts 20 to 25 years. Phase two is called the first primary recession, or postwar recession, and is characterized by a very short, sharp recession that usually lasts one to two years and ends the growth phase. The third phase, or plateau phase, is usually characterized by increasingly stagnant and deteriorating worldwide economic conditions. It typically lasts about 10 years. The fourth phase was called the depression phase by Kondratieff and is characterized by high unemployment and bankruptcy lasting as long as two decades. *The depression phase eliminates all the financial and economic excesses accumulated during the growth and the plateau phases.*

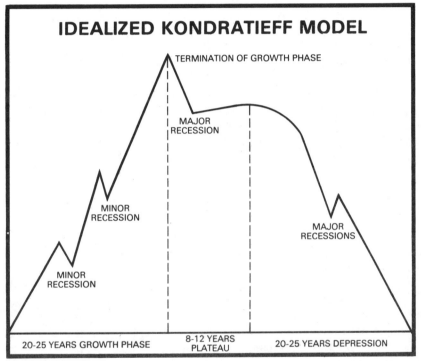

## IDEALIZED KONDRATIEFF MODEL

Figure 3.

## RIDING THE GROWTH PHASE

As the world economy springs forth from the depression trough of the previous Kondratieff Cycle, a 20- to 25-year period of economic growth and prosperity begins. The growth phase might be best characterized by relatively long periods of strong economic growth punctuated by a series of relatively mild and short-lived recessions. It can be broken down into two subphases: The "cautious" phase lasts approximately 10 years, and the "euphoric" phase approximately 10 to 15 years.

During the cautious phase, world economies continue to stagger from the negative effects of high unemployment and widespread bankruptcy generated by the depression. The public remains very conservative, having witnessed firsthand the financial hardships and havoc a depression can create. Prudence dictates the purchase of only those goods and services absolutely necessary for basic survival. Debt is avoided, and few new business ventures or investments are initiated. Banks and other financial institutions are equally unwilling to lend to anyone except the most credit-worthy borrowers.

During this period, the only broadly active participant in the economy is the government. There are no other entities of sufficient strength to operate effectively. Leaders are eventually elected who promise to restore prosperity by capitalizing on the vast legislative and money-printing powers of the government. Assistance to the unemployed is in the form of welfare and unemployment insurance and federal make-work projects. Weaker countries that are not politically or financially strong enough to achieve even limited prosperity during this period often succumb to civil violence and revolution.

Continued worldwide economic and political instability often initiates a major "trough war" in the first few years of a growth phase as the more violent and militarily powerful nations sublimate their economic and social frustrations by exploiting their neighbors.

By the end of the cautious phase, the world's economies are poised for a 10- to 15-year period of accelerating economic growth. The government has successfully injected significant amounts of money and credit into the economy by financing both make-work programs and the trough war. This printed money and credit are invested for the most part in bank savings accounts and government debt securities, and do not initially represent a sufficient causal factor in the fueling of inflation. Instead, they cause both long-term and short-term interest rates to fall to extremely low levels and plant the seeds for the emergence of the euphoric stage of the growth phase.

As the euphoric stage develops, society's confidence level begins to rise sharply, and the fear of depression is forgotten. Corporate earnings begin to rise dramatically as consumer demand picks up and labor productivity remains high. Federal and state tax revenues increase to the point that huge tax cuts, which greatly reduce tax burdens to both consumers and businesses, are legislated. Since interest rates are low and credit is readily available, the use of debt to finance both business expansion and investment becomes widespread.

As the growth phase matures and progresses toward the height of its euphoria, a general feeling of complacency prevails in society. Many of the newly affluent enjoy job security and promising business careers.

They buy their own homes and have a financial cushion of common stock and real estate investments that seems to magically appreciate in value.

## A RISING TIDE OF EXPECTATION

*To the public, the investment world appears almost riskless. This illusion begins to produce a profound change in ethical and moral values. Increasingly liberal attitudes come into vogue as the public shifts from orthodox and conservative to more radical and permissive values. Many new and unconventional religions spring up to accommodate this turn toward materialism. The liberal concepts also spill over into politics in the form of civil rights legislation and expensive government support programs for the less productive members of society.*

Business becomes increasingly more assertive in its expectations for continuing economic prosperity. Business ventures expand as rapidly as possible. After each new success, the desire to form new commitments to generate more wealth at an even faster rate accelerates.

Recessions are generally short-lived and mild. This is largely due to the implementation of government "safety net" programs such as unemployment compensation and government-contracted projects. Business activity always tends to greatly surpass the peak levels of each prior business expansion. Recessions are viewed by most business managers as ideal opportunities to capitalize on lower material and labor costs in order to expand capital investments.

The euphoria eventually spreads into larger segments of society. A greater number of people become entrepreneurs, indulge in leveraged investments, and sharply increase their levels of personal debt and consumption. As the growth phase matures into a full-fledged boom of apparently unlimited potential, the fear of a relapse into hard economic times and depression disappears.

## THE COMING OF WAR

Politically, many of the more economically and militarily advanced nations attempt to expand their power and prestige by suppressing their neighbors with force. This usually initiates a major international war, the costs of which greatly destabilize the already overburdened economies of the combatants. The war continues, inflation accelerates, and the demand for war materiel spurs the drive to build plants and equipment. Tremendous wealth is transferred from industrialized to commodity-producing nations to pay for their raw materials, assuming there will be heavy future demand for these commodities. Huge amounts of investment capital flow into these countries to construct additional production facilities.

## THE GROWTH PHASE BEGINS TO FALTER

At the height of the war, this huge demand for credit forces interest rates to sufficiently high levels to cause world economic growth to falter. In response, the business community begins to pressure government leaders to take remedial action. The government's initial response is to expand the availability of credit in the banking system. This immediately effects a temporarily sharp drop in interest rates and a significant upswing in business activity, the latter producing an even higher demand for goods and services. As demand eventually outstrips supply, prices are bid up to increasingly higher levels and accelerating inflation emerges on a worldwide basis.

After a brief respite, interest rates once again begin to rise in tandem with inflation as world credit demand accelerates to extremely high levels. The rise in prices begins to outstrip wage increases, causing the real standard of living of wage earners to fall. This in turn produces widespread labor unrest and a sharp falloff in productivity. At the peak of the growth cycle, many business ventures, faced with high operating costs and low labor productivity, begin to yield lower rates of return, thus increasing their risk of bankruptcy.

After the war, in response to growing public dissatisfaction caused by high interest rates and accelerating inflation, the government tries to remedy a politically explosive situation by restricting the volume of money and credit in the economy in an attempt to fight inflation.

Historically, these credit-tightening monetary policies cause high rates of unemployment, widespread business and personal bankruptcies, and crashes in world stock markets. This severe recession, which terminates the growth phase, was called the first primary recession, or postwar recession, by Kondratieff.

## SERIOUS RECESSION

As the first primary recession develops, certain highly leveraged sectors of the world economy are especially devastated by the force of contraction. These usually include residential and commercial construction firms, banks, mortgage lenders, farmers, transportation companies, and many manufacturing firms.

Commodity-producing nations particularly suffer from the first primary recession. The demand for their products drops sharply due to the severity of the business contraction. Because of their previous rapid expansion to meet inflation-induced demand, these countries are quickly saddled with huge debts that they are unable to repay. The economic and financial consequences of impending widespread defaults greatly stress the international banking system and significantly heighten the severity of the recession.

Even though the business and financial community has been severely strained, the recession proves to be sharp but short-lived. It leaves in its wake a significant reduction in the rate of inflation and interest rates. This in turn promotes a relatively stable political and financial base in which a period of slow but steady economic growth can once again occur. This was called the plateau phase by Kondratieff and historically lasts approximately 10 years.

## AVOIDING DANGERS OF THE PLATEAU PHASE

*Of the four phases of the Kondratieff Wave, the plateau phase is by far the most critical for investors.* According to Kondratieff, the primary function of the plateau is to allow an extended period of time for both businessmen and investors to appropriately restructure their assets and portfolios in preparation for the inevitable depression. *History indicates that those businessmen and investors who understand the intricate interactions of the various political and financial forces in the plateau period and can efficiently apply this knowledge to protect their interests, can significantly increase their chances of avoiding the destructive effects of the ensuing depression. For those who are less attentive, severe financial problems are almost guaranteed.*

In most nations, the sobering aftereffects of the shock of coming so near to financial collapse produce a widespread uneasiness and dis-orientation. The public tries to alleviate this stress by returning to the more traditional and conservative life-styles that proved so peaceful and comforting in the past. An initial tendency is to blame the hard times on the highly permissive public officials who ran the country during the latter years of the growth phase and the first primary recession. New leaders are elected who promise economic tranquility and a rapid return to good times. Historically, they legislate large personal and corporate tax cuts, reduce programs for welfare and defense, attempt to balance the budget, and promote a tight monetary policy.

These political decisions significantly reduce interest rates and inflation to levels not seen since the early stages of the growth phase, and tend to promote a feeling of economic stabilization. Since there is plenty of slack in the world economy at the beginning of the plateau period, a broad range of lucrative business ventures becomes available as business activity in most countries slowly gains momentum. However, for countries primarily engaged in commodity production burdened by massive debts accumulated from the excessive expansion that occurred during the growth phase, the prospects for recovery are almost nonexistent.

As the plateau progresses, leading international financial institutions begin to realize that most of the loans that were extended for economically unsound reasons during the growth phase will probably never be repaid. Additional high-risk lending is increasingly curtailed. Unemployment rises, and the resulting unstable political environment precipitates a huge outflow of risk capital into stronger countries whose economic and political situations are more stable. As a result, economic and financial polarization develops between the weak and strong countries of the world. By the end of the plateau, the weak countries are either bankrupt or near bankruptcy, and the strong countries have acquired most of the world's capital.

Since most of the transferred capital is initially confined to relatively low-risk and highly liquid investments, almost all of it is invested in the debt and common-stock markets of the strong countries. The combination of relatively low interest rates, steady inflation, and a booming stock market tends to delude investors and businessmen into a false perception of economic strength and stability. Ironically, even though the stock markets continue to surge upward, the overall business climate remains relatively stagnant, and unemployment remains surprisingly high.

During the latter years of the plateau phase, the weak economic foundation of most countries becomes more evident. By then, the most profitable business ventures have been exploited, and capital has shifted to more speculative ventures. Most of these new business ventures are undertaken when operating costs are high. Since businesses are unable to raise prices or increase demand, the level and quality of business activity decrease.

Eventually, the economies of the weaker countries become overburdened by the huge debt structure accumulated during the growth and plateau phases. They begin to stagnate and then falter. Inevitably, they experience accelerating unemployment and business bankruptcy that force them to either repudiate or default on their debt. This precipitates the first stage of the deflationary collapse called the depression phase by Kondratieff.

## THE "ROLE" OF THE DEPRESSION PHASE

According to Kondratieff, *the primary function of the depression phase is the removal of the economic and financial excesses accumulated during the plateau and growth phases.* This phase is divided into three substages: initial deflation stage, stagnation stage, and a final deflation stage.

In the initial deflation stage, world business activity rapidly falls to extremely low levels in response to the ongoing worldwide debt collapse. Unemployment accelerates, and since demand for goods and services evaporates, the prices of most products begin to decline. As the depression deepens, businesses are increasingly forced to liquidate their assets to maintain solvency. This widespread selling causes a sharp and substantial downward spiral in all markets that is most visible in common stocks and real estate. Most private wealth diminishes, and standards of living decline. Job security, so prevalent during the growth phase, evaporates. Most business ventures and investments appear very unstable and risky.

The prevailing fear of continued world economic instability motivates a restructuring of basic attitudes and conduct. Psychologically, attitudes of extreme caution and fear supplant hopefulness and confidence. When the psychological transformation is complete, any underlying desire to aggressively rekindle economic growth and prosperity is replaced by the widespread desire for protection from financial ruin. This attitude produces a self-feeding economic contraction to even lower levels, followed by a business climate in which few businessmen and investors are willing or able to risk their remaining assets on new ventures. Consumers purchase only the most necessary items to maintain a moderate life-style, and usually only cash transactions occur. Business owners begin to aggressively reduce their work forces in order to lower operating costs and repay debts.

In many instances, governments tax strong revenue-generating businesses in order to grant heavy subsidies to weaker ones. This prevents immediate bankruptcies but is eventually self-defeating. Once deflation begins to accelerate, it takes on a life of its own. *If governments attempt to support inefficient and noncompetitive industries to prevent unemployment, the situation is aggravated by forcing capital to be permanently withdrawn from the viable sectors of the economy.*

In fact, depressions are usually initiated by the weakest companies and industries going bankrupt. This creates a snowball effect as they pull the stronger ones down with them in a self-feeding spiral. As the deflation continues, most people resign themselves to accepting increasingly higher levels of unemployment and continued erosion of their net worth.

## THE SETTING IN OF STAGNATION

At the point of greatest psychological negativism, the initial deflation stage runs its course, and the stage is set for the stagnant phase of the depression—a protracted period of economic stagnation where countries attempt to adjust their economies to the deflated economic environment. During this period, governments attempt to stabilize the economy by major social legislation and support projects.

Typically, during the average 10-year period of the stagnant phase, unemployment reaches its highest levels. This creates intense social pressures and, in countries where the financial base is relatively weak, revolutions out of which despotic rulers often emerge. The financial trauma that weak countries suffer is greatly increased by a huge outflux of monetary gold from their banking systems to safer havens. By the end of the stagnant period, financial destabilization is severe enough to produce a second and even greater wave of bankruptcies.

As the international banking system cascades into the second and typically more violent phase of the deflationary depression, even the most stable countries approach a high level of instability and panic. At the height of the collapse, a large percentage of monetary gold and currency is withdrawn from all banking systems by demand depositors as the stability of even the most viable governments is questioned. *Economic chaos prevails as prices of most goods plummet to fractions of their former levels.*

At the height of the depression, most debts are finally liquidated by banks as they are forced to call in loans to raise cash. Thus, the run on banks that began in the previous phase intensifies in both scope and magnitude. By the end of this approximately five-year, second depressionary phase, the world economy is in a state of desperation. However, just when the downward spiral appears almost irreversible, natural market forces intercede first to stabilize the economy and then to initiate recovery. By the end of the depression, labor costs are again cheap, and raw material prices low, allowing inexpensive financing to again become available. Entrepreneurs and investors with a wide range of promising ideas again prepare to assume the risks of new business and investment ventures.

## BIRTH OF A NEW WAVE

Similar to the growth phase, the depression phase usually culminates when the cleansing process is complete. As a result, a new set of conservative values is instilled in society. As business profits begin to improve, confidence slowly returns and a new Kondratieff Cycle is born.


## CONCLUSION

Contrary to popular belief, the Kondratieff Wave described in this chapter is not an esoteric cyclical phenomenon that forces the economies of the world to expand and collapse in a relatively periodic manner. The Kondratieff Wave should be viewed as the interaction of world markets expressing a generalized picture of economic and financial overextension and underextension from an equilibrium position. As the world economy expands above this equilibrium level, the combination of the higher cost of money, debt accumulation, inflation, and social tensions begins to restrict the capability for continued economic growth.

Eventually, the sum of these natural market forces reaches such a high level of disequilibrium that the economy loses its upward momentum and begins to stagnate. Stagnation inevitably modulates into depression as the economy enters an extended period of negative growth until these excesses are purged. At this point, world interest rates, inflation, and aggregate debt levels are sufficiently low that a long period of positive growth can begin.

As we shall see in the next chapter, *the United States has experienced three complete Kondratieff Cycles and is now well into its fourth.* Each cycle, of course, is unique in that the degree of complexity of business and financial institutions increases and becomes more sophisticated in their inter-related activities. However, the basic structure of the Kondratieff scenario remains remarkably intact, regardless of the short-term distortions that may be imposed on it by powerful institutions.

In the end, the result is always the same. Economic distortions must be purged from the system before sustained growth can again proceed. This central thought should be kept in mind as we analyze the ebb and flow of depression and prosperity in the United States from the Revolutionary War to the present.

*"We are living in a period which all too readily scraps the old for the new. . . . As a nation, we are in danger of forgetting that the new is not true because it is novel, and that the old is not false because it is ancient."*

—Joseph Kennedy

# Chapter III
# Kondratieff Waves and the United States

## LESSONS FROM HISTORY

The best documented substantiation of the Kondratieff theory is the economic history of the United States from the Revolutionary War to the present. During this period, we have been able to identify three complete long-term cycles and a partial fourth cycle, each approximately 54 years in duration (Figure 4).

In each succeeding cycle, the structure of the world's economic system became more complex, often misleading investors into believing that the past is not a true representation of the future. Of course, governments and other powerful institutions can significantly interrupt the natural progression of a cycle for short periods of time. Ultimately, however, the cycles repeat in somewhat altered but easily recognizable form.

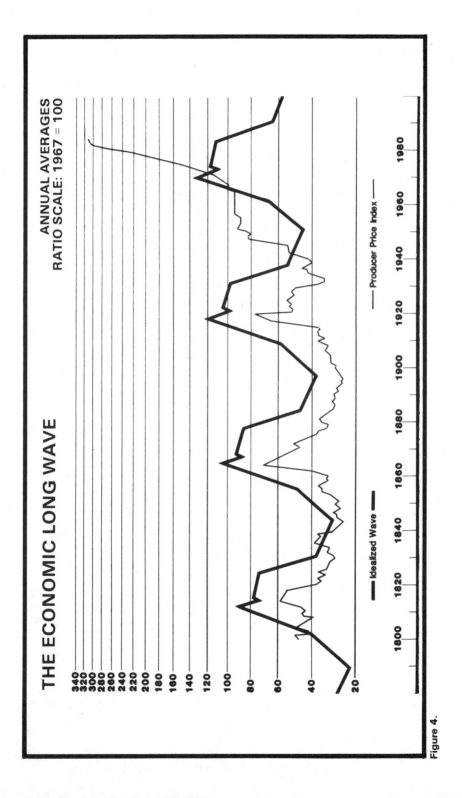

THE ECONOMIC LONG WAVE

ANNUAL AVERAGES
RATIO SCALE: 1967 = 100

Idealized Wave ▬▬▬

Producer Price Index ▬▬▬

Figure 4.

During the Revolutionary War, our fledgling nation was forced to borrow vast sums of money. In the early war years, cash was plentiful. After the Continental Army's first victory over the British at Saratoga, France, Holland, and Spain aggressively lent support with both arms and money. As the war continued, with no apparent victor in sight, many of these sources of capital began to dry up, forcing Congress to print currency to pay its debts.

After the final defeat of the British at Yorktown, euphoria spread nationwide. Because both state and government currencies were plentiful and there was a huge pent-up demand for European goods, credit was easily available with only nominal concern for its future repayment. This allowed the American public to go on a buying spree.

The credit binge was greatly aided by the creation of a large number of state-chartered banks authorized by Congress. Their function was to offer financial assistance to private businesses and farming communities. In reality, most of their loans went into various "get-rich-quick" schemes, particularly speculative real estate ventures on the Western frontier.

## THE FIRST DEPRESSION

By the mid-1780s, the economic boom began to lose momentum in spite of the emergence of a wide variety of promising new business ventures and the exciting and potentially rewarding development of the West. Interest rates were exorbitantly high and inflation rampant. By 1785, the country was enveloped in a full-fledged banking panic and depression. Tax revenues declined, putting the government under even greater pressure to pay its huge war debts. As the financial survivability of the government came into question, the value of the currency began to depreciate rapidly, causing a large volume of gold to flow out of the country.

Eventually, panic spread throughout the banking system, as a large portion of its long-term loans to land speculators and shaky business ventures began to default. A nationwide run on the banks ensued as both foreign and domestic depositors clamored for ready cash. Access to cash became of paramount importance to all businesses and financial institutions. Distressed liquidation of goods to raise capital severely depressed prices. Land was often sold at debtors' auctions for almost nothing, and newspapers were filled with notices of insolvency. In one county in Maryland, the public forced the suspension of all civil debtor suits; in another, they disallowed any bidding on land offered at sheriff's sales. In Massachusetts, the widespread discontent caused Shay's Rebellion, in which indebted farmers revolted against their obligations. Although the rebellion was put down, the state acknowledged this "injustice" and passed a debt moratorium.

By 1790, the depression succeeded in wiping out most of the excess debt and marginal business ventures built up over the Revolutionary War period. Business and commercial activity remained at a standstill, and the nation's financial and banking system was in shambles.

However, by 1791, prospects began to improve. George Washington won the Presidential election by a landslide, and Congress replaced the impotent Articles of Confederation with the present-day Constitution. On the same day the Constitution was ratified, Congress established the First Bank of the United States and issued a new currency fully backed by gold. With a new and widely respected federal government with full taxing powers, the nation was prepared to embark on a 25-year period of almost uninterrupted growth and prosperity (Figure 5).

## 25 YEARS OF GROWTH

Due to the depressed economic and financial condition of the country, interest rates declined to historical lows, and the prices of most farm and industrial products stabilized at pre-Revolutionary War levels. From the late 1780s to 1807, the economy progressed in a cautious but strongly positive manner. Infrequent and short-lived recessions were immediately followed by strong expansions. The country was at peace, crop harvests were plentiful, inflation was well under control, and interest rates remained low.

Although the lending capacity of the banking system was high, banks tended to remain very conservative and prudent. By 1800, the government had satisfied all its creditors and had even accumulated a small budget surplus.

In 1803, a war broke out between France and England. This stimulated tremendous demand in both countries for war materiel, and caused the volume of American exports to soar. European gold flowed into the economy, inducing a strong business boom, especially in the shipping and export industries. The industrial base also expanded rapidly, not only to accommodate war-related demand, but also to satisfy domestic needs.

Throughout the early 1800s, the westward movement began to gain greater momentum. Settlers poured into the Ohio Valley and Great Lakes regions in unprecedented numbers. From 1800 to 1805, the population of Cincinnati increased more than 30 percent and Chicago,

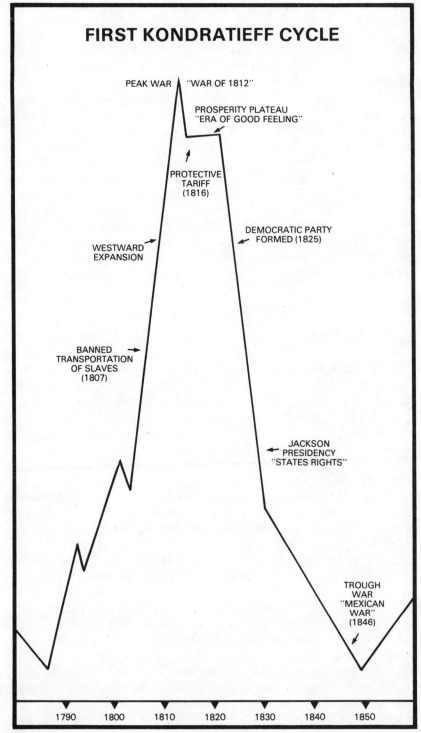

Figure 5.

more than 25 percent. By late 1806, these areas were beginning to experience the first signs of an immense land speculation boom.

In 1807, war between the United States and England began brewing. England blockaded European ports from southern France to northern Germany in an effort to prevent war supplies from reaching France. It became extremely difficult for American ships to reach their destinations due to provocative and often blatant harassment by the British. In 1812, the United States declared war on England, and within three years completely ran the British out of America.

## EFFECTS OF OUR FIRST "PEAK" WAR

The economic effect of this first Kondratieff peak war on the nation's debt-ridden financial structure was profound. The war was largely financed by wealthy individuals and state banks chartered by the First Bank of the United States. These state-chartered banks were allowed to issue their own paper currency in a fractional proportion to the amount of U.S. Treasury notes the bank was required to deposit as collateral. During the war era of 1812 through 1817, total state bank notes in circulation increased from $45 million to over $100 million, causing the prices of most goods to explode. From 1811 to 1815, wholesale prices in Philadelphia increased over 50 percent; in Baltimore, 68 percent; and in New York, 69 percent. During this period, the yield on U.S. government bonds increased from less than 6 percent to well over 8 percent.

Because interest rates were extremely high, banks and other lending institutions made huge profits that allowed them to extend credit even further to a profit-hungry public eager to participate in a wide variety of real estate speculations and marginal business ventures. In 1816, a liquidity crisis hit the banking system when it was realized that the overextended prices of commodities and real estate could not be sustained at their wartime levels. This crisis forced the banks to withdraw money from the system to raise cash.

The extreme scarcity of money drove the country into the first major financial panic and recession since the Revolutionary War depression 25 years earlier. Most state-chartered banks went off the gold standard. Migration into the Ohio Valley and Mississippi territories virtually ceased, and land speculators, who had purchased on credit, found it impossible to meet their obligations. Farmers suffered greatly, in many instances petitioning Congress to defer all cash payments due on public land. Domestic industries complained of high unemployment and liquidated their goods at prices far below cost. In Pennsylvania, real estate prices dropped more than two-thirds of their former values. *Before the end of this sharp but short recession, much of the speculative excesses built up during the growth period were purged.*

By 1817, the Second Bank of the United States had replaced the First Bank of the United States. One of its primary objectives was to reinstate a gold-backed currency. Since many of the shaky loans were washed out of the banking system, public confidence began to return, and the nation entered an eight-year plateau period of relatively stable economic growth called the Era of Good Feelings.

During this period, money in circulation increased only gradually and prices were remarkably stable. Land sales increased at a relatively uniform rate without a rekindling of the rampant speculation of the 1810 to 1815 period. Voters overwhelmingly elected President Monroe in 1817 and 1821 on a highly nationalistic platform called the American System. This promoted large-scale protective tariffs for manufacturers, and a home market and better transportation for farmers. It was a propitious time to raise tariffs since cries from domestic industries for protection came from almost every sector of the economy. Government-financed improvements for the farmers also included public works projects to build roads and canals.

In 1817, the New York Legislature authorized the construction of the Erie and Champlain Canals. Promoters and speculators in canal and road-building stocks bid share prices to exorbitant heights. Between 1815 and 1825, over 2,188 miles of roadway were laid in the United States. At the climax of the building boom that followed, canals and roads were constructed to link the Western states to the Eastern and Middle Atlantic States. All forms of interstate commerce grew as never before.

Many financial writers commented on the soundness of the banking system, in contrast to the rampant inflation and eventual price collapse following the War of 1812. The Earl of Liverpool, commenting to Parliament, stated, "America has increased its wealth in commerce, industry, population, and strength more rapidly than any other nation in the history of the world."

The Era of Good Feelings was a time of great national pride, prosperity, and widespread economic optimism rarely found in the history of Western civilization. Much of this increase in economic activity was financed by loans from European investors and American financial institutions.

Unfortunately, the huge government debts incurred during the War of 1812 were only partially repaid. By the middle 1820s, the massive debt accumulated by all sectors of the economy was beginning to threaten the economic and financial stability of the nation.

## END OF THE BOOM

By early 1826, the plateau boom was over, and the country began to experience the first stages of depression. This depression was characterized by a series of weak economic rallies immediately followed by periods of severe economic collapse and credit liquidation. By 1839, the European market for United States securities no longer existed. By 1840, most states had either defaulted or had omitted interest payments on municipal securities. The vast majority of both federal and state-chartered banks were either insolvent or on holiday.

Conditions deteriorated to the point that President Andrew Jackson recommended to Congress that the federal government assume many of the states' debts in order to save the nation's financial integrity. Michigan repudiated its debts, and most other states forced their creditors to accept pennies on the dollar for their paper. Illinois stopped all transportation construction projects and raised taxes to protect its credit rating. Most foreign loans to the U.S. were repudiated. The prices of railroad stocks dropped more than 80 percent from 1836 to 1843. The value of railroad bonds fell over 50 percent. In retrospect, this was one of the worst periods of deflation and loss of wealth the nation had ever faced. But similar to most depressions, the excess debt and inefficient business ventures built up during the growth phase of the cycle were eventually eliminated, so that by 1845, the economy again positioned itself to participate in the next upswing of the Kondratieff Cycle.

## A NEW PROSPERITY CYCLE

By 1846, America was eager to embark on its second complete period of long-term prosperity. In 1846, the war with Mexico resulted in the annexation of territories that included parts of the present-day states of California, Arizona, New Mexico, and Texas. Most Americans exuded a spirit of pride in the overwhelming strength of the nation. Economic and financial conditions stabilized, halting the downward plunge in the prices of most commodities. The financial system was very conservative, since most of the outstanding federal and state debts and currency of state-chartered banks were fully backed by gold.

Europe quickly became the largest foreign market for our grain products. This was due in part to England's repeal of its Corn Laws, which for many years imposed extraordinarily high tariffs on U.S. grain exports. From 1845 to 1847, the prices paid for most grains advanced almost 80 percent.

*Aided by the discovery of gold in California in 1848 and the public land grants of 1850, the U.S. was about to embark on one of the greatest and most prolonged eras of economic prosperity in its history* (Figure 6). Throughout the early 1850s, confidence in all sectors of society continued to improve. Banks slowly relaxed their tight credit policies. Business profits, especially those associated with transportation, farming, and international trade, began to rise dramatically.

Because interest rates were low and the currency sound, business soon enjoyed a significant inflow of risk capital from both domestic and foreign sources. Initially, most of this capital was invested in the construction and railroad industries, which were perceived as profitable participants in the continuing westward expansion. The popularity of these investments was reflected in the prices paid for railroad shares, which by 1852 had risen more than 70 percent from their lows of 1846.

The first stages of a real estate boom were also in progress. The demand for loans and credit to speculate in Western real estate and railroad common stocks and bonds was tremendous. The country greatly needed labor and time-saving devices and a means of traveling great distances in a short time. This era marked the emergence of basic inventions characteristic of late 19th- and 20th-century life-styles.

This same period also saw a resurgence of liberal political leadership as the newly affluent populace demanded and received a major transformation of social and civil rights laws. Congress initiated the Morrill Act of 1862, which called for the formation of state colleges and universities; the Emancipation Proclamation, which freed the slaves; and the Homestead Act, which gave free land to Western immigrants. More than 20 million acres of public land were granted as subsidies for new Western rail lines. In addition, the federal government began to greatly influence the financial market by borrowing huge amounts of money for public buildings, rivers, harbors, lighthouses, wharves, and canals.

By 1857, after 14 years of almost uninterrupted growth and prosperity, financial and economic conditions began to noticeably overheat. The gold discovered in California 10 years earlier had eventually found its way into the banking system to be used either as currency or loan collateral. With the banking system flush with gold and reinforced by a powerful economic boom, most lenders deemed it prudent to adopt a more aggressive lending posture. From 1850 to 1857, bank credit increased an astounding 55 percent.

By early 1858, government credit demands, especially for public works projects, had begun to conflict with those of business. The cost of money was forced to extraordinarily high levels so that by late 1858, interest rates on commercial paper in most of the large money center banks rose to over 30 percent.

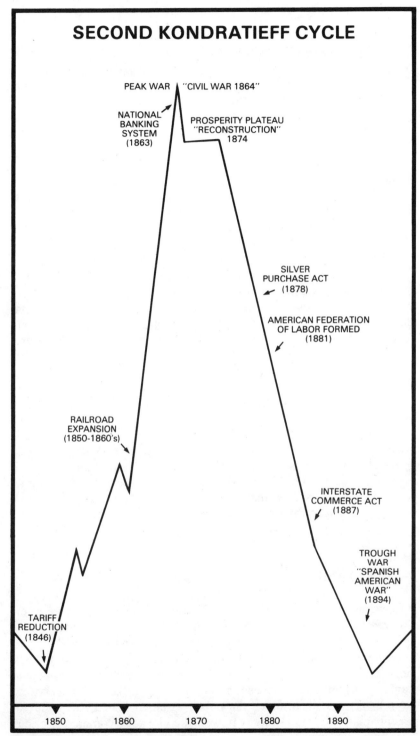

Figure 6.

## COOLING DOWN THE ECONOMY

The government responded to the overheated economy by buying gold in the open market to reduce the money supply. A sharp but short minirecession ensued. In 1859, however, the recession was cut short as the government was forced to again begin spending in preparation for the Civil War.

When war broke out in 1862, Congress immediately authorized the issuance of more than $450 million in new U.S. notes to cover war-related expenses. Additional government bonds were issued when it became apparent that it would be politically unfeasible to print greater quantities of currency not backed by gold. During the war period, the money supply increased from approximately $300 million to more than $900 million. *From 1862 to 1864, the price of most commodities almost tripled.*

By 1864, when victory by the North became assured, the government attempted to depress commodity prices to prewar levels in order to alleviate the economic and financial trauma brought about by inflation. As the Treasury began to tighten credit, state and national banks were forced to raise cash by calling in loans and hoarding U.S. bank notes, gold coins, and bullion. Such actions were taken in order to improve the banks' balance sheets and prevent a run on deposits. As the liquidity squeeze intensified, many businesses, especially those generating most of their earnings from war-related activities, slid into receivership or went bankrupt. Land sales declined by more than 84 percent, and farm prices collapsed. Huge losses occurred in the stock and bond markets as money became scarce and earnings plummeted. Unemployment reached its highest level in two decades when soldiers returning home could not find jobs. Fortunately, the painful postwar recession lasted only slightly more than a year.

## MONEY STABILIZED

Realizing the need to stabilize the nation's financial structure after the war, Congress passed the National Bank Act in late 1863. Its primary objective was to systematically abolish the prevailing state banking and currency system and replace it with a federal banking system under a single national charter. By late 1865, it became apparent that the national banking system would succeed, and by the end of the decade very few state banks remained. Since the public assumed that the new federal greenback would soon become fully backed by gold, commodity prices immediately stabilized. With public confidence restored, the nation entered a 10-year plateau period of stable economic growth and prosperity.

The reconstruction plateau period was characterized by a very rapid expansion of the railroad and farming industries, and a steady increase in international trade. In 1868, the prices of most commodities were stable and historically cheap. Business was good, and interest rates were moderate. As earnings began to improve, stock prices moved sharply higher. This was especially true of those associated with the ongoing westward movement and those involved in industrialization of the Northeast. The strong performance of common stocks was particularly due to huge purchases from Europe. An estimated $2 billion in European investment capital was transferred into the U.S. to participate in our booming equity and real estate markets. Foreign investment in our domestic markets was further encouraged in 1869 by the re-election of the staunchly probusiness Ulysses S. Grant.

## DEPRESSION SIGNS

Not all sectors of the economy were enjoying the same prosperity. Farmers and other major raw material producers, such as the mining and petroleum industries, were beginning to suffer under the burdens of falling prices and high debt.

Also under obvious stress throughout the plateau were those industries associated with world trade, such as cargo shipping and export/import businesses. These industries were being particularly hurt by the growing conservative factions of the government that were trying to economically isolate the United States from the rest of the world by the implementation of protectionist trade barriers. In 1861, their efforts were directed toward placing a maximum tariff of 24 percent on most foreign goods. By 1864, they had raised it to a prohibitive 47 percent.

The newly emerging labor unions and manufacturing firms in the Northeast significantly contributed to the political pressure placed on Congress to implement these severe tariff restrictions. The tariffs almost destroyed the economies of South America and Africa and forced most of the industrialized countries of Europe to implement retaliatory trade barriers. *By 1873, world trade had almost ceased, and the first major signs of the coming worldwide depression began to emerge.*

By late 1873, the positive, though sluggish, economic growth experienced by the U.S. during the reconstructive plateau began to lose its upward momentum. The government's massive debts acquired during and after the Civil War began to compete with public and business credit requirements. As money became scarce and the weaker links of the credit chain began to break down, the financial markets once again shifted to a more restrictive lending policy. This precipitated a major banking panic and depression. During the post-Civil War depression years of 1873 and 1879, prices declined more than 40 percent. The price of most metals and textiles declined more than 50 percent.

Railroad stocks also lost more than 50 percent of their value. As foreign demand for most goods plummeted, American exports fell more than 60 percent, causing widespread distress in the shipping industry. By 1880, as the depression grew more severe, political and social unrest increased, resulting in public demand for government relief. Congress responded by legislating price supports and free-trade measures aimed at restoring economic stability.

During the early stages of the depression, practically everyone suffered terribly at one time or another. As a group, the farmers in the West and South were affected the most. Encumbered with huge debts accumulated during the plateau boom and steadily falling grain and livestock prices, they championed price-support legislation. Such legislation was implemented by the government on the theory that the only way to buoy farm prices was to print additional federal notes and add more gold and silver bullion to the currency.

Opposed to the farmers were many of the so-called "sound money" advocates affiliated with the most prominent banking and financial institutions in New York and Chicago. They contended that long-term economic vitality depended upon a fully gold-backed currency, and, more importantly, upon the avoidance of destructive hyperinflationary policies like those used during the Civil War era. The fact that they held a large portion of their assets in currency and fixed-income securities that would be positively affected in a deflationary environment gave a personal impetus to their demands.

The New York bankers generally had their way until the early 1890s, when the depression became increasingly severe and the nation began to experience massive personal and business loan defaults with resulting political instability.

During the panic of 1893, the increasingly severe economic crisis in the U.S. caused Europeans to question its political stability and survivability. During the next three years, huge amounts of U.S. gold were transferred to the more stable political climates of England and Germany. This tended to reduce U.S. wholesale prices even more. To make matters worse, the American Midwest experienced a 10-year drought beginning in 1890, which further devastated the farming business and its associated industries. Farmers from all areas of the country began to intensify their demands for relief.

The first major victory by farmers was the Sherman Silver Purchase Act, which for the first time considered silver a monetary metal along with gold. By late 1893, more than $500 million in silver coins and silver paper certificates were issued. In order to inflate further, the Treasury began buying a huge volume of gold in the open market, monetizing it in the form of coins and certificates. In addition, from 1890 to 1896 (the last year of the depression), the annual increase in the currency in circulation averaged more than 20 percent, an unusually high figure for that era.

However, this new "pump-priming" monetary policy of the government proved ineffective as the depression's destructive forces again began to accelerate.

By 1894, more than 182 railroad companies, representing more than half of the nation's railroad capacity, went into receivership. The stock market collapsed. Unemployment grew.

## UNEMPLOYED MARCH ON WASHINGTON

Strikes and workers' riots became widespread. The Homestead strike in Pittsburgh, the Pullman strike in Chicago, and the march of Coxey's army of unemployed in Washington were the most violent. From 1873 until the depression was over in 1896, wholesale prices fell 50 percent—more than 60 percent below their Civil War peak. More than half of the nation's outstanding loans accumulated during the growth and plateau phases of the Civil War cycle were either in default or had payments of principal or interest discontinued. Most of the great fortunes amassed during the previous 50 years were either significantly reduced or completely wiped out. The nation's economy was at rock bottom.

By the late 1890s, however, conditions were such that the economy could once again begin to improve. Discoveries of gold in Australia, Colorado, and Alaska, and the expansion of gold and silver production in South Africa resulted in extremely plentiful supplies of these precious metals. Debt levels, inflation, and interest rates were once again at their cyclical lows, and political stability was slowly being restored.

## THE THIRD GROWTH PHASE

During the next 30 years of the third Kondratieff growth phase, the nation would experience the greatest period of economic growth and expansion in its history. It would be transformed from a medium-sized power into the strongest and most powerful economic and military force in the world (Figure 7).

With the defeat of Spain in the Spanish American War in 1898, the U.S., through the encouragement of Teddy Roosevelt, began expanding international trade into South American markets and the Far East. During this era, the Panama Canal was completed and experienced a huge volume of traffic. Not only did Roosevelt's imperialistic attitude greatly promote the economic power base of the country, it also inspired a feeling of national pride and confidence in the strength of the nation, and promoted a philosophy that any problem could be solved by sheer determination and aggressiveness.

During the first decade of the growth phase, recessions continued to be mild as business profits expanded to record levels. Economic growth was moderately robust. Food and commodity prices remained stable. Businessmen who were wiped out by the depression were replaced by a new generation of cautious, yet optimistic, entrepreneurs. This era marked the emergence of capitalism and big business. Business and personal income taxes were negligible. Labor unions were peaceful and inoffensive, since most present-day labor legislation did not exist.

As a result of these and other factors, public confidence soared. The legacy of the past depression was quickly forgotten. Businesses began investing in additional plants and equipment as consumer demand increased for a wide variety of innovative products. Interest rates remained low, credit was available, underlying economic and business fundamentals were sound. A renewed interest in investments emerged, especially in high-quality common stocks and urban real estate. By 1915, the economy was in a full-fledged boom.

Because of the expanding economy, businesses increased expenditures for new plants and equipment. Government loan demand was already high, due mainly to support given interstate road-building programs and extensive government office-building construction projects. At this juncture, interest rates and inflation were slowly rising, although not yet to debilitating levels. Excess industrial capacity was not developed sufficiently to warrant caution. However, due to huge debts run up from United States involvement in World War I, economic stability began to deteriorate.

The tremendous expense of conducting an overseas war provided the newly formed Federal Reserve System with its first significant opportunity to assist Congress in raising national debt levels. Huge treasury deficits were created primarily from bond sales to banks, financial institutions, and individuals. More than 90 percent of these bonds were purchased on credit from reserves made available by the

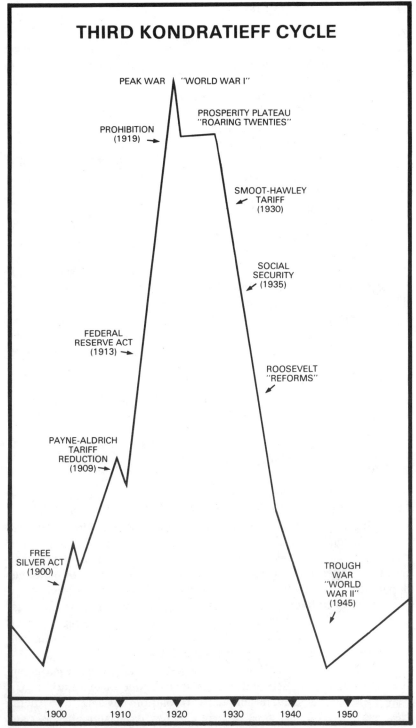

Figure 7.

Federal Reserve at preferential rates. Since bonds purchased by banks could fulfill reserve requirements upon which further bank loans could be made, the money supply skyrocketed and roaring inflation ensued. As this rapid injection of money entered the already euphoric markets, raw material and labor prices soared to historically high levels.

Wild inflation-hedge investing occurred. Goods were stockpiled. Future purchases were contracted for much more than was actually needed in order to insure the delivery of desired quantities. Producers in turn held back filling the orders, expecting even higher prices. This condition reinforced the belief that the real cause of inflation was a shortage of production capacity. A significant capital spending boom for plants and equipment followed that further increased demand for raw materials and labor. Government agencies also began to hoard strategic materials in the event of a prolonged war. As the buying intensified, hoarding and the bidding up of prices of unessential collectibles, such as art, gemstones, antiques, and uninhabitable real estate, became common. The higher prices went, the more consumer demand increased.

As the public became more aware of the loss of the purchasing power of the dollar in this hyperinflationary era, they found that one sure way to play the inflation game was to buy "real" items on the most leveraged credit terms possible with the hope of reselling them later at significantly higher prices. This strategy greatly increased the already euphoric credit expansion and forced interest rates even higher.

## THE LURE OF INFLATION

By 1919, as the public became speculatively oriented, it accepted the belief that the newly created Federal Reserve System with its unlimited money-creating powers would never allow prices or wages to fall because of the financial shock that would result. Reflecting this philosophy, the stock markets began to experience a brisk business as the public became an increasingly active participant. As it became more profitable and apparently less risky to expect inflation to push the highly liquid equity markets to even higher levels, investors began to speculate in the stock and commodity markets with increasing amounts of leverage. Money that was used to promote capital formation was now used to finance speculation in the supposedly permanent inflationary environment.

By late 1919, the President and Congress became concerned about the high rate of inflation and the speculative tone of the markets. On May 17, 1920, the Senate adopted a resolution advising the Federal Reserve that remedial steps be taken. A few days later, the discount rate was raised to a record 7 percent and kept there for a year. This step had an immediate negative impact on the markets. Almost overnight, the nation plunged into a severe financial panic accompanied by an equally sharp drop in the stock and commodities markets.

Although the resulting recession lasted slightly longer than one year, it was the most severe in more than 35 years and marked an end to the growth phase of this cycle.

During the postwar recession, most manufactured goods quickly lost more than 50 percent of their value. The price of basic commodities fell much lower. Corn dropped from $1.86 to $.41 per bushel, and potatoes went from $4.26 to $.61 per pound. The stock market lost more than 45 percent of its value as represented by the Dow Jones industrial average. Manufacturing output slowed to almost a standstill, and the gross national product fell more than 34 percent. Unemployment rose, and business failures were numerous. Major industries that could not liquidate their inventories quickly were the most seriously affected. The huge volume of inflation-hedge goods that was once hoarded made liquidations even more difficult. Conservative corporations with long records of dividend payments skipped their dividends and in many cases were forced to reorganize. Consumers sharply reduced their purchases, buying only the basic necessities.

By the end of 1922, the severe recession and credit liquidation ended, allowing a gradual improvement in business activity. The plateau period of the Roaring Twenties was about to begin. In the early 1920s, the nation was in a mild state of shock. Businessmen were very cautious in their lending policies. Fearing a sudden relapse of a recession, the Federal Reserve increased the money supply at a fairly rapid rate during 1921 and 1922, and then stabilized it for the remainder of the decade. The 1920s represented price stability and rapid business growth. Interest rates were moderate and stable. Unemployment was low, averaging only 7 percent during the decade.

By the fall of 1924, business activity was beginning to improve, and by the spring of 1925, a strong recovery was in progress. The stock market reached new highs with only mild corrections, and the American public was calm and secure. Businesses were once again producing a host of new and innovative products that promised to significantly enhance the quality of life. Electric washing machines and refrigerators were gaining rapid acceptance, as were electric and gas ranges. Radios were as common as present-day televisions and stereos.

As the decade progressed, consumers began to spend an increasingly greater portion of their income on nonessential goods and services. Many of these purchases were financed on credit, and the use of "installment buying" quickly became respectable. By the mid-1920s,

most conservative businessmen were offering "easy installment plans."
By 1926, nearly two-thirds of retail automobile sales and more than
three-quarters of furniture sales were on credit. Over half of all families
owned their own homes, usually financed by a mortgage. Since most of
these mortgages were for a maximum of 10 years, second and third
mortgages at very high interest rates were common.

Also by 1926, the stock market had been rediscovered by the investment community. With inflation quelled and the prices of real estate
and other commodities no longer rising, a rapid liquidation of inflation-
hedge investments and a transfer of funds into the stock markets became
widespread. By 1927, the Dow average rose more than 210 percent
from its low in 1921. Although much of this rise could be attributed to
the healthy economic climate and a general growth in earnings, a
significant portion of the rise came from a huge increase in leveraged
speculation.

The seemingly solid financial status of the United States relative to
the rest of the world also promoted the rise in the stock market. Due
to the fears of European investors, who continued to experience post-
World War I turmoil, more than $48 billion in gold (present-day dollars)
was transferred to America during the postwar years. This greatly
increased the value of the dollar. Between 1920 and 1926, the amount
of gold backing each printed dollar increased more than 34 percent.
These totals included gold in the United States national banking system
and excluded reserves held by nonfederal banks and private individuals,
which were estimated to have been substantial.

## WARNING SIGNS

By 1927, credit demands were beginning to greatly concern the Federal
Reserve. Interest rates were rapidly rising and foreign currencies were
beginning to seriously weaken. Because of the strong dollar, our exports
became increasingly uncompetitive and our manufacturing and agricultural industries noticeably depressed. In order to ease pressure on
the dollar, the Federal Reserve implemented a loose credit policy and
began pumping money into the banking system. Although this policy
did fulfill its purpose of depressing the value of the dollar over the
short term, most of the printed money eventually found its way into
the financial system to promote even further credit creation and stock
market speculation.

By the spring of 1929, interest rates were soaring to new highs,
primarily due to increased market speculation and consumer credit
purchases. As bank loans became increasingly unselective and risky,

the Federal Reserve began to tighten the money supply. By mid-1929, currency in circulation declined an astounding 20 percent from its 1928 highs. *The stock market stubbornly continued to reach new highs and credit continued to expand.* In late 1929, the discount rate was raised in several abrupt steps to 6 percent, a level sufficient to finally break the credit markets. In August, the commodity markets moved sharply downward. On Black Tuesday, in October, the stock market collapsed and the average stock lost more than 30 percent of its value in one day. The third Kondratieff depression had commenced.

When the economy finally ruptured, the financial shock was indescribable. Paper fortunes in the stock market disappeared overnight as investors were forced to liquidate their margined stocks for pennies on the dollar. The terrible realization that the country had not entered a new era of unlimited prosperity cast a pall over the populace that no optimistic statement from public officials could alleviate. During the next three years, the United States would experience the most rapid financial and economic collapse in its history.

Almost immediately coincident with the onset of the depression was the decline in prices of most raw materials and finished goods. This began to adversely affect the profits of many businesses associated with international trade. Extreme pressure was placed on Congress by the farming and labor lobbies to raise tariffs and eliminate "dumping" of foreign goods in the naive belief that high tariffs would support the price of farm and manufactured products.

In 1930, after a year of debate, Congress passed the Smoot-Hawley Tariff Act which increased the average duties on most imports to 40 percent. Although foreign nations and America's leading economists strongly protested this action, President Hoover reluctantly signed the bill into law. Undoubtedly, this act greatly increased the initial severity of the depression. In effect, other nations were put on notice that the United States was willing to adopt a course of selfish nationalism instead of cooperation. Many countries retaliated with even higher duties and import quotas. By 1931, a full-scale international trade war was in progress.

By 1932, the unemployment rate exceeded 25 percent. Many highly qualified men could not find work at any pay level. Since workers could not make mortgage payments, homes and farms were foreclosed on in record numbers. Many banks and financial institutions closed their doors. Each new wave of business and banking failures resulted in the destruction of bank deposits, causing an even more rapid contraction in outstanding credit. The eventual collapse of many well-established and trusted banks dramatically illustrated to the public the terrible seriousness of the depression.

By late 1932, the depression had become a nationwide financial panic. Individuals trying to maintain their former standard of living finally began to give up. People were beginning to take the law into their own hands by stopping foreclosures on farms and urban homes. A few states even passed laws prohibiting foreclosures and tax sales.

Regional bank failures were common. Unfortunately, there was apparently no federal guarantee or support forthcoming to provide security. As bank failures spread, deposits were shifted into safer New York banks, and later gold withdrawals were demanded as the panic became more severe. By the bottom of the first deflationary stage of the depression in early 1933, the stock market had lost more than 85 percent of its value, and many companies were bankrupt. Many high-quality state and municipal bonds forfeited interest payments due to a lack of tax revenues.

Internationally, those nations with large debts and weak political leadership repudiated their international obligations and fell into revolution. By 1933, all the world's currencies were taken off the gold standard, forcing what was left of international trade to virtually cease.

## POLITICAL STABILITY THREATENED

On March 6, 1933, as the panic began to threaten political stability, President Roosevelt ordered all banks and securities markets closed. In April, it was made illegal to own or transport gold out of the country. Coincidently, the newly elected President Roosevelt began to implement the New Deal, a wide range of government fiscal and monetary programs and policies designed to alleviate the nation's suffering. Roosevelt's first act was to request that the Federal Reserve greatly expand the money supply, which had been declining at a 10 percent annual rate for the previous three years. During the next two and one-half years, it increased more than 50 percent. In addition, he greatly increased the value of the Treasury's gold reserves by officially revaluing its price from $20 per ounce to $32 per ounce.

Simultaneously, the Federal Deposit Insurance Corporation and the Securities and Exchange Commission were created to suppress the fears of further bank and brokerage firm bankruptcies.

These programs had an immediate impact on financial institutions. By 1934, almost all banks that borrowed money from the Federal Reserve during the panic repaid their loans. By 1935, a considerable excess of reserves (more than $3 billion) was recorded in the banking system. Additionally, huge amounts of gold bullion entered the United States as European investors and institutions accelerated their transfer of capital due to domestic political and economic instability. An estimated $180 billion in gold bullion (present-day dollars) was transferred into the United States during the 1930s.

Roosevelt also legislated a wide range of innovative fiscal programs during the early 1930s. To support industry, Congress passed the National Industrial Recovery Act and created the Reconstruction Finance Corporation, which made inexpensive loans to hard-pressed businesses unable to obtain financing from normal sources.

To support farmers, Congress passed the Agricultural Adjustment Act of 1933, which assumed the responsibility of raising farm prices to predetermined levels by selectively reducing the supply of farm commodities on the market. Although the Supreme Court declared this act unconstitutional in 1936, it succeeded in raising the average farm commodity price by 130 percent, and raised farm income from $2 billion to more than $11 billion during the period from 1933 to 1937. In order to promote soil conservation and reduce unemployment, Roosevelt also enacted the Soil Conservationism and Allotment Act in conjunction with the Civilian Conservation Corps and the Works Progress Administration.

In 1935, the basis for the present-day Social Security System was legislated. This act, provided for a federal old age and survivor's insurance program as well as assistance to the needy and blind. In order to ease the international dislocations caused by the high tariffs resulting from the Smoot-Hawley Tariff Act, Congress passed the Recovery Trade Agreement Act that gave the President a period of up to three years within which he was authorized to implement substantial tariff concessions of up to 50 percent of the existing rates.

These federal programs eventually had positive economic effects. Hopes rose that the depression was over and that the massive monetary and fiscal plans of the government would pull the country out of its malaise. By 1937, the economy and the financial markets were apparently healthy and stable as business activity and confidence began to improve. Unfortunately, this was only an illusion.

By 1938, after more than five years of steady business recovery, the fragile world economy began to tumble. Much of the excess capacity accumulated from the early 1900s was not completely liquidated by the depression, and debt liquidation had not yet run its course. The strain of excessive government taxes on both consumers and businesses, coupled with a new wave of European loan defaults, initiated a second economic collapse and panic during 1937 and 1938.

While this represented the final downward phase of the depression, and was not as severe as the 1929 to 1933 period, it proved sufficiently severe to reignite fear in the financial markets and cause significant labor unrest in many of the already hard-hit basic industries. In the midst of this final stage of the depression, labor began to demand government protection from the disastrous effects of long-term unemployment. Congress responded by ratifying the Wagner Act of 1937, which allowed collective bargaining and forced business management to recognize and deal in good faith with bona fide labor organizations.

To further ease the plight of labor, significant progress was made in the area of social reform. The Fair Labor Standards Act of 1938 prohibited interstate commerce of any goods produced by companies employing minors under 16 years of age. It also set a maximum standard workweek of 40 hours and permitted overtime work at the minimum rate of time and a half.

The second and final downturn of the depression proved uncharacteristically short-lived as the government began to sharply increase the money supply in preparation for World War II.

During the war years, the government's primary objective was to insure the availability of funds necessary to support the conflict. From 1941 to 1945, the money supply increased from less than $40 billion to more than $100 billion. While this occurred the government imposed strict price controls and rations to stabilize prices. With no products to buy, most of this new money was eventually invested in United States government Treasury bills and Treasury bonds. As a consequence, the yield on Treasury bonds fell to 2½ percent and the yield on 90-day Treasury bills to ⅜ of 1 percent. *At no time in the history of the United States did the nation save at such a high rate as during World War II.*

As the war trough came to a close in 1945, the United States emerged as the unequivocal leader of the free world. It had a powerful and growing industrial base untouched by the war, while Europe and the Far East were in shambles. In addition, the U.S. possessed most of the world's gold and capital, a strong and stable currency, and a powerful and sophisticated military machine with the finances to support it. The United States was highly self-confident, and decided to capitalize its status in the postwar recovery.

## A NEW WORLD ORDER

The first priority of the U.S. government was to promote the reconstruction of Europe and Japan in order to protect itself from the threat of Communism. In addition, our government decided that it was imperative that the world monetary system be redesigned with the United States dollar, not gold, as the principal medium of world trade. It was rationalized that since the dollar was backed by a huge gold hoard it should be considered as good as gold.

By 1944, when it became apparent that the Allies would win the war in Europe, earnest preparation began for the reconstruction of Europe and the establishment of a new world monetary system. In late 1944, world political and financial leaders, led by the United States delegation, met in Bretton Woods, N.H., to establish the basis for a new economic order that was to remain intact for the next 25 years. After many weeks of debate, our allies reluctantly accepted both the economic and monetary proposals of the United States without amendments. Actually there was little choice, since they wanted to get their countries back to normal as quickly as possible.

*The new monetary system was to be an awesome responsibility for the United States. Each world currency would have its value tied to the value of the dollar, which, in turn, would be tied to the price of gold at $35 an ounce. In addition, the United States monetary authorities would be required to carefully control the volume of dollars in worldwide circulation in order to stabilize the price of gold within normal limits and fulfill its economic commitments to Europe.*

Immediately following the war, the U.S. government set about implementing the Bretton Woods agreement. In the first 10 years, the United States contributed over $40 billion in goods and services to its allies through a series of lend-lease programs that effectively removed most European war debts. The United States also directed an additional $8 billion toward relief programs through the United Nations and other international organizations. In 1947, Secretary of State Marshall proposed and helped pass a program calculated to make the 16 participating countries of Europe, including West Germany, economically and militarily self-supporting. During its first four years of operation, the Marshall Plan gave outright grants of nearly $12 billion to western Europe, which was largely used to rebuild plants and equipment in war-torn France, England, and West Germany. During the two decades after World War II, the United States gave a total of more than $8 billion in economic and military aid through the Marshall Plan. *Through these programs, America gained de facto* control of the world's financial and monetary purse strings, and set about exploiting this power.

By the early 1950s, the growth phase of the present Kondratieff Cycle (Figure 8) was well on its way. American business was beginning to emerge into the world arena on the coattails of United States power and prestige. As in all prior long-term cycles, however, economic growth took more than 10 years to gather momentum.

The decade of the 1950s might be generally characterized as a period of cautious growth in business and in the conservative economic and

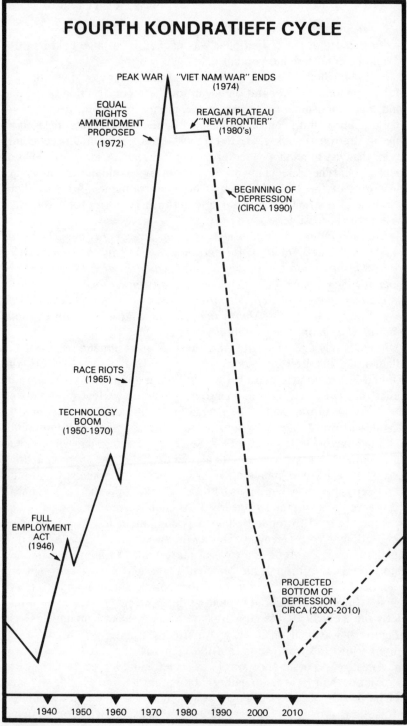

# FOURTH KONDRATIEFF CYCLE

PEAK WAR

"VIET NAM WAR" ENDS
(1974)

EQUAL
RIGHTS
AMMENDMENT
PROPOSED
(1972)

REAGAN PLATEAU
"NEW FRONTIER"
(1980's)

BEGINNING OF
DEPRESSION
(CIRCA 1990)

RACE RIOTS
(1965)

TECHNOLOGY
BOOM
(1950-1970)

FULL
EMPLOYMENT
ACT
(1946)

PROJECTED
BOTTOM OF
DEPRESSION
CIRCA (2000-2010)

1940    1950    1960    1970    1980    1990    2000    2010

**Figure 8.**

fiscal policies of the government. The Eisenhower Administration was primarily concerned with unwinding the world's monetary excesses generated by World War II and the Korean War.

There was a postwar inflation of double-digit proportions during the first two years of his administration, but by early 1954, it had fallen to the extremely low level of less than 1 percent per year. By the end of the mid-1950s the advantages to the United States of a dollar-based monetary system were becoming increasingly apparent. As we shall see in more detail later, this arrangement effectively enabled the dollar to be used as a reserve asset along with gold in both the Federal Reserve and foreign central banks. These dollars could only accumulate in foreign central banks as a result of net positive import purchases by American consumers.

*The United States immediately became the only country in the world that could run balance-of-trade deficits and not experience a drain on gold bullion reserves.*

Since dollars pay no interest to foreign central banks, most of them preferred to hold United States Treasury bills and Treasury bonds as reserve assets. This arrangement thus enabled foreign central banks to help pay for our domestic budget deficits and resulted in a sharp reduction in U.S. interest rates. *The major misgivings of most foreign leaders accepting this plan were that at some future date U.S. authorities would abuse this privilege by running large foreign trade and domestic budget deficits and that too many dollars would be printed, causing worldwide inflation.*

Throughout the 1950s, the average yield of long-term U.S. bonds rarely exceeded 2½ percent, and 30-year home mortgages were easily obtainable at a rate of 3½ percent or less. These low rates were achieved even though the Federal Reserve kept the growth of the money supply well below 2 percent during the Eisenhower Administration. With interest rates low and inflation mild, confidence returned and the massive industrial capacity of the U.S. began to slowly expand in domestic and foreign markets. By 1957, U.S. exports reached over 20 percent of total world exports. However, when the unemployment level reached a national average of more than 6 percent during the 1958/1959 mini-recession, demands began for a more aggressive monetary posture.

## THE RETURN OF LIBERALISM

In the 1960 election, the basically conservative position of Eisenhower was largely duplicated in the campaign platform of Vice President

Richard M. Nixon. Presidential candidate John F. Kennedy's platform was in full opposition. His campaign centered on a theme of "getting the country rolling again" and portrayed Nixon's ideas as being indifferent to the needs of the poor and disadvantaged and complacent regarding the threat of Soviet expansion internationally. His proposed New Frontier program employed Keynesian economics to further solidify American world leadership, using the monetary and fiscal policies of the U.S. to solve the world's problems. Kennedy stated that economic growth, not tax increases, would provide the massive federal revenues necessary to accomplish these plans.

Immediately after winning the election in 1960, Kennedy instructed the Federal Reserve to significantly loosen its tight credit policy. During the three-year period of his presidency, the money supply rose 50 percent faster than it did during the Eisenhower years. In addition, Kennedy initiated new fiscal policies. His social programs increased welfare transfers and public works projects. Investment tax credits and generous depreciation allowances stimulated business and lowered import tariffs, which enhanced world trade. These measures, combined with the tax cuts of 1963 and 1964, gave the economy a euphoric boost and "proved" to doubters that the key to endless, noninflationary prosperity was found in the sophisticated, well-timed use of monetary and fiscal policy. Although it required about two years to become visible, the Kennedy and Johnson Administrations were to see major domestic and international booms lasting virtually unchecked from 1963 to 1970. This was one of the greatest boom eras in American history.

World trade increased with the general relaxation of trade barriers. The Trade Expansion Act of 1963 and the increasing demand for foreign imports by the American consumer created new import/export businesses in the U.S. These primarily included international banking concerns based in the financial district of New York and its environs.

By the early 1960s, the U.S. began to run huge international balance-of-trade deficits. These were incurred primarily to finance NATO rearmament, commitments to developing Third World nations, and investments by American businesses abroad. The last was chiefly in the form of real estate and stock ownership in western Europe. Huge dollar balances were accumulated by overseas financial institutions and foreign central banks. In 1963, it is estimated that of the $40 billion in balance-of-trade deficits the U.S. accumulated since the war, $31.5 billion was used to buy our Treasury bills and Treasury bonds by public and private foreign institutions to largely fund our many domestic welfare programs. This large and growing investment figure, which exceeded $6 billion in 1964, became a source of great concern since many European leaders feared the Americanization of Europe.

In 1963, when Lyndon Johnson replaced the assassinated Kennedy, business activity was just beginning to accelerate. With the tax cut of 1964 increasing capital expansion in business, consumer spending, and the growth in state and local government for Johnson's Great Society public welfare programs, the nation's economy was showing the first signs of financial instability.

## THE VIETNAM WAR "BOOM"

With the expansion of the Vietnam War in 1966, the situation became progressively worse. In 1967, defense spending increased by more than $15 billion and, for the first time since World War II, totaled more than 10 percent of the gross national product. By late 1968, with increased war expenses and the accelerating costs of maintaining a wide range of social programs, government credit demands began to conflict with those of business. Rates on long-term bonds and Treasury bills approached 7 percent, and the rate of inflation approached 6 percent.

The economy was in a huge economic and speculative boom. Housing prices were advancing sharply, and the stock market was exceeding all-time highs almost on a monthly basis. Brokerage firms could not keep pace with the heavy volume of trading as both institutional investors and the public were buying stocks in record amounts. Most respected economists assured the public of the soundness of Keynesian economic principles and of the safety precautions taken by the Federal Reserve that would continue to allow the nation not only to solve its domestic problems but also the problems of the rest of the world.

Immediately after the election of President Nixon in 1968, a mild recession was orchestrated to try to cool the overheated economy. This recession was quickly truncated by the increasing financial demands of the war and social spending programs. When the Federal Reserve again pumped both currency and credit into the economy, a surge in consumer buying was ignited, based on the fear that inflation was out of control. This rapid infusion of currency and credit continued until 1973, causing worldwide prices of commodities and labor to accelerate to historically high levels. From 1970 to 1974, the price of copper went from $.50 to $1.50 per pound; soybeans advanced from $3.50 to $12.90 per bushel; and sugar advanced from $.05 to $.66 per pound. Inflation-hedge investments in real estate, diamonds, gold, silver, antique art, furniture, and most other "real" items became highly popular with investors.

Companies purchased large quantities of raw materials in far greater amounts than their needs on the assumption that there would be greater shortages later as goods became more scarce. This reinforced the perception that the real cause of inflation was a shortage of production rather than an overabundance of demand. This in turn caused a worldwide capital spending boom and further heightened the costs of labor and materials. *Labor unions demanded and received huge wage increases and automatic inflation adjustment clauses in their contracts. When the labor unions realized that inflation was consuming these wage increases, they felt cheated. The labor force became resentful and labor productivity declined sharply.*

As the prices of most goods and services continued to rise to higher levels, many investment "experts" began recommending greater use of leverage as a method of counteracting the destructive effects of inflation. Horror stories such as the great German hyperinflation of the early 1920s were told to add credence to their theories. The panic-stricken public ceased rational investing and started speculating.

It became common during this period for investors to heavily buy "real" items, especially residential and commercial real estate, leveraging with 10 to 20 percent down payments in anticipation of being able to sell in the future at significantly higher prices. Banks made huge profits on these deals and encouraged speculation. In the California residential home market, it was not uncommon for a qualified person to buy millions of dollars of real estate using only a signature as collateral. *This widespread purchasing on credit greatly aggravated the already over-extended financial markets and forced the cost of money to the highest levels in American history.*

## THE POSTWAR RECESSION

By early 1973, the Federal Reserve was becoming greatly concerned. The U.S. had been running huge balance-of-trade deficits during the war years, and the dollar was sinking to new lows on a regular basis. American prestige abroad was at a postwar low, and there was widespread discussion of replacing the U.S. dollar as the unit of world trade with a combined basket of currencies from the strongest nations. The cost of the Vietnam War and the resulting social unrest continued to tear the nation apart both emotionally and economically.

Beginning in the spring of 1973, the Federal Reserve began to systematically withdraw funds from the banking system in an attempt to cool off the economy. It was not until early 1974 that this policy had any noticeable effect. Inflation stubbornly persisted above double-digit levels, and though interest rates were climbing to new highs, the nation's credit demands remained undiminished. To make matters worse, Organization of Petroleum Exporting Countries (OPEC) increased the price of crude oil by more than 400 percent. At the same time, the Watergate scandal was about to force Richard Nixon out of office.

By the summer of 1974, the combination of tight Federal Reserve credit policies and the weaker financial position of the economy broke the markets. The resulting 1974/1975 Kondratieff primary recession represented two of the most traumatic years the American public had ever experienced. Stock and commodity markets crashed with startling quickness, causing a panic in the business community. Those who were highly leveraged were particularly hard hit. The gross national product fell sharply. Unemployment reached more than 8 percent, the highest level in more than 20 years. The government's "safety net" of unemployment programs became a severe drag on the economy as a sharp decline in government tax revenues ensued. Copper fell from $1.50 to $.50 per pound, and sugar fell from $.66 to $.08 per pound.

The stock market eventually lost more than 60 percent of its value. The real estate market dried up since there were few buyers, even at greatly reduced prices. Finally in mid-1975, the economy was sufficiently cleansed to allow it to enter the plateau period of the cycle.

For fear of severe political disruptions, the 1975 recession was prematurely ended with the massive money-creation policies of the Federal Reserve. The economy had reached the panic stage, and the public demanded relief from this unaccustomed suffering. Taxes were cut, and huge foreign loans were given to England and Italy to help stabilize the international situation. New York City was bailed out by federal loan guarantees.

## THE CARTER DEBACLE

Starting in mid-1975 and continuing through 1976, national confidence began to slowly re-emerge. The stock and bond markets made good upward progress and both long- and short-term interest rates fell to significantly lower levels. The dollar strengthened, and the inflation rate retreated to less than 6 percent—down from its 12 percent high in 1974.

In late 1976, Jimmy Carter was overwhelmingly elected on a Populist Conservative platform. He promised to significantly reduce government spending on both defense and social programs, balance the federal budget, and bring inflation under control. The public was now convinced that government could no longer solve the nation's economic and social problems by printing money and by spending for welfare programs. It longed for the past when inflation was low and life did not change so quickly. President Carter's prescription for positive economic growth to heal the ailing nation was simple: 1) reduce government interference in the economy to the lowest possible level, and 2) reinstate autonomy in the markets to private enterprise and the individual.

However, by 1977, it was evident that the Carter Administration was not going to fulfill the mandate of the electorate. Whether Carter was influenced by the still strongly liberal Congress, the international banking lobby that had become immeasurably powerful during the past two decades, or by his lack of understanding of either the nature of or the solution to the problem, he perpetuated the highly inflationary monetary and fiscal programs of the previous three Presidents. *The Carter era marked a series of seemingly irrational programs that alternately expanded and contracted the economy, eventually producing unprecedented inflation, huge trade deficits, a deteriorating dollar, high oil prices, and, ultimately, worldwide economic chaos.*

Domestic expansion was fueled by the familiar combination of federal budget deficits and easy credit policies with their highly inflationary consequences. Carter rationalized his change of heart by stating that since the unemployment rate averaged higher than 8 percent and the nation's gross national product averaged no less than expected levels, intolerable social burdens should not fall upon those weak sectors of the economy least capable of bearing them. During the four years of the Carter Administration, the country experienced a combined federal deficit of more than $18 billion, an inflation rate of over 17 percent, a prime rate of 20 percent, a level of unemployment over 8 percent, and a price of gold that climbed from $100 to $850 per ounce, with the coincident depreciation of the dollar.

Foreign reactions to this American debacle ranged from "outrageous" to "almost criminal." There was increasing disparagement abroad because of America's lack of discipline and its decline in geopolitical power. By the end of the Carter Administration, American prestige and influence overseas were at their lowest level in 60 years.

## THE REAGAN ERA

In 1980, Ronald Reagan, elected by a landslide, reflected America's disappointment with Carter. Reagan ran on a platform of 1) reducing federal interference in the domestic economy, 2) balancing the budget, 3) strengthening the dollar, 4) lowering interest rates, and 5) reducing the inflation rate. These represented all of Carter's promises and his failures.

During his first six years in office, Reagan made significant progress in solving many major economic problems. The rate of inflation fell from 17 percent to less than 1 percent. The prime rate fell from 20 percent to nearly 7 percent. The stock market almost doubled its old high of 1050 established in 1968 and early 1973. Reagan's only significant unsolved task during his second term in office was the reduction of the federal deficit and the resolution of the international trade imbalance.


## CONCLUSION

We are well into the latter stages of the fourth Kondratieff Cycle in the United States. All the basic indicators are in place. The current cycle's growth phase, which began with the termination of the Great Depression by World War II, ended with the Vietnam War peak inflationary blow-off in 1974. The post-Vietnam War recession in 1975 was typically severe and served as an economic introduction to the present plateau period. *During this plateau, we have experienced, as expected, the reinstatement of a conservative government, the steady abatement of inflation, the rise of isolationism and protectionism in world markets, and generally stagnant world economic growth. Internationally, we are presently in the midst of a debt crisis in which most of the credit extended to weaker countries is no longer being repaid. We are also witnessing the first stages of a major flight of risk capital from increasingly unstable countries into stronger countries, especially the United States.*

Similar to all final stages of the plateau period, much of this investment capital is presently finding its way into the stock markets of the strong countries. As we shall see in the next two chapters, this, of course, will have a negative impact on inflation-hedge investments, such as real estate, precious metals, and most commodities, which reached their peaks earlier in the cycle.

Our projections indicate that this plateau period will last until the late 1980s, when a serious international financial panic and depression should develop. Depending upon the final level of overextension, our best forecast is that the world economy should be able to remain intact until 1987 or 1988. However, it is virtually impossible to predict the exact termination date of a plateau. In any event, prudence in investing and conservative life-styles are strongly recommended for the duration of this cycle.

*"Oh, the farmer is the man,*
*the farmer is the man*
*Lives on credit till the fall.*
*With the interest rate so high*
*It's a wonder he don't die*
*For the mortgage man's the one*
*That gets it all."*

—Populist Song, 1896

# Chapter IV
# Power Cycles and Real Estate

## THE "BEST" INVESTMENT

It is estimated that real estate comprises more total value and public participation than all other investments combined. This is largely because, during the present Kondratieff Cycle, the financial rewards of investing in real estate have been truly outstanding. It is estimated that during the past 40 years, the average commercial and residential properties increased on average over 1,000 percent on a nonleveraged basis. Since most properties were bought with a mortgage or some other form of leverage, many real estate investors achieved even greater gains.

Beyond its obvious financial rewards, the popularity of real estate as an investment is greatly enhanced by the wide range of financial and legal options available to the investor. Because real estate investment is usually free from most of the controls and regulations of federal and state government agencies, both the method of ownership and the financial terms of buying and selling property can often be creatively structured without costs or delays.

Perhaps even more important is the strong emotional appeal that real estate generates in the minds of property owners. To many investors, the financial rewards of real estate investment are of secondary importance to the feelings of stability and power achieved by ownership. This is no doubt a direct result of the evolution of property ownership in Western civilization. From the times of the earliest civilizations, land holdings were always equated with power and wealth. This was especially true during the feudal period in Europe when all properties were held by either the nobility or the church. It was then broadly recognized that only by the private ownership of land could the common man hope to further his standing in society and protect himself and his family from the unpredictable whims of a landlord.

With the evolution of democratic forms of government, the dream of private ownership of property became a reality. In fact, many early constitutions demanded that the public always be guaranteed the right of private ownership of land, along with the right to vote and the right to a fair trial.

The public often pressured government to grant special dispensations in the areas of taxation and financial incentives to a wide range of real estate interests. It was rationalized that only by broadly based private ownership of land could hard-won freedom be assured. This is especially evident in the history of real estate ownership in the United States.

In 19th-century America, strong government support for real estate ownership was especially evident in the settlement of the Western states. As government offered farmland to the public at low prices, legislated protective tariffs to reduce foreign competition for our farm products, and supported the building of a vast array of roads, canals, and railroads for the distribution of farm products to the Eastern states, real estate and real estate-related investments prospered above all others.

As society progressed from an agricultural to an industrial base, the emphasis on government support for real estate shifted from farms to cities. Throughout the 20th century, both federal and state governments systematically granted generous tax subsidies, passed lenient building codes, and issued government-guaranteed loans to a wide variety of urban property developers and residential homeowners. In this rapidly changing society, homeownership was increasingly looked upon as the stable foundation upon which the family was based. It was rationalized that if families could attain a respectable place to live, all society would benefit. It eventually became accepted as a duty of governments to provide each individual the opportunity for home ownership.

Through these government-backed incentives, commercial and residential real estate construction grew to become the largest industry in the United States. As a result, huge fortunes were made in real estate investment. A careful perusal of one of the most recent issues of *Forbes* magazine, featuring the 500 wealthiest individuals in the United States, confirms that the largest percentage of individuals who made the bulk of their fortunes over the last 30 years did so in real estate.

Mesmerized by the size and scope of these huge profits, real estate investors have deluded themselves into believing a continuation of the boom in real estate is virtually assured. Many used the last recession to buy up bargain properties on high leverage in anticipation of a resumption of an inflation-induced rise in prices. *However, most of these investors are unaware of the fact that real estate investments have long-term boom-and-bust cycles that closely parallel the long-term economic cycles of the Kondratieff Wave.*

## THE CYCLICAL NATURE OF REAL ESTATE

To better understand the cyclical nature of real estate prices, it would perhaps be useful to carefully examine the real estate component of the Kondratieff Wave.

In the idealized real estate cycle (Figure 9) that begins at the lowest point of the depression phase of the Kondratieff Wave, prices and investment in most sectors of the real estate market are at historical lows. The nation is attempting to regain confidence after the financial and social devastation caused by the depression. Real estate acquires an extremely bad reputation as an investment since the vast majority of people with real estate holdings were severely hurt as prices dropped. Although most forms of real estate are selling at a small fraction of previous values reached during the last cycle peak, investors are either financially unable or too frightened to make investments. With long-term mortgage rates in the 2 to 3 percent range, and many properties priced at historically low levels, the real estate market eventually stabilizes and a new cycle emerges.

Initially, real estate activity lags behind overall economic recovery because of the glut of distressed properties that stubbornly continue to depress the market.

As the real estate cycle progresses further into the cautious stage of its growth phase, residential activity begins to lead the real estate market out of its long period of relative stagnation. The public slowly regains confidence, emphasizing the upgrading of family standards of living by

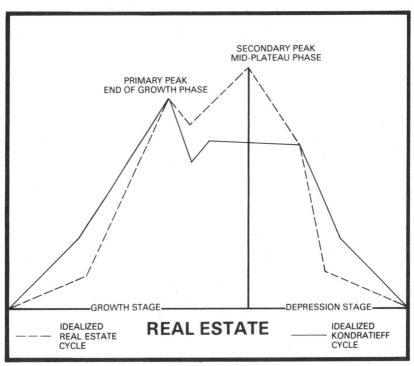

**Figure 9.**

buying a new home. In this initial stage of the cycle, homebuyers are often aided by government-subsidized mortgage loans and low-cost housing projects.

As the economy continues to expand into the second decade of the growth phase, business activity measurably increases and unemployment levels reach historically normal levels. With confidence restored and money to spend, a widespread buying spree for products of all kinds soon envelops consumers. As the demand for goods eventually outstrips supply, shortages begin to appear in key sectors of the economy and deliveries become delayed. This increased demand eventually produces a massive building boom as plant capacity is increased to meet demand. Capital spending for manufacturing plants and commercial offices is greatly assisted by a general relaxation in the monetary and credit posture of the government, allowing financial institutions to expand their lending base. *The prime beneficiary of this credit expansion is the real estate industry.*

By the middle stages of the growth phase in the Kondratieff Cycle, the real estate markets are starting to show the first signs of euphoria.

In the residential markets, consumers continue to purchase new homes at an increasingly accelerated pace since employment levels remain high and debt accumulation low.

On a value basis, home purchases are at their highest level in the long-term cycle because mortgage rates remain at their cyclical lows and land, construction materials, and labor continue to be relatively inexpensive.

Investment in commercial construction also becomes increasingly attractive. Business continues to expand, building sites become more scarce, and commercial real estate values are forced to continually higher levels. Also increasing the attractiveness of real estate is the fact that the rate of inflation significantly exceeds the rate of increase of both long-term interest rates and property taxes.

## SPECULATION RUNS RAMPANT

As the top of the growth phase approaches following some 20 years of sustained prosperity, real estate investment begins to become more speculative. Prices continue to advance with only mild corrections, and the prospects for continued business expansion appear bright. This encourages bankers to lend money to an even broader spectrum of real estate projects. These loans increasingly require smaller and smaller down payments and in many cases use only the building and underlying land as collateral. The confidence of lenders is usually reinforced by the growing support of the real estate industry by the government. These government-sponsored incentives usually include guaranteed, low-cost mortgages for the needy; favorable capital gains and investment-tax incentives for apartment and residential construction projects; and an even wider variety of large-scale, government-financed or guaranteed construction projects.

As the economy enters the last stages of the boom, speculation in real estate accelerates, inducing additional waves of optimism. Businessmen, investors, and even formerly conservative mortgage bankers become caught up in the euphoria. A conservative rate of return is no longer the criteria for the purchase of real property, since a continuation of price appreciation is taken for granted.

This self-feeding trend of continually higher levels of real estate prices proceeds in a fairly orderly manner until the accelerating inflation of the peak war. Peak wars always cause a sharp escalation of real estate prices and mortgage interest rates in a relatively short period of time. With the outbreak of war, labor costs accelerate as the most productive members of the labor force are reassigned to war-oriented occupations. In order to accomplish war-related objectives as quickly as possible, the government must significantly increase the nation's money supply so that higher wages can be paid. Of course, the results are high inflation rates and an increasing scarcity of labor and building materials.

The prices of real estate eventually skyrocket, especially those of undeveloped land and marginal business properties that had heretofore not participated in the boom. Eventually, credit demands by the government to finance its massive spending programs begin to conflict with the credit needs of businesses and consumers. This forces the costs of mortgage rates, construction, and labor to record levels, causing many formerly profitable development projects to become economically unfeasible, and sets the stage for the downward adjustment of real estate in the postwar recession.

Immediately after the war, the nation experiences a sharp but short-lived recession as the government attempts to combat inflation with tight monetary and fiscal policies. The postwar recession is especially devastating to the real estate industry as the prices of all real estate investments fall sharply from their speculative highs. Many of the more "aggressive" investors and businessmen, burdened with little cash and highly leveraged properties, are quickly forced into bankruptcy.

As the economy moves into the plateau period, it soon becomes apparent the real estate boom is far from over. Because of a general fall-off in construction as a result of the wartime shortages of men and raw materials, there is a shortage of commercial and residential buildings to support the needs of returning soldiers and businessmen flush with war profits. Furthermore, interest rates and construction costs have fallen to levels not seen since the middle years of the growth stage cycle. With both personal and business debt at relatively low levels and the financial system flush with money, homes are easy to buy and buildings easy to construct.

Residential construction is especially aided by the exceptional increase in the consumer's buying power as food costs fall much faster than both retail costs and wages because of the sharp decline of commodity prices at the wholesale level.

The revival of the residential real estate markets soon spills over into the commercial real estate markets, precipitating a second and usually more powerful real estate boom than the one that occurred at the cessation of the growth stage. Business activity recovers, and general prosperity returns. This further encourages individuals to buy their own homes. Near the final peak of the real estate cycle, most new home-owners incur high-cost mortgages on overvalued properties.

Usually near the middle of the Kondratieff plateau, the real estate markets again become saturated and begin to selectively turn down.

As we shall see, the California boom of 1865, the Florida boom of 1925, and the most recent California real estate boom of 1978 reached their peaks in the middle of postwar plateaus in the last three Kondratieff Cycles.

Throughout the remainder of the plateau, real estate prices continue to soften primarily as a result of high mortgage rates and low inflation rates. Eventually, as the plateau slips into depression, the high level of personal and business indebtedness begins to create severe problems for most mortgage holders. Since real estate is typically an illiquid investment, the process of mortgage liquidation is agonizingly slow. Both borrowers and lenders tend to hold on to their properties, assuming that the depression is only a sharp correction characteristic of the mild recessions of the growth phase.

*Most of these investors have never seen hard times and are completely dumbfounded. Many are unaware that real estate prices are declining, since there are no market quotations for residential or business property. Weaker interests face immediate foreclosure. Most of these properties are reluctantly taken over by banks or other financial institutions holding the mortgages. Properties in somewhat stronger hands continue to be held because of owner unwillingness to take a loss and the expectation of a market reversal.*

As the slow process of mortgage liquidation occurs, only a handful of new building projects are initiated, and unemployment in the building trades greatly surpasses the national average. Attempts to stimulate construction by deunionizing the labor force and reducing wages only result in further bankruptcies. These occur because reductions in the costs of new building reduce the values of older properties, which were built in a time of higher material and labor costs.

Near the end of the depression, many holders of unprofitable real estate throw their properties on the market in panic. At this point, real estate prices become so low that in many instances they fall below the value of tax payments due on the properties. This causes even properties that were unencumbered to be liquidated. Patient investors typically can purchase these properties for pennies on the dollar. Eventually, when the excesses of the real estate market accumulated during the growth phase are washed out and a new set of values are instilled in society, the market stabilizes and enters the next long-term up cycle.

## AMERICA'S FIRST REAL ESTATE CYCLES

In the first complete real estate cycle starting in the early 1790s and reaching its peak around 1820, the primary thrust of real estate activity revolved around the settlement of the frontier territories through population growth and expansion. Two significant governmental policy decisions helped this migration.

In 1793, in a final moment of bitterness for its loss of America as a colony during the Revolutionary War, England refused to forfeit most of its forts and outposts located in the Great Lakes region of the Northwest Territories. In August 1794, the United States militia, under the leadership of General Anthony Wayne, overwhelmed an alliance of Indian and British soldiers at the Battle of Fallen Timbers and drove the alliance into Canada. In its aftermath, America and England signed the Treaty of Greenville, which officially ceded to the U.S. most of what is now Michigan, Wisconsin, Illinois, Indiana, and Ohio, together with 16 enclaves, including what are now the cities of Detroit, Chicago, and Cincinnati. For the first time, the frontier east of the Mississippi River was free of all threats of British or Indian encroachment. American pioneers and farmers immediately began to swarm into the West in unprecedented numbers.

In order to facilitate an orderly settlement of the West, the Public Land Act of 1796 was ratified. This act called for the systematic surveying of the frontier into townships, sections, and acres, and effectively set the pattern for the settlement of the American West. It also stipulated that no land could be sold unless it was properly surveyed and had legal title. With a sound legal system for the private ownership of property, and the promise of a new life with unlimited opportunity, droves of Americans moved West. In the next two decades, a major portion of the Northwest Territory was settled. Its cities grew rapidly in both numbers and size. By 1805, the populations of Chicago and Detroit increased over 100 percent, and by 1812, they more than doubled again.

In early 1802, due to the Napoleonic Wars, France was experiencing severe financial difficulties. In order to raise money, Napoleon transferred ownership of the Louisiana territories of the western Mississippi Valley to the United States. The $10 million price of the Louisiana Purchase was perhaps the greatest land bargain in American history, and succeeded in opening up the nation's heartland. Settlers quickly began pouring into the Mississippi Valley at an even faster rate than the migration into the Northwest Territory. Aided by generally rising prices during the growth phase of the real estate cycle, farming quickly became a profitable business, causing premium prices to accrue to choice farm properties.

By 1810, many of the most popular areas of the Mississippi and Ohio River Valleys were beginning to experience a real estate boom of historic proportions. In the major cities, well-situated properties were becoming scarce, forcing the prices of commercial and residential real estate to continually higher levels.

Real estate investments soon became speculative as bankers from the East lent money to increasing numbers of marginal borrowers for a wide variety of building projects. Collateral requirements were sharply eased, and conservative rates of return no longer became the criteria for the purchase of real estate investments. As speculation on price appreciation accelerated, properties were often bought and sold several times in one day.

With the advent of the War of 1812 and the high demand both in England and France for war-oriented raw materials, the nation's inflation rate skyrocketed. This sent the already overextended real estate markets into a speculative frenzy that was not to abate until 1815. From 1810 to 1815, the average price of a farm more than doubled, and select farm properties increased many times more.

In early 1815, banks became so overextended in speculative real estate loans that by the end of the year, a liquidity crisis that eventually initiated the next postwar recession ensued. Frontier immigration ceased abruptly. Many real estate properties experienced foreclosures. Farmers were especially hurt, suffering a sharp drop in property values, as well as a fall in crop prices. From 1815 to 1818, the wholesale prices of farm products dropped over 60 percent with most of the decline occurring in the first two years.

By late 1817, the financial panic subsided as the nation entered the postwar plateau. Migration resumed its westward thrust, this time aided by government-sponsored canal and road-building programs. During this plateau, money in circulation increased only gradually, and the rate of inflation was remarkably stable. Crop prices actually declined, and the prices paid for farm and business properties remained relatively constant.

By 1826, the economy again slipped into depression. Real estate prices declined sharply in a self-feeding spiral characterized by forced sales and foreclosures. Prices continued to decline until the late 1830s, when a brief speculative flurry of real estate activity in Chicago and Cincinnati turned into the panic of 1837, one of the most severe real estate crashes in American history. Prices were to continue downward until the bottom of the depression in the late 1840s.

The second long-term real estate cycle began near the trough of the Kondratieff Cycle of 1846. After the culmination of the short war with Mexico, the U.S. added most of what is now Texas and California to the Union. A migration into these territories soon followed. The migration into northern California and Oregon territory was spurred by the discovery of gold and silver in 1848 and 1849. Backwoodsmen and farmers who could not find a livelihood on the prairies and arid high plains packed up their covered wagons and headed for the Pacific states via the Oregon Trail in the North and the Gila Trail in the Southwest deserts of Arizona and New Mexico.

By the early 1850s, over 10,000 wagons and more than 42,000 people had registered at Fort Laramie in Wyoming to begin the westward trek. In 1850, the government greatly aided the westward movement by passing a bill to make a wide range of land grants to railroad companies, enabling them to construct a vast railroad network in the West. *It is estimated that from 1850 to 1856, more than 20 million acres of choice Western land were granted to these railroad companies.* The total trackage in the West increased from 9,000 miles in 1850 to over 25,000 miles by 1857. This program opened up the vast riches of the Western states to the markets of the world, and set the stage for the great land boom of the Civil War era.

As the railroads interconnected farming, mining, and ranching production in the West with the consuming industrial interests of the East, the wealth of the nation grew exponentially. As a reflection of this prosperity, credit needs became immense as consumer demand for goods began to increase the costs of money and raw materials.

## LAND PRICES SHOOT UP

The rising costs of real estate property were particularly evident. Public land prices in many of the key Western states increased over 600 percent between 1850 and 1857, while real estate loans more than doubled. Even the former unfarmable plains states were beginning to develop into highly productive grain-producing centers as new irrigation and harvesting techniques were perfected. The prospects of farming appeared especially bright due to the steady rise in prices of most crops. Between 1857 and 1859, the average price of a bushel of wheat rose from $.93 to $2.50. Farms were also selling for record prices. By the advent of the Civil War, the nation was in the midst of a real estate boom of record proportions.

By 1860, the financial system was beginning to overheat. Mortgage rates exceeded 10 percent, and inflation was beginning to run out of control. When the Civil War broke out in 1862, the government proceeded to immediately triple the money supply in the banking system. The prices of most products, including most real estate investments, increased correspondingly. Throughout the country, and especially in the newly developed Western states, land speculation ran rampant. This was especially true in those cities and towns destined to benefit from the building of the first transcontinental railroad.

In July of 1862, President Lincoln signed the Pacific Railway Act, which provided for the railroad's construction by the Union Pacific and the Central Pacific railroads. The contract stated that as partial payment for building the railroad, the government would pledge alternate sections of public land from 10 to 20 miles wide on either side of the track and loans of $16,000 to $48,000 per mile for every mile completed. By the end of the war, railroad fever ran high. Property speculation accelerated in communities located in the path of the railroad.

After the Civil War ended, the nation was forced into a typical postwar recession. The Treasury tightened credit, and a severe banking crisis was precipitated. The value of land declined over 50 percent, and farm prices collapsed. By 1867, however, the economy had stabilized and entered the reconstruction plateau. The real estate boom was once again under way, this time fueled by an increasing level of European capital flooding into the real estate markets, and an increasing demand for homes and farms by returning soldiers.

However, by late 1869, real estate speculation again peaked, and the prices of most properties began to slowly decline. Four years later, the entire economy began to turn down as massive debts began to stifle economic activity. Money became scarce, and the economy drifted into a depression that lasted until the turn of the century. From 1872 to 1879, real estate lost over 59 percent of its value, and by 1880, over 70 percent. Once again, farmers were especially hard hit as the old problems of declining land and crop prices played havoc with their profits. This time the problem was greatly magnified by the huge glut of farm produce entering the market from the large number of new farms started during the real estate boom of the previous two decades.

Throughout the depression, government fiscal and monetary stimulation implemented to raise crop prices had little effect. When it became obvious that even massive federal support could not hold up property prices, the real estate panic of 1892 began. This crisis lasted until 1896 and forced the prices of most properties down to pennies on the dollar. Over half of the nation's farms and many real estate investments fell into receivership. The property market was once again at rock bottom.

## BEGINNING OF A NEW CYCLE

When the post-Civil War depression bottomed out around 1896, the real estate market was once again positioned to begin the next up-leg of a new cycle. Debt levels were historically low, and mortgage rates were in the 2 percent range. Real estate prices were low because of the many distressed properties flooding the market.

A radical change in the demographic structure of the country was also becoming apparent. The U.S. initially evolved from a predominantly rural-agrarian economic base. The emphasis was now being shifted to heavy industry and an urban-based economy. Thus, the general focus during this real estate cycle shifted from farming and the settlement of the frontier to urban commercial and residential properties.

From the beginning of the cycle through 1910, building construction expanded fairly rapidly. The construction of new commercial buildings and apartments grew about 10 percent a year. This demand was greatly enhanced by a huge influx of immigrants from Europe and western Asia and the migration of many unsuccessful farmers from Southern and Midwestern rural areas to the cities in search of work.

In New York, Chicago, Philadelphia, Detroit, and Boston huge urban housing projects were relatively easy to finance, since mortgage rates continued to remain low and credit was easily obtainable. By 1915, the nation, especially its Eastern cities, was in a massive real estate boom.

When the country began preparing for World War I, property rentals and the prices of real estate investments began to move up sharply because of a shortage of acceptable accommodations. The boom was greatly aided by a huge increase in credit that had been generated to finance the war effort. As the resulting inflation hit the already euphoric real estate market, the prices of choice properties doubled and even tripled. By 1919, most people became real estate speculators to some degree, and many were using very high leverage.

As the inevitable postwar recession hit in 1920 and 1921, the real estate boom was temporarily dampened. Mortgage rates were forced to historically high levels, and money became scarce. However, by the end of 1922, the recession was over and the boom was once again in full swing. Soldiers returned from Europe in need of homes, and businessmen were ready to expand. With usable buildings in such short supply and the cost of money and credit relatively low, prices began to rise.

From 1921 to the peak of the building cycle in 1925, the volume of new building construction increased almost 400 percent. Much of this construction was financed by the growing use of highly leveraged, long-term mortgages. By the end of the real estate cycle, one-half of all families owned their own homes through a mortgage. Since the maximum mortgage period was 10 years, second and third mortgages were commmonplace.

By 1925, the demand for real estate was satiated, and the pace of building construction began to turn down (Figure 10). From 1926 to

1929, the volume of construction fell over 30 percent. With the inflation rate in the 1 to 2 percent range and mortgage rates at historically high levels, investors began to transfer their capital away from real estate and into the exploding stock market.

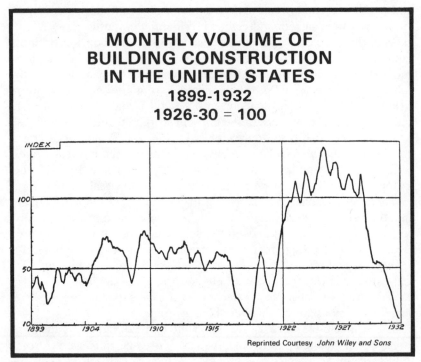

**MONTHLY VOLUME OF
BUILDING CONSTRUCTION
IN THE UNITED STATES
1899-1932
1926-30 = 100**

Reprinted Courtesy *John Wiley and Sons*

**Figure 10.**

With the onset of depression, marked by the panic of 1929, the real estate market was already in trouble. From 1926 to 1929, buyers became increasingly scarce and mortgage money extremely tight. Many lower-quality or heavily mortgaged properties could not be sold at any price. The real estate market had almost dried up. During the next three years, prices continued steadily downward with only weak and sporadic rallies. By 1932, the first and by far the worst wave of the depression was over, leaving in its wake a host of lost real estate fortunes.

Residential and commercial real estate prices fell to less than 20 percent of their former values. Foreclosures on all types of property were common. With the election of Roosevelt and the implementation of the New Deal, the government immediately attempted to aid financial institutions holding shaky mortgages by monetary and fiscal stimulation. It also tried to assist investors who lost an unprecedented amount of equity in their real estate holdings. In 1932, Congress created the Home Loan Bank, which provided liquidity in the form of money and credit. Investors, in turn, used their mortgage portfolios as collateral for the loans.

In 1933, Congress provided direct aid to most homeowners threatened with foreclosure by creating the Home Owners' Loan Corporation. This provided low-cost direct loans to those who were unable to maintain mortgage payments and were about to lose their homes. In 1934, Congress passed a bill to allow for the creation of the Federal Housing Administration (FHA) to guarantee the mortgages of a wide variety of qualified potential homeowners. This program effectively reduced the cost of home ownership and significantly reduced the risk of lending for financial institutions holding the mortgages.

A few years later, the Federal National Mortgage Association (FNMA) was formed to create a secondary mortgage market on a national scale. FNMA agreed to purchase mortgages from privately owned national mortgage associations, such as insurance companies and corporate pension plans. FNMA not only furnished the depressed real estate market with much needed liquidity, but more importantly, it also "institutionalized" the mortgage market on a national level.

Unfortunately, the continuing severity of the depression counteracted most of the immediate benefits of these programs. By the late 1930s, most real estate prices remained near their lowest levels. There were still plenty of excess mortgage debts that needed liquidation.

## POSITIVE EFFECTS OF WAR

With the involvement of the United States in World War II in the early 1940s and the Korean War a decade later, the stagnation stage of the depression was prematurely terminated. Historically, trough wars are characteristically mild conflicts and tend to marginally reverse the downtrend in general price levels. However, both of these wars proved to be very expensive, requiring a vast amount of financial, human, and material resources to resolve them. This huge and rapid injection of money and credit into the economy had the effect of shortening the depression and prolonging the subsequent growth phase by about 10 years. This effectively stabilized the collapsing real estate market and set the stage for one of the greatest and most prolonged real estate booms in American history.

As with all prior long-term real estate booms, this one started out slowly. The 1950s were typical first years of the long-term real estate cycle. The country was, for the most part, cautious and conservative. Because of the huge increase in the nation's monetary base, most of the world's economic and political leaders expected a new postwar depression similar to the one occurring after World War I. Because of this, Congress legislated the Full Employment Act of 1946, in which the government assumed responsibility for maintaining full employment regardless of the prevailing economic conditions.

In addition, Congress embraced the economic theories that advocated the use of the full fiscal and monetary powers of the government to "manage" the economy by stimulating it out of the recession at the first hint of difficulties. These programs were very effective during the early phase of the growth stage. Debt burdens and interest rates remained low, and liquidity high, creating a strong underlying demand for real estate investments.

In effect, the period of the 1950s and early 1960s was a time of social and economic tranquility not seen since the early days of the 1900s. During this phase of the cycle, real estate investments were generally stagnant. This was because inflation remained in a range of 1 to 2 percent, and there was still a glut of vacant properties on the market.

The only real impetus for investing in real estate came from the wide range of federal tax incentives and mortgage underwriting programs for homeowners legislated during the depression. Because the yields on most mortgages were extremely low by historical standards, financial institutions preferred to continue investing in more lucrative areas, such as the stock market and the reconstruction of western Europe.

However, in the middle stages of the growth phase—the early to mid-1960s—the real estate boom began to accelerate. It was greatly aided by the unique combination of a postwar baby boom of unprecedented proportions and a massive migration from the cities to the suburbs. This stimulated a great demand for residential and commercial construction projects. For political expedience, the Kennedy and Johnson Administrations decided to favor real estate in general and residential housing in particular as prime beneficiaries of their relatively accommodative monetary and fiscal policies. To accomplish the goal that every American should have adequate shelter, both Presidents initiated programs encouraging the purchase of commercial and residential properties. Aided by the housing lobby led by the National Association of Home Builders, the U.S. Savings and Loan League, and supported by a heavily liberal Congress, a series of Congressional acts aimed at direct subsidization of residential housing was quickly passed.

In 1965, the Department of Housing and Urban Development was created to administer programs such as the Government National Mortgage Association (GNMA), which created securities out of private pools of mortgages fully backed by the United States government and insured by the FHA and the Veterans Administration (VA), and the Housing Act of 1968, which gave special treatment to low- and moderate-income families. Under Section 235 of the Housing Act, which applied to housing, and Section 236, which applied to apartments, interest payments were largely subsidized. Many poorer families purchasing their homes under this program paid only 1 percent of the average 7 percent mortgage rate. This essentially made a gift of residential homes to the vast majority of welfare recipients. *In order to pay for these housing projects, the government aggressively printed money, substantially increasing the national debt level.*

In addition, investors in high-tax brackets used Section 236 in commercial building projects as a tax shelter because of the accelerated depreciation allowed. These advantages encouraged the creation of a huge new tax-shelter industry, and induced a growing number of institutional investors and individuals in high-tax brackets to use their assets to meet the demand for funds to finance real estate purchases.

By the end of the decade, so much money and credit was pumped into the system that inflation began to accelerate the rise in both construction costs and land values. Investors were beginning to buy real estate solely for its appreciation potential. As an example, between 1964 and 1970, home prices nearly doubled.

Just when it seemed there would be no end to the real estate boom, the economy began to show signs of financial stress.

By the early 1970s, it became apparent that the economy was in severe trouble. The costs of the Vietnam War and the government's social reform programs overstimulated the economy, and significant financial disintegration in several key areas was obvious. As the war intensified in the early 1970s, both Congress and the Nixon Administration became reluctant to reverse spending levels, and inflation began to explode. Interest rates soared to prohibitively high levels as it became evident that the government was losing control of the economy.

In response, the government desperately tried to stabilize the economy by implementating monetary ease, credit crunches, massive budget deficits, and a sharp depreciation of the dollar. With the dramatic oil price increases in 1973 and 1974 by the newly formed OPEC cartel, inflation exploded in a speculative frenzy not seen since the postwar hyperinflation of the early 1920s. As a result, the average price of a home again doubled by 1974. In desperation, monetary authorities subjected the nation to a particularly painful postwar recession beginning in late 1973 and lasting until the early months of 1975. Unemployment rose to very high levels, and many of the more leveraged and under-capitalized business and real estate ventures declared bankruptcy. New York City nearly went bankrupt. However, the postwar recession eventually ended in 1975 with most real estate properties showing remarkably minor price declines.

## CHANGING ATTITUDES

As mentioned earlier, one of the characteristics of a real estate cycle is a subtle but definite shift in basic attitudes toward life. The liberal values of the growth phase become conservative during the plateau phase. As mentioned in Chapter III, the growth phase of the current cycle was much longer than that of the three previous cycles due to the brevity of the depression stage. This accommodated a much greater than expected overextension in long-term debt accumulation in the real estate market and other areas, such as municipal bonds and international credit. As a result, many of these powerful, politically sensitive sectors became institutionalized. Lobbies were created to prolong easy credit policies at all costs. In effect, Jimmy Carter was elected President in 1975 on a populist-conservative platform promising to reform government spending policies and alleviate suffering brought on by the destructive effects of runaway inflation.

After only a short time in office, Carter was overwhelmed by these special-interest lobbies, and reinstated the promiscuous monetary and fiscal policies of his predecessors. Within a short time, the midplateau real estate boom was once again in full swing, greatly aided by the demand generated by returning Vietnam War veterans seeking home-ownership.

Second-generation individuals of the post-World War II baby boom who reached the prime home-buying ages of 25 to 35 also contributed to this demand. The demand, coupled with a new concept of real estate as an increasingly popular inflation hedge and supported by a wide array of favorable tax breaks, seemed to almost guarantee that it would be a highly lucrative investment venture.

By early 1976, the average price of a new home rose to over $45,000, a 12 percent gain from the prior year. Real estate speculation was becoming a major topic of conversation at many social gatherings. Even inaccessible and arid parcels in the deserts of Arizona and New Mexico were bid up to record prices on the assumption that land was becoming increasingly scarce.

By 1976, the volume of mortgage loans offered by savings and loan associations exceeded $60 billion per year from their cyclical lows of less than $5 billion in 1950. Many of these loans were offered with exceptionally good terms, such as small down payments and greatly reduced income requirements. These were justified by the fact that price appreciation was greatly exceeding the rise in wages.

With the general economic recovery relatively stagnant and corporate and personal loan demands relatively low, financial institutions, flush with money, continued to put an ever-increasing percentage of their available funds into diverse real estate mortgages and building projects. By the end of 1976, the economy had completely recovered from the postwar recession, and real estate speculation was again expanding to record levels.

High-rise office-building projects in the sunbelt states of California, Arizona, Texas, and Georgia were common. Limited partnership interests in other projects were greatly oversubscribed, making huge profits for real estate developers and promoters. Closing sales was easy since buyers had only to witness the astounding price appreciation of the past decade to accept the financial viability of a project. Multimillionaire developers and general partners abounded. Enrollments in real estate schools rose to record levels as individuals wanting to "get rich quick" flocked into the real estate profession.

In 1976, the government was becoming increasingly concerned by the excessive speculation in the real estate markets. The purpose of the social welfare legislation of the 1960s—to enable all Americans to own their own homes—was being destroyed by the massive inflation-induced price appreciation of residential housing. Under the assumption that most of this excessive appreciation was caused by speculation, a desperate Congress passed the Tax Reform Act of 1976.

Perhaps the most significant feature of the Tax Reform Act was the ruling that interest and taxes paid during construction could no longer be deducted as a current-year expense. Instead, companies were forced to deduct their expenses over 10 years on a straight-line basis. This immediately reduced the number of investors in high tax brackets who used the initial tax write-off benefit in most tax-shelter programs. Secondly, the act reduced the remaining maximum interest expense deduction from $25,000 to $10,000 per year and cut the maximum capital loss to only $10,000 a year. This particularly hurt those investors currently buying residential income properties as investments, since these properties do not usually yield a positive net income before taxes.

A third feature of the act forced all depreciation in excess of that determined using the straight-line method to be taxed as ordinary income when the property was sold. This effectively discouraged many tax-shelter projects that employed accelerated depreciation as a key promotional feature.

These features, along with significant reductions in initial write-off provisions in limited partnership arrangements and the tightening of rules regarding the expensing of vacation homes, dampened the investment appeal of many real estate projects. However, the real estate boom still contained a great deal of upward momentum.

By 1977, the real estate market was euphoric. The median price of homes reached over $73,000 and was expected to go higher. Many mortgages were now being offered to those buyers who had not qualified a few years earlier. Financial institutions were beginning to develop a wide range of schemes to increase the attractiveness of mortgages. Such creative financing as gradual-payment mortgages, with small down payments and large balloon payments in later years (when it was assumed the price of the house would be much higher), were devised. Other mortgage packages were created with the buyer assuming second and even third mortgage commitments.

Perhaps the most innovative scheme was the mortgage pass-through developed by the Bank of America for the active California housing market. In essence, it packaged mortgages in the form of bonds that were sold to the public much like Real Estate Investment Trusts (REITs), a real estate investment vehicle made popular on Wall Street in the middle to late 1960s. These and other money-raising schemes provided an almost limitless source of money with which to finance the continued boom, and major participation in its expansion shifted from the institutions to the public. In 1977, the average price of a home in Orange County, California, skyrocketed from over $55,000 to $83,000, a gain of 50 percent from the previous year.

With the phenomenal increase in prices, the real estate market became a haven for speculative capital. It was common practice for investors to "trade up" by using their increased equity as a down payment on a new and more expensive home. Some investors became multihome-owners, renting the bulk of their properties for below market rates in anticipation of selling the properties at higher future prices. The degree of leverage used in these deals was as astounding as the profits. Many banks issued loans with no down payment, using only the underlying building as collateral.

By 1978, the frenzy that until this point was confined to the major metropolitan areas now spread to small cities and towns. Condominiums and undeveloped raw land began to replace commercial and residential real estate as the area of major interest. The real estate markets were becoming greatly overpriced and speculative, especially in view of the sharp increases in interest and the inflation rates.

In response to this frantic upsurge in real estate prices, Congress passed the Revenue Act of 1978, designed to further dampen speculation. Although the Revenue Act included special allowances for older home-owners by lowering the age and increasing the amount at which a once-in-a-lifetime exemption on capital gains tax could be exercised, its real purpose was to shift investment appeal from real estate to other areas, such as the stock and bond markets. A significant reduction of capital gains taxes on all personal investments and a corresponding reduction of corporate tax rates opened up many new areas for venture capital that were previously disadvantageous from a tax standpoint. This sharply increased corporate profitability and earnings, and gave a further impetus for capital formation, especially for venture capital in many newly emerging high-technology industries.

## THE FED STEPS IN

In addition to these fiscal policies, the government asked the Federal Reserve to exert its influence by tightening the amount of credit available to the public for real estate speculation. By the end of the spring of 1980, mortgage rates exceeded 18 percent and credit became available to only the most credit-worthy borrowers. The midplateau peak of the real estate market for this cycle was at hand.

In late 1980, the nation overwhelmingly elected Ronald Reagan President on a hard-line conservative platform, which included as its key points, reduced government spending, tax cuts for business, reduced interest rates and inflation, and deregulation measures that removed a great deal of government control over the economy. More importantly, tight credit policies initiated by the Reagan Administration in 1981 and 1982 squeezed out many of the economic and financial excesses of the Carter era and accelerated the downtrend of real estate prices that had gradually started in early 1980.

## CONCLUSION

During the past few years, all indications suggest that the real estate cycle in the United States completed its midplateau peak in 1980 and made rapid progress into its predepression mode. As expected, both the inflation rate and business activity stabilized at much lower levels, and much of the excessive optimism that assumed continued price appreciation of real estate properties started to evaporate. This is most visible in the huge glut of office space and unsold or uncompleted homes in the suburbs of high-growth areas.

In the residential real estate market, it is estimated that over 15 million homeowners bought new and resold homes during the peak years of the real estate boom of the late 1970s and early 1980s. (Figure 11). Many of these new homeowners paid highly inflated prices at historically high mortgage rates. Based on long-term economic analysis, we estimate that at present the average residence is approximately 40 percent overvalued, financed mainly with high-risk mortgages using a wide variety of "creative" financing methods. Presently, many of these homeowners, especially those who purchased their homes at high leverage as a speculation on capital appreciation, are finding it increasingly difficult not only to make mortgage payments, but also to resell their homes for amounts close to purchase prices. For many owning the more "aggressive" creative mortgages, balloon payments are beginning to come due, raising payment rates and forcing many homeowners into foreclosure and bankruptcy.

These investors are beginning to realize that the real estate market is suffering from the great number of for sale signs visible everywhere. Many of these signs have been there for a long time. They are also beginning to become aware of the increasing number of magazine articles focusing on the outstanding potential of the stock and bond markets, and increasingly downplaying real estate investments. A periodic drop in mortgage rates is still able to generate a flurry of activity by anxious homebuyers easily coerced by increasingly desperate real estate salespersons encouraging home purchases in a "last chance opportunity" before home price and mortgage rates go higher, but an even larger number of potential new homeowners are beginning to realize that the outlook for substantial price appreciation is diminishing as inflation continues to remain low and mortgage rates remain at near-record levels.·

The commercial real estate market also seems to be experiencing severe stress. Vacancy rates of office buildings in many of the major cities of the nation are approaching the 40 percent level, as the market becomes glutted from the record number of new buildings erected during the peak years of the cycle. As a result, net rents in cities across the country have declined anywhere from 5 to 60 percent.

Even more importantly, many of these commercial projects are designed to initially produce a negative rate of return on the investment even if fully occupied, based upon the assumption that expected future price appreciation from inflation will result in an eventual overall profit. As the normal upsurge in inflation that usually accompanies the recovery in the economy has failed to materialize, there is a growing feeling by many property developers that something is amiss.

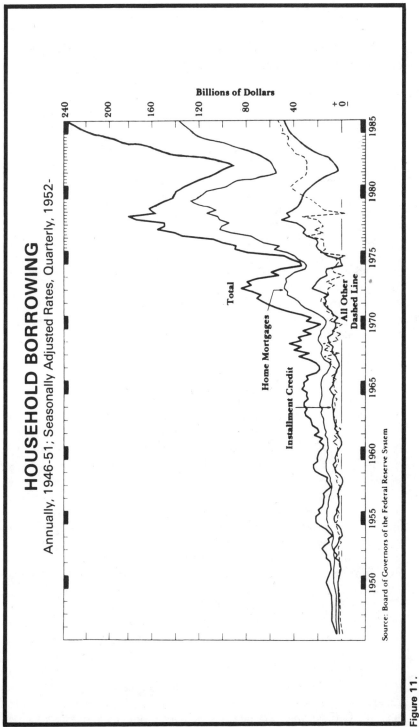

# HOUSEHOLD BORROWING

Annually, 1946-51; Seasonally Adjusted Rates, Quarterly, 1952-

Billions of Dollars

Total

Home Mortgages

Installment Credit

All Other
Dashed Line

240

200

160

120

80

40

+0−

1985

1980

1975

1970

1965

1960

1955

1950

Source: Board of Governors of the Federal Reserve System

Figure 11.

Of particular concern to these investors is the historically high rate of interest that most of them must pay to service their debts and finance their day-to-day operations. Let's assume the real rate of interest is the prime rate minus the rate of inflation. If the prime rate is 11 percent, and the prevailing inflation rate is 4 percent, the real rate of interest is 7 percent. Historically, whenever the real rate of interest exceeds 3 percent, borrowers are paying premium prices for financing. With the prime rate presently at 8 percent and the inflation rate at a minus 1.5 percent, the real rate of interest is an historical high of 9½ percent. This places tremendous pressure on most of the marginal and highly leveraged commercial properties.

*In the immediate future, we expect the real rate of interest on mortgages to increase to even higher levels as market risks become more pervasive.* This should cause many real estate projects to become even more financially unfeasible and effectively discourage the formerly huge inflow of domestic and foreign capital into them. Most of this new money will probably enter an alternative investment, such as the money markets, where the rate of return is higher with much less risk. Many real estate investors are beginning to realize the advantage of liquidity after having been caught with a leveraged property in the 1980/1982 real estate panic. The virtual impossibility of finding either a buyer or mortgage money even in a modestly bad recession will not soon be forgotten.

*Of equal importance to the expected decline in real estate prices could be the rapid decline in the flow of new capital from institutions involved in limited partnerships and tax shelters.* During the past seven years, it is estimated that the total volume of tax-shelter investment has increased over 500 percent.

We are now seeing a significant reduction in the tax benefits these projects generate. This year, it is highly probable that both Congress and the Internal Revenue Service will enact more stringent rules regarding depreciation methods. In that event, many existing partnerships would not be able to collect the remainder of their scheduled contributions. This, of course, would spark a round of defaults that could result in a collapse of the tax-shelter industry similar to the REIT collapse in the early 1970s.

At present, many investors are surprised when they receive Internal Revenue Service notices stating that their real estate tax-shelter deductions are being disallowed. This is in accordance with the new tax laws passed by Congress in 1981, 1982, and 1986, which gave the Internal Revenue Service power to end tax-shelter abuse. This was especially apparent in the recently passed Tax Reform Act of 1986. Although the act failed to completely cancel the investment attractiveness of tax-shelter investments, it did go a long way toward closing many of the cherished tax loopholes that have allowed the industry to thrive over the past 15 years.

Perhaps the most important feature of the new tax bill is its treatment of accelerated first-year tax deductions. In prior years, syndicators were allowed to take big deductions for accrued interest that was not actually paid until the underlying mortgage came due. Hefty deductions for future costs to the partnerships could also be written off in the first year.

The new law replaced nearly all of these "front end" writeoffs primarily by changing the rules regarding depreciation. Beginning in 1987, the use of accelerated depreciation for non-residential property will be replaced by the mandatory use of straight line depreciation. In addition, the former 19 year depreciation schedule will be replaced by 27½ year schedule for residential and 31½ year schedule for commercial real estate.

To make matters worse, the rules regarding losses from both commercial and residential real estate ventures are no longer deductible against taxable income from interest, dividends, or other sources of income. This will be especially unfavorable in view of the decline in the deductions against a maximum tax rate of 28% and 34% as opposed to a maximum rate of over 50% under the 1984 tax act, and the rise in the capital gains tax rate from the former 20% to the 28% to 34% brackets.

Owner-managers are permitted one valuable exception. A loss of up to $25,000 yearly is deductible from "passive" income, defined as that from interest, dividends, and labor, provided the owners adjusted income, at the bottom of the first page of Form 1040, is less than $100,000. The deduction lessens as income rises from $100,000 to $150,000, where it disappears.

From our analysis, the enactment of this bill forced commercial property values down between 15% and 20%. We expect the long-term effects to be even more devastating as investors begin to assess the financial damages incurred in real estate tax shelter investments and seek remedies in the courts. The effects of such broad-based litigation should be sufficient to make both lenders and potential investors cautious enough to greatly diminish real estate activity for the duration of the plateau, and of course, well into the depression phase of the cycle.

## WHAT THE FUTURE HOLDS

For the remainder of the plateau, we expect that the average real estate investor will become increasingly uncomfortable with owning a nonincome-producing property and begin reducing the price, hoping for a sale. As prices continue to stagnate and in many cases decline, the small number of buyers who are able to purchase properties will begin to postpone their purchases, waiting for even lower prices. Formerly optimistic investors will show less urgency and adopt a wait-and-see attitude. Many formerly aggressive mortgage-lending institutions will become more selective in their lending practices and begin to require larger down payments and more stringent income requirements. Many investors who hold on to their properties may consider renting in order to ease their losses. This will persuade many would-be buyers to rent and will tend to reduce demand even further. As prices continue to decline, properties will be increasingly placed on the market as anxious investors actually begin to experience an equity loss. In panic, these investors will attempt to dump their properties at the purchase price.

However, buyers at that price will not be easy to find, causing many owners to be stuck with unsalable properties. Any consideration to further reduce the price of their investments will be postponed, since losses incurred by selling below the purchase price cannot be recovered. The option at this juncture is to keep the property and hope for recovery or foreclosure. Those long-time property owners who have experienced equity appreciation during the previous period (50 percent and more) will not be greatly affected in the early stage of the collapse and will not contribute to the initial real estate crisis. Since they represent the majority, mortgage loan companies will view early foreclosures as a temporary problem. Even builders and developers who are holding large blocks of unsold homes will not panic, since they have witnessed all this before. Bankruptcies will be as numerous as they typically are in recessionary economic times and will not cause great concern.

Unfortunately, during the economic transition from the plateau to the depression phase, these concepts will abruptly change when the real estate market spirals into chaos, causing prices to plummet in response to reduced economic activity and high unemployment. Investors and homeowners will begin to walk away from their properties in increasing numbers. Banks and other financial institutions will be stuck with properties they cannot dispose of and which are losing value at an increasing rate. As their portfolios of unsold property begin to build up, the management practices of most financial institutions will begin to be intensely scrutinized. Many who are undercapitalized or have made too many bad loans will be forced into bankruptcy.

As the news of these banking problems spreads to the public, large deposit withdrawals will increase, putting even greater pressure on finance companies, leading to even more failures. Particularly hard hit will be mortgage lenders specializing in second and third mortgages, and the construction industry. The availability of financing for construction will cease to exist, and all but a handful will not survive even the first year of the crisis. With no demand for these inventories of unsold homes and buildings and an almost nonexistent supply of money to finance projects, the building trades, along with the wide range of associated businesses, will disappear. Historically, the highest level of unemployment of all industries during depressions is found in the construction industry.

Somewhere near the bottom of the first and probably most severe downwave of the depression, the government will be forced to interfere to halt the financial ruin that the real estate market and the economy as a whole will be experiencing. Up to this point, the government will not have realized the severity of the problem. *Governments usually correct problems only after the fact, long after most of the damage has already taken place.* In effect, most of the government's early attention will be concentrated on the problem of feeding the populace and providing adequate medical care.

As a first step, in order to boost public confidence, the government will probably greatly increase coverage of FDIC and FSLIC insurance, consolidate many distressed institutions into their stronger competitors, and begin to supply funds to the banking system in increasing amounts. In order to relieve pressure on the homeowner, some form of mortgage assistance, especially for the elderly, poor, and unemployed, will undoubtedly be passed. Since interest rates will probably be somewhat lower than the actual mortgage rates for most homeowners, government-backed refinancing schemes will become popular. On the state and local levels, property taxes will undoubtedly be greatly reduced. Large tax credits for new homebuyers might be employed to support the building industry. There is no doubt that the real estate industry will come under increased scrutiny and regulation, similar to the securities industry during the last depression.

Eventually, these programs will prove effective and the rapid decline in real estate prices should moderate. By this time, we expect most properties might be purchased at discounts of over 80 percent of their predepression prices for those investors with cash or acceptable collateral. Since it is probable that after an extended period of economic stagnation lasting up to 10 years, the real estate market will resume its plunge to new lows, most conservative investors might elect to continue to shun real estate for an indefinite period no matter how attractive property prices and financial terms appear.

By the start of the next growth phase, low-risk purchases should again become commonplace, and long-term commitments will again be prudent. At this point, select investments in high-quality properties should again allow the conservative investor to make sizable profits throughout the duration of the next upswing in the long-term real estate cycle.

*"Civilizations maintain their strength and stability as long as the gold content of their currency remains relatively uniform. Only during the latter years of their existence, when they begin to debase the gold content of their monetary units, do they lose power and prestige and fall to ruin."*

—Douglas Kirkland

# Chapter V
# How Gold, Currency, and Credit Affect Investment Opportunities

## THE POWER OF THE GOLD STANDARD

In the most primitive civilizations, the primary method of exchanging goods was simple barter. As society progressed, a more efficient method of trade became necessary. The principle of using a single commodity as a medium of exchange between buyer and seller was eventually conceived. This "money" represented a significant step in the development of a standard measure of value for trading purposes.

Commodities, such as cattle, salt, tobacco, and seashells represent a few of the numerous instruments that at one time or another assumed the role of money. Eventually, gold became the most popular form because it possessed all the natural physical and chemical properties necessary to give it a stable value. It was extremely durable, easily transportable, and could be divided into smaller portions without altering its value. Its high market value gave it a great intrinsic value allowing large transactions to be conducted with relatively small amounts. Above all, gold could not be created on demand, having to be extracted from the ground at a high cost. Governments thus had great difficulty increasing their money supplies, thus causing the artificial stimulation of their economies through inflation. For these reasons, gold became essential to the stability of early civilizations.

As economies increased in complexity, gold coins and gold bullion formed the basis of commercial trading systems. Gold was either coined in a pure or nearly pure monetary unit and used in the actual exchange process, or melted into bars as a store of value in conjunction with other mediums of exchange, such as grain, cattle, silver, or nonprecious metal coins. These developing civilizations recognized that a basic requirement of money was that its intrinsic value be kept constant. Eventually, all of the major civilizations of the pre-Christian era used gold as their basic form of money. So popular and widespread was its use during that era that there evolved a remarkable standardization of size and weight of gold coins in many culturally and geographically separate nations. Nearly all of the 20 major civilizations that existed during this period determined a standard weight ranging between 120 and 140 grains of gold per gold coin, with over half being exactly 130 grains.

Many other forms of monetary exchange, including barter, were used extensively alongside gold. Still, gold was always preferred as the medium of exchange whenever it was available. These civilizations maintained their strength and stability as long as the gold content of their currency remained relatively uniform. Only during the latter years of their existence, when they began to debase the gold content of their monetary units, did they lose power and prestige and fall to ruin.

As trade expanded, gold increasingly became the principal medium of exchange in international transactions. One of the first dominant participants in world commerce was the Byzantine Empire. At the height of its power around the 10th century, the Byzantines dominated world trade from the Atlantic Ocean on the West to China in the East. One significant reason for their success was the widespread respect for the quality of their basic monetary unit, the gold solidus. Eventually, world trade was largely integrated under a single system via their gold coins.

The Byzantines were a wise people. They understood that the continuation of their political and economic power depended on a solid monetary system based upon the use of gold coins and gold bullion. Their domination of international trade evolved in two phases. First, great efforts were exerted to establish and maintain a continual supply of gold from mining. Second, high-quality gold coins were allowed to directly interact with other coins in world markets. If a competing nation attempted to corrupt its coins' value, traders would refuse them, accepting instead the solidus. Thus, corrupt governments were soon discredited, isolated from social and economic interactions with their neighbors, and eventually drifted into financial chaos and revolution.

By the start of the second millenium, most of Europe and the rest of the civilized world had adopted the Byzantium-based gold standard as their principal method of domestic and international trade. However, due to the frequent reduction of the gold and silver content of many of the nations' gold coins by ruling monarchs, dwindling confidence in many of the existing governments retarded economic stability and prosperity. After numerous instances of monetary corruption, the public rebelled and in many cases forced the monarchs to preserve the value of the currency by maintaining a more constant weight of gold and silver. By the middle 1500s, most powerful nations were on a strong and stable gold- and silver-based monetary system in which gold was used almost exclusively to settle trade imbalances between countries.

As the world entered the age of mercantilism and industrialization, nations progressed to higher levels of social and economic sophistication. It gradually became necessary to expand the exclusively gold-based system to include paper currency. Initially, paper currencies were written promises to pay in gold or silver on demand and were used strictly to facilitate large domestic transactions. In this system, the gold and silver backing the contract was safeguarded by the issuing financial institution. As the volume of the transactions became greater, government-backed gold and silver paper currencies became popular. In time, practically all transactions were conducted in paper currencies, with most of the gold and silver held in government treasury vaults in bullion form.

Since it was assumed that not all notes would be redeemed simul-taneously, the issuance of paper currencies soon exceeded the amount of gold on deposit, and the fractional reserve banking system was born. The amount of paper currency that could be circulated without being fully backed by gold depended on the political and economic stability of the issuing bank or government. If a paper currency was printed irresponsibly, investor confidence would be shaken and the populace would redeem their deposits for gold and silver to an extent that the issuers could not meet the demand. In this instance, the issuer was forced to either suspend redemption and close its doors, borrow gold from another source to supply the demand, or suspend the issuance of additional paper currency. Thus, when a nation employed a gold-backed currency, gold acted as a discipline against the indiscriminant printing of paper money.

As more extensive trading developed, so did the fundamentals of an international gold exchange standard. In a gold exchange standard, the currencies of all participating countries are redeemable in gold at a fixed price. When a country imports more than it exports, it runs a balance-of-payments deficit, causing gold to flow out in settlement. The subsequent reduction in the domestic money supply causes a contraction in the internal demand for goods that in turn causes the prices of goods and imports to decline and economic and political instability to increase. Over time, the level of exports rises as goods become cheaper and gold flows back into the country, setting an economic recovery in motion. In this way, the gold exchange standard creates discipline in world markets and effectively promotes economic and political stability.

Periodically, countries were forced to go off the gold standard, such as when vast quantities of paper currency were printed to finance a war. The result was inflation, which devalued the currency and increased the value of gold and other commodities. International trade was disrupted because currencies no longer had a fixed value and were subject to wide fluctuations and manipulations by governments. Eventually, a gold standard was by necessity re-established, allowing stability to return to the world financial system.

Understanding these interactions of money in the form of gold, currency, and credit is perhaps the single most important driving force underlying the Kondratieff Wave. In the following idealized cycle of currency, credit, and gold, it is instructive to watch how these three investment mediums interact to create the monetary basis for the idealized Kondratieff Cycle presented in Chapter II.

## THE THREAT OF COLLAPSE

During the final and usually most violent stages of a depression, the nation's economic and financial structure is often on the verge of collapse. Since government leadership is completely discredited, there is usually a widespread concern for the political survivability of the country. Unemployment is at record levels, keeping many workers from finding jobs at any wage rate. Labor unions lose power and are considered ineffective. Business and personal foreclosures and bankruptcies are at record levels. Banks are under intense pressure as huge withdrawals of gold and currency threaten their solvency. Since the public is too frightened to keep its assets in banks, hoarding of both currency and gold becomes common. In some cases, gold is shipped overseas to more stable havens. As gold and currency are redeemed from the banking system, banks begin to close their doors at an increasing rate. Eventually, even the strongest are threatened with bankruptcy. Here the natural market forces of the gold standard begin to exert stabilizing counter-cyclical influences on the collapsing economy.

To see this more clearly, assume most of the world is on a gold standard, and that the price of gold in terms of other currencies, including the dollar, is held at a fixed price. Also assume that other commodities, such as wheat and silver, are allowed to fall to much lower levels in accordance with the reduced supply and demand characteristics of the economy. This makes both the dollar and gold greatly overvalued in both domestic and international markets. In other words, the amount of goods that both the dollar and gold can buy is historically large.

The increased purchasing power of gold gives the gold-mining industry a tremendous financial incentive to explore for new deposits or mine low-grade deposits that were previously economically unfeasible. This also produces an era of new mining and ore-processing inventions that facilitate the recovery of gold from low-grade ore. By the end of the depression, gold production is soaring to record levels. This production quickly finds its way into the banking system, providing urgently needed liquidity and stability. With this new injection of gold, the government justifies the creation of additional paper currency since the integrity of a gold-backed currency is more strongly assured.

In the first few years of the expansion, the legacy of the depression casts a generally negative influence on political and financial leaders. Government becomes increasingly liberal, and preoccupied with legislation that will prevent a depressionary relapse. This legislation takes the form of measures to insure that in the event of a relapse, the banking system has sufficient authority to print currency and provide credit. This is rationalized by the belief that depressions are primarily caused by falling prices. Additional legislation is directed to the punishment of alleged depression profiteers. Usually, powerful private banks and large industrial businesses are singled out for censure and reform. *The central government always gains significant power at the expense of the private sector and the free market during the early growth stage of the Kondratieff Wave.*

As the recovery expands, the general euphoria of prosperity translates into even higher expectations. Since paper currency continues to be fully backed by gold, the government and private sectors increasingly favor more expansive monetary policies and less stringent lending practices in the public and private sectors. These easy-money policies usually do not cause weakness in the dollar because both interest rates and inflation remain low and monetary gold plentiful. Credit extension in the banking system tends to remain moderate.

By the beginning of the second decade of the recovery, the economy becomes euphorically positive since depression horrors have been forgotten by the majority of the work force. Debt levels and taxes are low, allowing the use of credit to become increasingly popular. Labor unions remain peaceful and inoffensive, employment levels are high, and wages continue to rise, allowing entrepreneurial enterprises to emerge.

But as the economy enters the second decade of the growth phase, the monetary system begins to show the first signs of stress. Consumer and wholesale price indexes start to accelerate, and the government's ability to maintain the gold standard is severely tested. Prices rise as the economy approaches full capacity, and demand for raw materials puts upward pressure on manufactured goods and labor costs. As the resulting inflation eventually forces the price level of most goods to equal and eventually exceed their parity price level with gold, it becomes undervalued in world markets for the first time in many years.

Because the purchasing power of gold is now less than most other commodities, such as silver and copper, there is decreasing incentive for gold exploration and the mining of marginal ore bodies. This causes production to decline. In a pure gold exchange standard, world production fluctuates to maintain a stable commodity price level. If gold stocks increase more rapidly than the production of other commodities, prices rise. If they increase less rapidly, prices fall. With the level of gold production rapidly slowing at this stage of the cycle, the self-correcting nature of the gold standard begins exerting downward pressure on prices, forcing the economy to contract.

In order to keep prices from falling, both the government and the private banking system encourage the formation of credit-creating schemes. Since the economy has experienced exceptional upward momentum during this period, these policies are easily implemented, causing a continuation of the economic boom.

By the latter stages of the growth phase, the credit-creating capacities of the economy reach their limit, and the economy begins to show signs of instability.

As credit extension to the banking system is sharply increased and government debts greatly expand to help finance the peak war, the dollar rapidly declines and gold begins to be redeemed from the banking system and hoarded by depositors. This puts tremendous pressure on banks to call in loans.

At this point, a nation has two options if it decides to remain on the gold standard. It can attempt to fix its basic price level with such schemes as wage and price controls, rationing or allocating goods and services to the market, or it can suffer the deflationary consequences of natural corrective forces that result from maintaining a gold standard until commodity prices fall to much lower levels. History shows that national debts incurred both prior to and during a war are so massive that the only logical avenue for the country is to suspend gold payments to depositors and remove it from the monetary system. When gold is removed, the nation is immediately liberated from the discipline required to maintain a gold standard. This allows currency and credit expansion to rise to significantly higher levels.

Exponential inflation soon follows. Since gold is now relegated to the status of a pure commodity, its price tends to immediately align with the prevailing commodity price level. This upward explosion in the price of gold is often spectacular, especially if the government appears unstable because the war involvement is more extensive than anticipated. *Countries that choose to remain on the gold standard usually experience an influx of gold from those countries that leave it, and prices tend to rise. Through this mechanism, inflation at the peak periods of the Kondratieff Wave translates into a worldwide phenomenon.*

## THE RESULTS OF INFLATION

Rampant inflation is very disruptive to most business interests. Initially, businessmen fail to understand the cause of inflation and thus have no precedent from which to derive logical decisions to cope with the problem. Most are accustomed to the stability and security accruing to contracts requiring payment in gold of a specified weight and fineness, only to see these contracts declared illegal by law. Compounding the dilemma is the popular opinion that high prices are the result of shortages. Thus government agencies are created to administer food prices and allocate consumer goods and products. In weaker countries where inflation is particularly rampant, civil disruptions occur. Often, strong centralized leadership is required to provide national stability. The rise of dictators and military control are common during this period. In such an unstable environment, gold virtually disappears (except in black markets where it usually commands a sizable premium).

Eventually, the economic and social disruptions brought on by inflation begin to abate as the war comes to a close. For most countries, the postwar recession is usually traumatic but short-lived. The recession often ends with a deflation of prices to an approximate alignment with the price of gold. In a smoothly functioning economy, this usually takes one to two years.

The public accepts the need for a cleansing recession since it believes that the economy is much too inefficient and overextended in debt. In order to correct for these perceived excesses, a conservative political leadership is elected that promises a return to an environment of economic stability and reduced inflation. The solution is usually a return to the discipline of the gold standard that stabilized the economy so well in the past.

Unfortunately, the implementation of this policy proves more difficult than expected. Of primary concern is the growing disparity in the ownership of gold bullion between the strong and weak countries of the world. As economic and political instabilities increase in the weaker countries from the massive accumulation of debts and financial aftershocks of the war years, an even larger share of the world's gold is steadily transferred to more stable nations.

In many cases, weaker countries actually transfer their physical gold into the banking systems of stronger countries for safekeeping even after they have acquired full ownership through the settlement of international trade balances. This accumulation of gold in the banking systems of the stronger countries often causes a sharp increase in their money supplies. The overexpanded money supplies often force interest rates to artificially low levels, promote stock market speculation, and generally give the public the delusion that the visible economic prosperity so characteristic of the plateau period is more solid than economic statistics indicate. Perhaps the most apparent difficulty is that this influx of money tends to keep the currency of stronger countries artificially overvalued relative to their weaker neighbors. A strong currency tends to promote imports over exports, and a severe balance-of-trade problem quickly develops.

By the latter half of the plateau, most of the financially strong countries return to a full gold standard. Consequently, world demand for the production of gold remains extremely high. Those financially weaker countries that must continue to employ a paper currency standard find it easy to sell but difficult to buy in the gold currency-based countries. This causes currency instability to accelerate to critical levels as the plateau advances toward its conclusion.

As goods produced by the strong countries remain uncompetitive in the world markets, high levels of business failures and unemployment soon begin to develop. In reaction, political pressures for trade protection arise. Concepts of nationalism and isolationism are adopted by the newly installed ultraconservative, probusiness government leadership. Significant retaliatory trade legislation soon follows. Ultimately, an accelerating trade war of devastating proportions spreads throughout the international markets. Because of the resulting collapse of international trade and commerce, debts become increasingly difficult to repay, and the likelihood of international debt defaults is greatly heightened. The fear of default forces an even more rapid transfer of foreign capital into the strong countries, causing their currencies to become even more overvalued.

Increasingly stronger trade measures soon follow these events. Eventually, when one or more of the weaker countries default on a significant portion of their international loans, the world spirals into the first stages of actual depression.

It is our observation that the depth and severity of the resulting depression is directly proportional to the level of debt and economic inefficiencies built up during the preceding growth and plateau periods. Particularly noteworthy are the size and level of world involvement in the peak war, the level of international loan commitments by both the public and private sectors, and the aggregate, domestic, long-term debt levels of business and investment interests.

When these areas of overextension are moderate, the depression tends to be an extended affair characterized by a slow but steady decline in economic activity and level of unemployment. The basic economic and social structure of the country remains intact so that social and political unrest becomes a significant problem only during the final years of the depression. In this type of depression, the gold standard is relatively easy to maintain since the participating financial interests are given ample time to adapt to the slowly deteriorating economic conditions.

Since the present generation has little direct experience with previous deflationary periods, it tends to fear inflation much more than deflation. This attitude accommodates the continuation of the conservative policies legislated during the plateau in which the chief concern is a strict adherence to a fully gold-backed monetary system. As the depression deepens and tax revenues become sharply reduced, the government makes great efforts to balance the budget by curtailing government-spending projects and interference in the economy.

These depressions are characterized by balanced budgets and a sound currency. Many business enterprises actually thrive during all but the most violent phases of the depression. As time passes, prices continue to drift down, and gold becomes steadily overvalued. Near the peak of the gold cycle, an ounce of gold might buy only 10 bushels of wheat. Near the bottom, however, it could buy 50 bushels.

## THE TRAUMATIC END

As the depression progresses into its final and most traumatic stage, severe economic and financial contractions begin to disrupt the already weakened economy. Most commodity prices continue to decline and give no indication of reversing their trend. Basic commodity producers, especially in the farming and mining industries (except gold mining), are particularly hurt, often going bankrupt. These bankruptcies spread to other industries and eventually produce a nationwide credit collapse of accelerating severity. As the panic engulfs banking and financial interests, massive withdrawals occur. Initially, most withdrawals consist of paper currency. As the panic heightens, gold and silver withdrawals accelerate.

At the height of the liquidity panic, the public demands a more inflationary posture by the government to relieve the nation's suffering. Efforts are directed toward increasing the amount of currency in circulation either by printing more paper currency or adding a second form of hard currency, such as silver, to the monetary reserves. Usually, efforts to print more paper currency are met with stiff opposition due to the fear that printing excess currency may become uncontrollable, again forcing the country off the gold standard. When currency inflation does occur, gold usually disappears from the market and is either hoarded or transferred to safer, more stable havens overseas. Attempts to use silver or some other commodity are usually met with less resistance. But this invariably produces only a moderately positive effect. These and all other reflation techniques have little efficacy compared to the natural, countercyclical effects of the gold standard.

Near the bottom of the depression, in those countries still on the gold standard, the value of gold is historically high, and new mines are rapidly being discovered. This newfound gold soon filters into the banking systems and provides the financial markets with much needed liquidity and stability. This helps drop interest rates in both the mortgage and bond markets to historically low levels, making them very attractive to entrepreneurs seeking long-term capital. Eventually, as economic and financial stability evolves, credit again becomes available, and the nation begins to experience the first stages of recovery and transition into the next growth phase of the cycle.

By contrast, in those depressions that begin from extremely over-extended economic conditions where large domestic and international debts are high as a result of a more extensive wartime involvement, extremely violent depressions can occur. The overall price level often plunges precipitously as a rapid contraction of the debt structure causes both the money supply and business activity to decline sharply.

Instead of requiring 15 to 20 years for widespread business and personal bankruptcies and bank failures to reach a critical stage, violent depressions reach this point in two to three years. Rapid depressions cause immediate high levels of unemployment, general strikes, and widespread social and financial discontent. Business activity quickly contracts. No businessman or economist could have envisioned in former times such pervasive destruction and wealth transfers in such a short period. Competent workers are unable to find jobs; creditors cannot collect on their debts, and mortgage foreclosures are common. Changes occur so rapidly and values are destroyed so swiftly that the public becomes bewildered and immobilized. Federal and state tax revenues dry up, and government institutions can barely function even at marginal efficiency.

In extreme depressions, financial industries suffer greatly. Bank failures are most common in areas far removed from the major money market centers, especially in the farming regions. Corporate and individual customers begin to withdraw their deposits from banks in these outlying regions and are only willing to conduct business with banks in the largest and safest cities. The volume of deposits in large money centers grows rapidly, giving these banks a false sense of confidence. In reality, this "growth" is merely an indication of fear. These deposits actually put the large banks in serious danger as the next wave of withdrawals, often led by foreigners and institutions, first in currency and later in gold, eventually hits them also. When it becomes evident to the remaining depositors that these money center banks are near default, a general run on the banks develops and bank holidays are declared in most states.

In desperation, the public looks for leadership to deliver them from these difficulties. Since the private sector is immobilized, the only available leadership is the government. Invariably, the political party in office is too conservative or "shell-shocked" to function in a strong leadership capacity. Thus, it is usually voted out of office or overthrown by revolution. The public often favors a leadership that represents absolute power and control. Justification comes from the belief that the previous government was a failure and that heightened government involvement is necessary for recovery.

## THE DESPERATE STAGE

The degree of public desperation cannot be overemphasized. Little consideration is given to the potential loss of freedoms that results from this decision. The new leadership accepts the mandate of the people for change and aggressively initiates a series of government-sponsored programs to relieve the crushing burdens of the deflationary depression.

The primary focus of the recovery programs initiated by the new government is most often in two specific areas. Since the major impediment to short-term economic recovery is believed to be the large debt levels still existing, it is determined that they must be reduced to much lower levels. The most immediately available avenue is depreciation of the value of currency to the point that the outstanding debt is reduced in real terms. Of course, this avenue severely hurts creditors. Yet, it is rationalized that their loans would not be repaid anyway, and it is to their advantage to be repaid in cheaper dollars rather than none at all. Historically, this scheme has proved moderately effective in the short run, but has devastating long-term implications. Currency devaluation destroys the confidence of a society and is usually never completely regained. In future crises, when the public recalls that in the past the government resorted to such radical steps, the withdrawal of gold and currency from the banking system occurs with much greater speed.

It must be remembered that the major function of the gold standard is to promote the trust and stability of a currency in the world markets. By maintaining a gold standard, society knows that corrective natural forces eventually stabilize the economy and set the stage for future prosperity. When a nation resorts to manipulating the economy for a short-term gain, it is viewed as a sign of weakness by the investment community and eventually promotes the permanent flight of capital to less risky areas.

The second major policy by the government to promote recovery is an attempt to boost the wage and price levels by a series of government interventions. Such government-sponsored programs include the implementation of tariffs to reduce imports and to support domestic production, make-work projects, farm quotas, and tax increases.

These programs are always costly. In the more stable depressions, budgets are usually in balance. During these severe depressions, huge budget deficits exist, often hindering the recovery. As a result, after a few years of short-term recovery, even more severe depressionary conditions arise. These periods closely resemble the earlier depression phase except that financial difficulties are more pronounced. There are also new debt burdens and a debased currency, leading to more extensive social unrest and a deeper distrust of government. At this point, many governments resort to an international military conflict to export their civil unrest.

Barring a complete breakdown in the political structure, the war usually fulfills its intended objective of stimulating the economy out of recession and re-employing the idle labor force. While these major trough wars typically serve their intended function of shortening the duration and depth of the depression, they also tend to create severe, long-term, structural imbalances in the economy. By cutting the depression short, the natural cleansing forces of the Kondratieff Cycle and the gold standard are kept from completing their work, allowing many structural debts and inefficiencies built into the system to remain intact throughout the next growth phase.


## THE GOLD STANDARD IN WESTERN CIVILIZATIONS

This encapsulization of the idealized, long-term, monetary cycle is based upon the financial history of gold, currency, and credit of the international financial system from the beginning of recorded history to the present, with special emphasis on the United States. While we recognize that no two Kondratieff Waves are perfectly alike, it is still easy to recognize many remarkable parallels in the interactions of money and society, regardless of advances in the sophistication of governments and financial institutions.

As we shall see in the following monetary history of gold in the United States, our country seems destined to repeat the same mistakes that invariably lead to financial panics and depressions. We begin our historical survey in England just as it was emerging from the Dark Ages.

By the mid-1500s, England was well on its way to becoming a world power and required a stable and uniform currency to support its ambitions. At that time, it maintained a relatively stable currency that was selectively corrupted over the years by the ruling monarchs so that no definitive backing by a fixed amount of gold and silver existed. In order to create a more uniform currency and bring order to the chaotic monetary system, Queen Elizabeth, in 1560, mandated that all coins be reminted and restandardized to contain a fixed weight of gold and silver. Although gold was a part of the English monetary system for over 300 years, it was considered too precious even in small amounts to be used in circulation.

Silver was the preferred metal used in day-to-day transactions, the pound sterling being valued at its weight in silver. Gold, except for that used in relatively infrequent large-scale transactions, was usually stored in the vaults of wealthy landowners and the government treasury.


## GOLD AND FOREIGN TRADE

With the rise of mercantilism in the early 1700s, the use of gold in both large-scale domestic and international transactions was preferred in the burgeoning arena of world trade. Since merchants needed coins in large denominations to buy increasingly larger shipments of goods from merchants and farmers, silver-dominated currency was eventually replaced by gold. By the early 1700s, international transactions were principally conducted in gold, and the English guinea became the principal unit of currency in England and the preferred international unit of exchange.

In 1717, Parliament issued a proclamation requiring that the value of the guinea be fixed at 21 shillings. This fixed the price of gold at 3 pounds, 17 shillings, and 10½ pence. The value of most world currencies was indirectly tied to the value of the pound through the international markets, so that in reality the world had adopted a gold exchange standard. For the next 200 years, the value of the pound was to remain virtually constant in terms of gold. During these years, England dominated the world, both economically and militarily, largely due to the strength and stability of its currency. By the middle of the 18th century, England was the undisputed leader in trade and commerce, with London the center of world banking and finance.

As might be expected, there were several instances in which the government was under tremendous pressure to devalue the pound in terms of gold. Usually these efforts to debase the currency were involved with either the trauma of financing an international war at a peak period or with pressures to inflate during the depths of depression. Fortunately, all attempts to devalue the currency were quickly met with strong opposition from intellectual, financial, and conservative interests in the Parliament. In each instance, the value of the pound was maintained. It was decided that the integrity of the government, shown through the stability of its currency, far transcended the short-term desires of the public. In retrospect, these decisions proved correct as natural market forces eventually enabled the economy to correct its inefficiencies and allowed the financial condition of the nation to improve.

Since England was the center of world trade and the pound the premier international currency, all other foreign countries, including the American Colonies, were forced to emulate the disciplined adherence to a stable gold-backed currency in order to effectively compete in world markets. This was not difficult for the Colonies since they were largely populated by former English citizens who were accustomed to a gold-backed currency.

Prior to the American Revolutionary War, bartering was the predominant form of trade in the Colonies due to the shortage of gold and silver coins in circulation. In fact, England did not allow the Colonies to mint gold coins in any form in order to insure their economic dependence. Nevertheless, by the start of the Revolution, a significant number of gold and silver coins and bullion were in reserve in the Colonies, primarily as a result of our maritime trade with the Spanish West Indies, Mexico, and South America.

Since these countries were able to mine gold and silver in great quantities, they preferred to trade bullion and coins for products the Colonies offered. The Spanish silver dollar later gave both its weight and name to the first American currency. Smuggling, pirating, and the slave trade also contributed to the silver hoard in the Colonies.

As the struggle for independence began to intensify, the restrictive economic and financial policies imposed by the English governors on the Colonies began to meet strong resistance. As pressure increased, the British Parliament finally allowed the State of New York to mint a small number of gold and silver coins and print a limited issue of interest-paying paper currency called "bills of credit," the equivalent of today's Treasury bills. Within a few years, most of the urban states began to print their own currencies, and by the start of the Revolution, approximately $12 to $20 million in currency was in circulation throughout the Colonies, half in the form of gold and silver coins and the remainder state-issued bills of credit.

With the outbreak of war in 1775, the newly formed government was immediately confronted with the task of financing the war effort. Since the Continental Congress was delegated only weak taxing powers, it was difficult to raise money from the general public. Since the new nation was considered a high-credit risk by both domestic and foreign leaders, it was also very difficult to borrow sufficient amounts of hard currency from the financial markets. In desperation, it was decided that the war would be financed by the only other means available— issuance of paper currency.

In 1775 Congress passed a resolution allowing the issuance of $2 million in paper currency. This currency was called the *continental* and was backed by the full faith and credit of the colonial government. The resolution also provided that each paper dollar was to be fully redeemable in exactly three Spanish silver dollars from the Treasury. Acceptance of the bills for the conduct of business was mandated by law, and failure to accept them as legal tender was punishable by severe fines and penalties. The first issue was highly successful and greatly assisted in financing the war effort. It was so successful, in fact, that an additional $14 million were issued later that year.

As the war became increasingly costly and drawn out, Congress was under great pressure to continue financing the war regardless of the inflationary consequences. Disregarding sound judgment, it elected to print even more paper currency. By 1779, over $240 million in continentals were printed. It was estimated that only about $10 million

Spanish dollars existed in reserves at that time, so the ratio of continentals to hard currency greatly exceeded the statutory limit.

As might be expected, a drop in value of the continental began in 1776 and accelerated throughout the remainder of the decade. Due to growing public awareness that the new currency was rapidly losing value, most gold and silver coins were quickly withdrawn from circulation. By 1777, the continental was virtually a worthless scrap of paper. Internationally, the new government was completely discredited. Foreign trade came to a standstill. Merchants accepted payment only in gold and silver. Since America had not yet become commercially independent of Europe, the Colonies suffered badly.

In order to re-establish its credibility in world markets, Congress resorted to a series of desperate programs to recompense the injustice caused by the continental fiasco. In early 1780, it voided the continental as legal tender and initiated a program in which the Treasury was required to redeem worthless continentals for a few cents per dollar denomination. In addition, Congress enacted the "scaling laws" to allow for a more equitable settling of debts during the years the continentals were in circulation.

The scaling laws required debtors to more fairly compensate creditors who lent money during the period of severe inflation and had loans repaid in drastically cheapened currency. In order to re-establish a free trading relationship with foreign countries, laws were enacted requiring all of their claims to be repaid in gold and silver upon demand. Although these measures resulted in additional financial hardship for the Colonies in the postwar era, the re-establishment of both domestic and international credibility was essential to the future growth of the nation. If these steps had not been taken, it was recognized that the development of the United States would have been retarded for several generations.

## FIASCO OF A NEW CURRENCY

From a broad historical perspective, the continental fiasco was one of many instances in history where an extraordinary hyperinflation swiftly and utterly destroyed a currency. The inflation-based destruction of a currency is characteristic of an economically backward nation governed by weak leaders with no knowledge of the true nature of money or its relationship to the social and moral stability of the country.

Hyperinflation undermines respect for the legal system, promotes counterfeiting, fosters a wide variety of fraudulent and speculative investment schemes, and opens tremendous opportunities for shrewd profiteers. Hyperinflation almost incited a revolution against the new government. America almost lost the Revolutionary War, not due to an unwillingness to fight, but because of the resulting chaos and loss of respect for government leadership caused by a discredited currency. Fortunately, the error was acknowledged sufficiently early to allow a fresh start to be made before irreparable damage was done.

With the reinstatement of the foundation for a relatively stable monetary system, the gold, silver coins, and bullion that were hoarded by the public were quickly recirculated throughout the monetary system. In addition, most major countries began to resume trade with the United States. Particularly noteworthy was the great demand by both France and Spain for the Colony's products. Since France and Spain were both on a strict gold standard, all payments were made in gold coins and bullion.

In addition, England indirectly contributed to the transfer of gold to the United States. In order to resume trade, Britain was required to pay reparations for the damages done to the citizens of the Colonies. Since these payments were required to be based exclusively in gold and silver, the Colonies were soon flooded with gold currency and were well on their way to restored credibility and economic recovery.

With the monetary system now stabilized by virtue of a solid foundation in hard money, the Colonies were both psychologically and financially ready for expansion. Banking and financial interests were exuberant over victory in the war and began to rapidly expand the scope of their business activities. Since the government opposed the issuance of a new federal currency, it remained the responsibility of state banks to create one. Almost immediately, the urban states issued a wide range of state-denominated currencies, usually fully backed by both gold and silver. In addition, banks in these states proceeded to issue loans for a variety of business ventures chiefly associated with the shipping, road-building, and farming industries. In more rural areas of the country, a large volume of loans was issued for real estate speculation.

By 1784, it became apparent that credit extension was again out of control. Even though the state currencies were still considered fairly stable and most were fully redeemable in gold or silver, the loan portfolios of banks proved otherwise, and the nation suffered a relatively severe postwar banking and liquidity panic.

Although traumatic for many, the crisis proved to be short-lived. By the early 1790s, the banking panic began to subside. Most of the excesses built up during the postwar years were reduced to acceptable levels and interest rates fell considerably. The newly elected President, George Washington, decided to take a series of positive steps to help promote the credibility of the monetary system. In 1791, at the insistence of

Washington, Congress appointed Alexander Hamilton to lead a delegation of prominent citizens in formulating suggestions for banking reform.

The delegation quickly split into two opposing factions. On one side were the advocates of a strong central bank who believed that the unifying effects of a nationally chartered bank were essential to the stability of the nation's economy. This faction was championed by Alexander Hamilton. Opposed to Hamilton was the state banking lobby led by Thomas Jefferson. This faction reasoned that a strong central banking system had always led to inflation and corruption and, therefore, should be avoided at all costs. They cited the recent continental debacle as a typical example.

After a heated debate, Hamilton's faction prevailed, and in 1792, Congress established the First Bank of the United States. In addition, Congress passed the Coinage Act of 1792, which, for the first time, required the maintenance of standard denominations for gold and silver coins.

The primary function of the First Bank of the United States was to issue government notes payable in gold by the federal government. The amount of gold and silver reserves needed to supply redemptions was the sole responsibility of the bank's administrators. From its inception, the First Bank of the United States was a great success and expanded rapidly into all areas of business. More importantly, the strength and stability of the bank contributed greatly to the credibility of the newly formed government from both foreign and domestic perspectives.

The Coinage Act was also very popular. By this act, the U.S. dollar became the basic unit of currency and was defined solely in terms of gold and silver in which 37¼ grains of silver and 24¾ grains of gold constituted redemption equivalence. To solidify the strength of the dollar and quantify the number of dollars in circulation, the act further provided that any holder of foreign silver or gold coins could have his holdings reminted in U.S.-denominated coins free of charge. Interestingly, the silver dollars in circulation today still contain 37¼ grains of silver.

With a strong currency and a respected federal government, the nation was prepared to enter the growth phase of its first complete Kondratieff Cycle.

At the bottom of the cycle, the prices of most products were historically cheap. Interest rates were low, and the debt levels of the country were nominal. Since the purchasing power of gold was at its highest level in the short history of the United States, a huge influx of European gold and silver soon purchased a broad array of products and investments.

## A PERIOD OF PROSPERITY

During the next two decades, there was prosperity throughout the Colonies. With prices steadily increasing, it was almost impossible to not make a profit in business or to make a bad investment. Prosperity was greatly aided by the Napoleonic Wars being fought in Europe. Even though the demand for our war-related raw materials increased steadily throughout the first decade of the 1800s, it was not until about 1810 that demand climbed to truly significant levels. Since most foreign purchases assumed payment in gold and silver coins or bullion, the money supply began to expand rapidly.

By 1811, the mint, under the Coinage Act, coined over $5 million, a huge sum in those days. The volume of these new coins, added to the already large volume of gold in the Colonies as a result of the flourishing foreign trade, began to cause an accelerating inflation. The huge amount of paper currency and credit beginning to flood the markets also contributed.

Between 1800 and 1810, the population of the country nearly doubled. This put great pressure on the banking system, since the amount of money in circulation had not kept pace with the population growth. In order to keep prices from falling, the First Bank of the United States and most of the state-chartered banks were forced to initiate large-scale programs to increase the money supply in the form of credit and paper currency. By the start of the War of 1812, a monstrous paper money machine existed.

This huge expansion of credit was largely caused by the state banks. Although the states were not constitutionally permitted to issue paper currency, they were allowed by law to charter state banks that could do so. By 1810, states greatly increased the numbers of these charters, which were soon issuing currency and loaning money for a wide variety of risky business ventures. By the start of the War of 1812, paper currency flooded the market, most of it backed by little or no gold assets. Inflation and speculation were beginning to accelerate. Just as this was occuring, the charter for the First Bank of the United States came up for renewal but was turned down. This was a critical decision by Congress, because the government lost its primary vehicle for financing wars.

Already overextended, both state banks and private lenders were able to only partially fill war-financing needs. To compound the problem, over $15 million in gold and silver coins had to be returned to the original stockholders and depositors of the bank. Since most of these coins were quickly removed from circulation and hoarded by the public due to paper currency inflation, the banking system began to experience redemption difficulties.

In addition, the heavy withdrawal of gold from the banking system by foreign interests was causing problems. To help finance the war with the British, the United States had to run a significant balance-of-trade deficit with Europe. Since most of these foreign purchases required payments in gold, the gold reserves of the nation steadily declined.

By 1814, during the postwar recession, a broadly based liquidity crisis developed and a run on the banks ensued. As a result, all banks eventually suspended gold and silver withdrawals, and the economy began to tumble. Gold and silver disappeared, and there was a widespread shortage of cash. States passed laws delaying payment of gold and silver in all business contracts and legal judgments (Figure 12).

In order to stabilize the situation, in 1817, Congress chartered the Second Bank of the United States. The bank immediately began issuing a new currency fully redeemable in gold and silver. Since the war was over and the currency was once again fully backed by gold, inflation quickly abated, and the economy entered a postwar plateau.

The plateau period lasted until the middle 1820s when the U.S. economy began to experience the first stages of rapid deflation. Although the initial impact of the deflation was very severe and created a second postwar banking crisis, the ensuing depression was comparatively mild. Business activity declined only moderately, as both consumer prices and credit extension contracted at a slow but steady rate. The depression remained very orderly until 1838, when a serious financial crisis began to develop.

In a delayed reaction to the destructive effects of the inflation following the War of 1812, the voters proceeded to elect a series of conservative Presidents. In 1824, Andrew Jackson was elected by a narrow margin. He promised to decentralize the banking system away from Washington and toward the states. It was a popular belief that the inflationary upheavals experienced both during the Revolutionary War and the War of 1812 were primarily the result of an excessively powerful central government.

It was Jackson's opinion that "hard money", in the form of gold and silver, should be the primary form of money, and all currency and credit-creating functions should remain the responsibility of the states. Strongly opposed to Jackson were increasingly vocal business interests devastated by the deflationary effects of the depression. These business-men advocated an "easy money" policy, in which significantly more currency should be issued to support prices and terminate the depression.

During his first term in office, Jackson solidified his plan for a transfer of power to the states. In addition, he steadfastly refused to increase the money supply under any circumstances. By the end of his first term, the Jacksonian faction was firmly in power. After a resounding

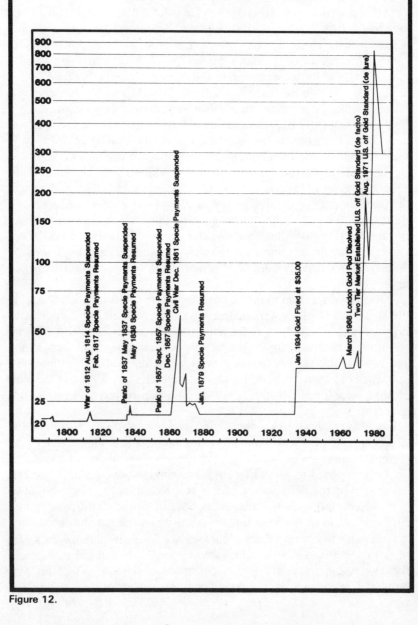

Figure 12.

victory in the 1828 election, Jackson implemented the first step in his overall plan. Through Presidential authority, he refused to renew the charter for the Second Bank of the United States. He then ordered that its assets be dispersed and deposited among various state-chartered banks of his choosing. These banks were located chiefly in the Midwest states where his political support originated. Many of these banks did not know what to do with this huge windfall of assets. Eager to use the money, they soon began to issue loans for a variety of real estate schemes located largely in the areas that are now Chicago and Cincinnati. A roaring speculation soon developed in canal real estate, road-building properties, and securities.

Additional state-chartered banks soon sprang up to accommodate these speculators. Foreign interests joined in purchasing properties and securities with gold and silver. This increased the hard money assets in the banks and fostered even more speculation. It was quite common to see investments double in a short period of time at the height of the frenzy.

Jackson eventually became concerned about the rapidly developing inflation and instructed Congress to enact the Specie Circular, which required that all public land in the West be purchased exclusively with gold and silver. Land was no longer permitted to be purchased on credit. The collapse in values of already extremely overpriced land was immediate and devastating.

Since most of the land speculation employed very high leverage, prices collapsed immediately. Farm prices fell even faster as the debt burden of farmers was compounded by a severe drought throughout the West. A massive run on the banks ensued, and all gold and silver redemptions were suspended. By late 1837, all banks were off the gold standard (Figure 12).

During the resulting depression that lasted until 1846, more than 600 Western banks failed, and the volume of currency of state-chartered banks changed from $149 million to $59 million. Compounding the problem was a huge outflow of gold and silver from America to Europe in the latter years of the decline. This was due mainly to the increased fear of political instability. Federal tax revenues dried up, and riots began in some urban areas. By the end of the depression, the financial and economic base had collapsed to the lowest levels in history. The existing conservative government was completely discredited and immobilized.


## THE COMEBACK OF GOLD

There was one area, however, that grew stronger as the depression deepened. Due to relatively high fixed gold prices, and the general need for gold assets in order to increase the degree of solvency in the banking system, the gold-mining industry enjoyed almost unprecedented prosperity. In this way, the natural function of the gold standard brought about slow but steady economic recovery.

By the late 1840s, gold was discovered in California, and the proportion of gold in the monetary base of the banking system began to increase dramatically. From 1847 to 1850, gold production rose from less than $1 million per year to over $50 million per year, and remained at that level for the rest of the century. Because of the deflationary depression, commodities and manufactured goods were available for purchase at fractions of their former values. This stimulated foreign interests to begin purchasing our products and investments. By 1850, the United States was well on its way into the growth phase of its second complete Kondratieff Cycle.

As the naturally countercyclical effects of the gold standard began to influence the economy, the revival of business activity proceeded steadily. When the newly minted gold coins became available, the general price level rose sharply, and the banking crisis quickly abated.

The 1850s represented a typical middle stage of the growth phase of the Kondratieff Wave. Money and credit became increasingly plentiful, interest rates were low, and businesses flourished.

Throughout most of the 1850s, both U.S. currencies and gold remained relatively undervalued, while our products enjoyed increased demand in world markets. As the growth phase progressed, the credit-creating function of the banking system became more liberal in its policies. With so much gold in circulation, in conjunction with an expanding economy, the state-chartered banks became extremely profitable. During the decade of the 1850s, when their number tripled to over 1,600, these banks began to issue paper currency and credit in prodigious amounts.

During the latter part of the decade, the principle of "free banking" also became increasingly popular. The free-banking laws allowed almost anyone to form a bank without having to be chartered by either state or federal institutions. Reserve requirements and currency-creating regulations were lax, and in most instances not enforced. Well before the Civil War, speculation in a wide variety of new businesses and investments was expanding rapidly.

By 1860, inflation had again become a problem. The prices of most items were three to four times their earlier levels. Both market interest rates and wages rose sharply in reaction to this inflation. As prices rose to meet and then exceed the fixed price parity of gold, mining activity began to level off and in some instances decline. Gold no longer flowed into America from abroad to buy our products. In fact, significant gold outflows to Europe occurred due to our growing balance-of-trade deficits. The banking system was in the initial stages of distress.

The problem was greatly compounded by the beginning of the Civil War. In April of 1861, fighting between the Confederacy and the Union began with the battle of Fort Sumter. It was a widespread belief in the North that the South would be unable to endure more than a few months of fighting. The initial months of war were financed by private loans from wealthy institutions, individuals, and a slight increase in federal taxes.

By late 1861, the war was nowhere near its end, and a subtle uneasiness began to spread throughout the North. This was partially due to the uncertainty caused by the war and concern about the highly illiquid banking system. Depositors eventually began to accelerate the redemption of their assets in gold and silver.

By December 1861, most banks, including state-chartered banks and free banks, suspended gold redemption. Many of the weaker state-chartered banks quickly went out of business as their paper currencies became discredited. Since most of the remaining banks were in a precarious position, the federal government was forced to go elsewhere to finance the rapidly expanding conflict. In order to forestall a crisis, the government resolved to issue over $150 million in U.S. notes, more popularly called greenbacks. These notes were initially redeemable in gold-backed notes also issued by the Treasury. But by 1863, when the total volume of greenbacks issued was raised to $450 million, the gold redemption feature was cancelled.

As the newly issued currency entered the markets, inflation exploded. Since the new greenbacks were required by law to be accepted as legal tender for payment of all debts, gold and silver coins and bullion quickly disappeared from circulation. From April 1861 to mid-1863, while the banks suspended payment in gold, the price of gold on the black market rose from $20 to $60 per ounce, a 200 percent gain. The value of the greenback dollar depreciated proportionally (Figure 12).

The Civil War resulted in great political and social tensions in the country. The Northern states were severely polarized by the issues involved, and many people thought the government was in jeopardy. By 1864, the outcome of the war was still in doubt. Due to high inflation rates and political unrest, foreign interests began transferring their gold and silver assets out of the country. In order to stem the outflow of gold, the U.S. government resorted to a series of currency-exchange controls. These attempts proved futile as the foreign currency markets quickly went underground. Even the domestic banking interests removed their gold from the monetary system for hoarding in safer havens. This was fairly easy to accomplish since the loose regulatory controls of the state-chartered banks and private banking interests did not anticipate these actions.

These were desperate times for the nation. The economy and the financial system were out of control. Without sound money to back the large volume of existing paper currency, commerce and trade became disrupted. Foreign commerce virtually ceased. In desperation, Abraham Lincoln assumed almost dictatorial powers to restore order.

His first move was the systematic abolishment of the state banking system and its replacement by a national one. In 1863, the National Bank Act was legislated and quickly implemented. The act effectively gave the federal government exclusive power over all banks. Its charter stipulated that any qualified group of persons could form a bank under a national charter and engage in all the necessary activities of a conventional bank. Specifically, a national bank could accept deposits, issue notes, and make loans. In addition, there were relatively strict reserve requirements placed on deposits. Up to 25 percent of all deposits were required to be collateralized with federal notes and bonds. In order to reduce the power of the state-chartered banks, a prohibitive surtax of 10 percent was charged to each state deposit not redeemed. By 1865, over $100 million of new national bank notes were in circulation and most of the state-chartered banks either converted to national banks or were forced out of business.

## THE LIBERAL GOVERNMENT BLAMED

After the war, the public began to assess the damage of wartime inflation and the subsequent postwar recession. Most blamed the rapid loss of their wealth on the liberal leadership of the government, and especially on those who advocated a removal of the gold standard. The response was the election of a more conservative national leadership whose primary goal would be to prevent inflation and quickly reinstate the gold standard.

In the 10-year plateau period following the war, these goals were largely accomplished. Since the general price level had climbed to approximately 107 percent of the purchasing power of gold at prewar levels, it was necessary for the price of the average commodity to decline by 50 percent to reach parity with gold. This was largely accomplished by 1873. Since money in circulation remained relatively constant during this period, much of the decline in prices was attributed to the general contraction of credit levels in the financial system.

By early 1873, the United States returned to the gold standard on a
*de facto* basis with the free-market price of gold at $24 per ounce,
while the fixed price remained at $20 per ounce. However, this forced
deflation put a terrific strain on the economy since war debts and a
rush of overseas loan defaults placed great burdens on the already shaky
banking system. Late 1873 marked the transition from the plateau to
the beginning of depression.

In 1872, the nation overwhelmingly re-elected the staunchly conservative Ulysses S. Grant. Grant campaigned on a platform that asserted
the nation's ills largely stemmed from the huge amount of paper currency
still circulating throughout the economy. Immediately after the election,
he persuaded the strongly conservative Congress to pass the Resumption
Act of 1874. This effectively required the Treasury to redeem all the
wartime greenbacks in gold and silver in anticipation of a resumption
of a fully gold-backed monetary system. By January 1, 1879, all national
banks were required to resume full payment of withdrawals in gold
coins, and the United States had returned to a fully operational gold
standard.

The resumption of the gold standard was very deflationary for the
economy. Not only did the Resumption Act remove a great deal of
much needed liquidity from the banking system by the large-scale
retirement of paper currency, it also forced a large portion of monetary
gold to be used as bank reserves.

Deflation was particularly severe in the commodity-producing industries. Those engaged in farming and mining silver were especially
hard hit. The demand for silver especially declined as a result of the
stagnant business conditions brought on by the recession and the
movement to eliminate the use of silver in favor of gold from many
world monetary systems. In order to partially relieve this distressed
sector of the economy, the Bland-Allison Act of 1878 was passed,
allowing $2 million in silver coins to be minted. This gesture proved
entirely inadequate in relation to the ongoing credit and price collapse.
By 1885, the price of silver had fallen to 82 cents per ounce. By 1890,
the price was 70 cents per ounce.

As the deflationary effects of the depression began to intensify, the
government came under strong pressure to boost general price levels
by a series of inflationary tactics. In July 1890, the Sherman Silver
Purchase Act was passed, obligating the Treasury to buy a minimum of
4.5 million ounces of silver per month and use it to back a new issue of
Treasury notes. This action was perceived as potentially highly inflationary, and investors quickly began exchanging paper money for gold.
Uncertainty, then fear, soon gripped domestic and foreign investors as
the resulting redemptions escalated. By early 1893, the Treasury's gold

reserves had declined to a little over $100 million, just above the statutory minimum set by Congress. By late 1893, the crisis had reached the panic stage, and gold was again hoarded out of circulation. By early 1894, a panic was in full force, and banks failed by the hundreds.

The populace was near rebellion. In all sectors of the country, people sought an explanation for their suffering. Financial institutions were severely criticized as more and more people demanded tighter regulations and reform in the banking system. The Democratic Party championed the downtrodden, demanding immediate inflationary measures be taken by the Republican Party in power. Farmers and labor unions were particularly vocal, since they could not find work at an "acceptable" wage. In desperation, Grover Cleveland, the newly elected Democratic President, secured a loan of over $100 million from a consortium of large New York banks to increase the Treasury's gold reserves and maintain reserves for further gold redemptions.

When these steps proved ineffective, Cleveland, under the advice of J.P. Morgan, undertook a project in which a special issue of 4 percent gold-secured U.S. government bonds was sold to European financial institutions in exchange for gold. This effort brought $65 million in revenues to the Treasury and made Morgan a small fortune in fees. However, financial pressures continued to intensify as it was perceived by many foreign interests that the U.S. was in grave political trouble. By early 1896, as the heavy outflow of gold abroad resumed, the depression deepened, causing more business failures, labor strikes, and riots.

## THE POWER OF GOLD

Just when it seemed that there would be no end to the difficulties, the countercyclical influences of the gold standard began to again turn the economy around. As was true at the cyclical bottoms of each of the other major depressions, the purchasing power of gold was once again at an historical high. With gold fixed at $20 per ounce and the price of products and investments selling for fractions of their former values, gold was considered extremely expensive with respect to most historical standards.

The first indication that the depression was nearing an end was the almost frantic resumption of business activity in the gold-mining industry. Prospectors combed the world exploring for new deposits of the metal, which was artificially overvalued. Old mines were reopened, and new and innovative mining techniques were developed. In 1898, significant gold and silver discoveries were made in Alaska and Colorado. In addition, the cyanide gold extraction process was developed, making it possible to extract gold inexpensively from low-grade ore. By the turn of the century, a huge supply of newly discovered gold began flooding the economy with much needed liquidity. The nation was prepared to enter its third complete Kondratieff Cycle.

The revival of the economy was almost miraculous in its speed and breadth. Price levels began to climb, due mainly to increasing business activity and a sharp increase in the gold supply. Greatly contributing to the rise in business activity were large-scale purchases of our products and investments by foreign interests. Since both the dollar and gold possessed an historically high purchasing power, U.S. assets were seen as bargains now that depressionary conditions abated. With interest rates at extremely low levels and a high degree of credit availability, many purchases, especially the acquisition of companies and large-scale commercial real estate properties, were facilitated through long-term loans.

Since gold reserves were at extremely high levels, and because it appeared that gold production would continue indefinitely, the government gave gold center stage in the monetary system. In 1900, Congress enacted the Gold Standard Act, which formally put the United States on the already operational international gold standard. With a strong and widely respected currency, world confidence in our economic strength and stability was quickly restored, fostering an extended period of growth and prosperity.

Because of the severity of the depression, the nation's political stance became increasingly more liberal. The public elected a host of easy money advocates who promised to prevent a depressionary relapse and to punish special interest groups who had "unfairly" exploited the depression for profit.

One of their first actions was the legislation of a series of reform measures designed to greatly liberalize the currency- and credit-formation procedures within the banking system. Money supply growth parameters were relaxed or increased to significantly higher levels, reserve requirements were lessened, and minimum capital requirements to open new banks were sharply reduced. In the first decade of the new century, the volume of bank notes in circulation more than doubled to $716 million, excluding over $600 million in new silver certificates and $1 billion in new gold certificates. These policies did not affect the rate of inflation since the economy was far from overextended in credit, and the demand for most products was low.

Reform legislation focused particularly upon the big banking interests in New York, which were symbolized by J.P. Morgan and Co. A widespread belief was held that Morgan and his group were primarily responsible for the depression. They were subsequently attacked by the liberal press as callously disregarding the national interest during the depression. Teddy Roosevelt and a reform-oriented Congress passed legislation to insure that private banking establishments could no longer "control" the pursestrings of the country. In this same context, the anti-trust acts, the Federal Reserve Act, and the Income Tax Act were legislated in 1913 and 1914.

The Federal Reserve Act was to become the most significant body of law affecting the future course of U.S. monetary history. The original purpose of the Act was to increase the flexibility of the existing monetary system in order to meet the financial needs of the business community. In order to accomplish this objective, the Federal Reserve was designed primarily to manage the money supply by providing extra money when the business sector needed capital for expansion, and reduce the money supply if less capital was needed. It was hoped that by controlling the money supply, the Federal Reserve could eliminate depressions.

The second important function of the Federal Reserve was the authorization of the issuance of a more stable form of money. This was designated as the Federal Reserve note. The note was to be backed by 40 percent gold and was to be fully secured by commercial paper held at the district banks. National banks were allowed to use these notes as reserves to make loans but were required to keep at least $35 in notes as reserve for every $100 in loans extended. Leadership of the Federal Reserve was exercised by the Board of Governors, each of whom was appointed by the President for a 14-year term. For the first time in U.S. history, the federal government assumed *de facto* control of the financial and monetary structure of the nation.

From the mid 1890s to the start of World War I, the nation experienced a fairly typical Kondratieff growth phase. Credit became increasingly plentiful, allowing interest rates and consumer prices to trend steadily upward at their normal rate. By 1911, raw commodity prices once again reached a basic equilibrium with the fixed price of gold so that dollar-related investments were generally fairly valued. International trade balances were also in approximate harmony with the dollar.

America was justifiably self-confident. Business activity and profits were flourishing and standards of living were at cyclical highs, making it difficult to lose money on almost any investment. The advent of World War I was to quickly shatter this stability.

In 1914, war broke out in Europe as Germany invaded France. In order to raise money to finance the increasingly costly war effort, a large volume of American-based common stocks and U.S. government securities were sold by foreigners. The proceeds of these sales were then redeemed for gold, which was also transferred to Europe. This caused a sharp but temporary decline in gold reserves, which reduced the money supply. A sharp recession followed. As the war intensified, this outflow of gold was soon reversed as risk capital re-entered the U.S. in record amounts. In 1915 and 1916 alone, over $2 billion in gold flowed into the country. *By 1918, the United States owned over 40 percent of the known world gold reserves, with the Federal Reserve owning nearly $1 billion of that total.*

During the war years of 1917 to 1919, the monetary base of the banking system expanded rapidly. When the U.S. entered the war in 1917, the Federal Reserve was forced to issue additional notes to assist government war financing. During the war years, over $3 billion in new notes were issued. This issuance, in conjunction with the huge inflow of more than $48 billion (present-day dollars) in gold, caused the money supply to triple from its prewar levels. By 1920, the average article cost three times its prewar price.

For the first time, the Federal Reserve exerted its power, becoming an engine of inflation. By 1920, the inflation rate became intolerable. In desperation, the Federal Reserve increased the discount rate from 4 to 7 percent. This immediately caused the nation to fall into its third Kondratieff postwar recession. Wholesale prices declined over 40 percent in one year. Afterward, the economy rapidly stabilized.

As the nation entered the postwar plateau, the dollar emerged as the world's strongest currency. With the huge injection of gold into the U.S. banking system, every dollar of currency was now fully backed by over $.34 in gold. The war had been costly. By its end, the total credit outstanding exceeded $15 billion, a level that was to cause economic difficulty throughout the plateau.

The end of the 1922 recession marked a period of prosperity and economic growth typical of all previous plateaus. European gold continued to flow into the U.S., but at a greatly diminished rate in relation to wartime levels. The growth of the money supply was relatively modest throughout the remainder of the decade.

Internationally, the world, particularly central Europe, was re-establishing political and economic stability. Germany suffered the destruction of its currency, setting the stage for the rise of the Third Reich. France was in severe financial trouble and required massive loans to survive as a nation. England was attempting to regain its former status as the financial center of the world through a return to the gold standard and a reinstatement of the value of the pound in terms of gold to its prewar level.

The world desperately needed liquidity and stability in order to achieve political harmony and deter a rise of Communism. In order to realize these objectives, the world's former gold-exchange standard was modified at the Geneva Convention of 1922 for the first time to permit government-backed paper (currency, Treasury bills, Treasury bonds) to be used in addition to gold as a reserve asset for central banks. Since the pound sterling was the primary currency of international trade and commerce, it was determined that, as a temporary expediency, only British pounds and pound-denominated debt could be used in this capacity. It was assumed that other currencies could eventually obtain this privilege.

This modification of the gold-exchange standard effectively resulted in a tremendous expansion of England's bank reserves, largely in the form of government securities. Since these debt instruments could now be used to settle international trade balances in lieu of gold, the expansion of international liquidity was also greatly facilitated.

All parties were pleased by the arrangement. England, of course, enjoyed an almost insatiable demand for its domestic debts. Foreign central banks received much needed liquidity in addition to interest-paying reserves of high-quality issues. This marked the beginning of both structural inflation and Socialism in England. It was now able to repay its domestic budget and balance-of-trade deficits with printed money without being constrained by a disruption of its gold reserves. *With these acts the world had effectively taken its first large steps toward abandoning the discipline of a strict gold standard and had unwittingly accepted the long-term inflationary consequences.*

Throughout the early years of the 1920s, credit availability remained relatively plentiful and interest rates remained low in the United States, since most financial institutions were rich in cash assets. A significant cause of this excess money was the huge influx of capital from other areas of the world, which were still in a state of political and economic disorder following the war.

## FOREIGN MONEY

Why did so many foreign interests transfer so much money and gold into the United States during the 1920s? The primary reason was the desire to transfer assets from a higher- to a lower-risk environment. European countries and others around the world that were directly involved in World War I were greatly overextended in debt and in a precarious political and financial situation. Germany, France, and many smaller European nations, such as Belgium and Austria, were desperate for loans to finance the rebuilding of their war-torn industrial base.

The reconstruction of Europe, especially Germany, was largely financed by bond sales to American citizens and institutions.

As time passed, it became evident that the principal and interest on these bonds would never be paid. This caused all additional lending to these countries to be curtailed. Without additional capital to promote growth, economic activity turned increasingly negative, and political and social unrest began to surface. Labor unions and industry began to demand protectionist trade barriers. Currency controls were erected to protect exports. This greatly concerned free-market-oriented investors who quickly shifted their investments to less restricted markets of the United States.

By 1925, a huge volume of foreign capital flowed into the United States from Europe. It is estimated that from 1920 to 1925, we accumulated over $150 billion in foreign currency (present-day dollars). Since this currency had to be exchanged into dollars before it could be invested, the dollar became greatly overvalued. This overvaluation continued through the 1920s. As the economic conditions in these countries continued to deteriorate, unemployment soared. In response, the weaker foreign governments imposed additional trade barriers on their neighbors as they struggled for economic and political survival.

Regardless of these mounting problems, England and most major European countries remained determined to reinstate their currencies on the gold-exchange standard. Most government leaders felt that the remonetization of gold would result in a return to harmony in international trade and economic stability. However, this objective was extremely difficult to realize due to the exceptional strength of the United States dollar.

In order to correct this imbalance, the Federal Reserve decided to artificially drop interest rates by injecting currency and credit into the banking system (Figure 13, A, B). It was hoped that by reducing interest rates, the relative attractiveness of the dollar in world currency markets would be reduced to such a degree that the fragile European currencies, including the pound, could be stabilized. Currency stabilization was considered a prerequisite for the successful remonetization of gold. This policy was moderately effective so that by 1927, most major currencies were again convertible with gold at the prewar gold price. Unfortunately, this stability was only temporary.

In the United States, the rapid injection of money into the economy caused a severe strain on our financial system. Rather than utilizing the employment of this money for productive purposes, the vast bulk of it went into stock market speculation. Concerned that speculation was getting out of control, our financial leaders abandoned their international currency stabilization program.

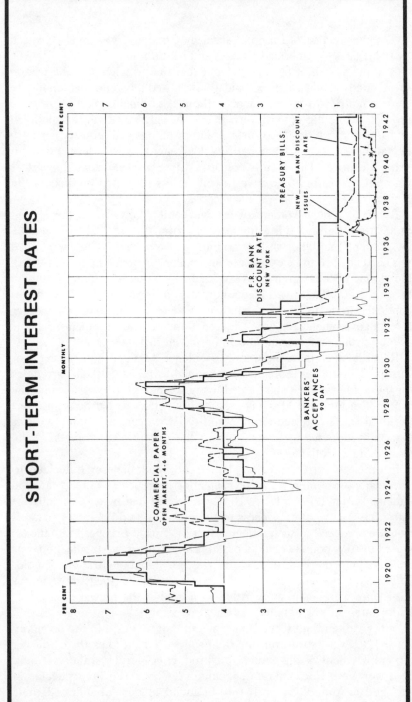

# SHORT-TERM INTEREST RATES

PER CENT

MONTHLY

COMMERCIAL PAPER
OPEN MARKET, 4-6 MONTHS

F.R. BANK
DISCOUNT RATE
NEW YORK

BANKERS'
ACCEPTANCES
90 DAY

TREASURY BILLS:

BANK DISCOUNT
RATE

NEW
ISSUES

1920  1922  1924  1926  1928  1930  1932  1934  1936  1938  1940  1942

Figure 13A.

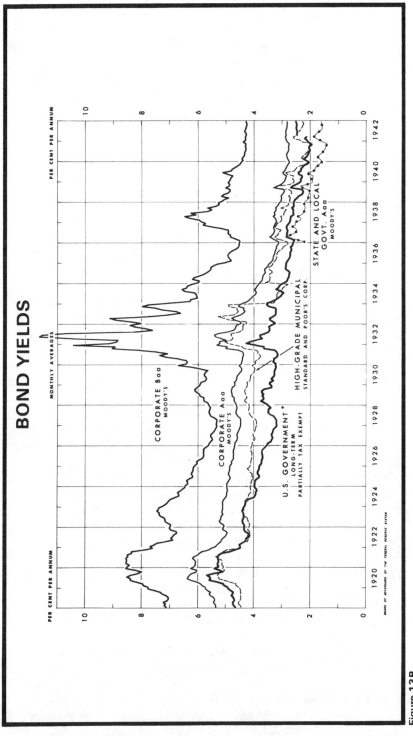

Figure 13B.

Interest rates immediately exploded upward. The value of the dollar soared, and the flow of foreign capital into the United States accelerated. This was very deflationary to most European countries. Their financial markets began to selectively turn down. By 1929, the situation was so severe that many governments began defaulting on their debts. The world began to experience the worst depression in recorded history.

As the depression deepened, most countries rapidly suspended gold payments to depositors who increasingly demanded redemptions in gold. In 1931, England was the last European power to suspend gold payments. Since the United States held most of the world's gold, its payment policies did not change until later. However, by 1932, over 20 percent of U.S. banks suspended gold payments, and depositors from all parts of the country were beginning to withdraw their savings. Political and economic strife was widespread. Over 25 percent of the U.S. population was unemployed, and the other 75 percent was extremely unsure of its employment prospects.

In late 1932, as the panic intensified, depositors were no longer satisfied with paper currency withdrawals, demanding gold coins, gold certificates, and bullion. Efforts at seeking gold redemptions by U.S. citizens were quickly joined by an increasing number of foreign depositors. Bank moratoriums were widespread. An increasing number of them suspended gold payments. By early 1933, over 40 percent of the nation's banks had closed their doors (Figure 14).

At the height of the panic, people were sufficiently desperate to sacrifice almost anything to provide for themselves and their families. This fear resulted in the 15-year term of Franklin Roosevelt as President and the abandonment of the world gold standard.

On March 4, 1933, Franklin Roosevelt was inaugurated. Acting on the advice of his chief economist, John M. Keynes, he persuaded the disillusioned Congress to grant him virtually dictatorial powers to radically transform the social and financial fabric of the nation and the world. On March 8, 1933, in a special session, Congress adopted the Emergency Banking Act. In summary, it provided for huge money-supply expansion, the confiscation of all public and private gold and gold certificates, and a major reform of the banking industry.

The objective sought by forcing the Federal Reserve to increase the money supply was essentially the increase of consumer wealth and spending, allowing demand to increase. This was expected to result in increased productivity and employment. Retail business would of course benefit from higher consumer demand, and commodity producers would benefit from higher prices.

Acknowledging the fact that these programs would be perceived as inflationary by the investment community, Roosevelt sought to prevent

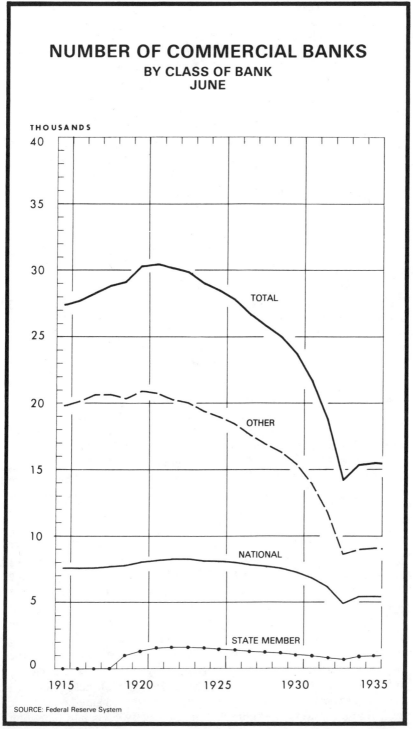

# NUMBER OF COMMERCIAL BANKS
## BY CLASS OF BANK
### JUNE

THOUSANDS

TOTAL

OTHER

NATIONAL

STATE MEMBER

1915    1920    1925    1930    1935

SOURCE: Federal Reserve System

Figure 14.

another episode of gold hoarding. This was accomplished by confiscating all gold and gold-related investments owned by businesses, individuals, and foreign interests. In addition, the transfer of gold out of the country was outlawed. Simultaneously, once it was determined that the government could remove most of the gold from the system, Roosevelt promptly revalued the dollar upward in relation to gold almost 70 percent, i.e., from a value of $20.67 per ounce to $35 per ounce (Figure 12).

The monetary system was now adequately protected against a further run on the gold supply. Of course, this was a meager consolation to domestic and international creditors who held gold-payment contracts that were currently payable only in significantly cheapened dollars.


## A UNIQUE EVENT

The devaluation of the dollar in terms of gold was a unique event in world history. Never before was a devaluation used to raise the general price level after a long and sustained period of deflation. Previously, devaluations always resulted from long periods of inflation. Logically, if a country tried to artificially raise the price of gold to higher levels, it would be purchased in the free markets of the world and sold to that country for artificially cheap currency. This currency would then be used to buy the country's products at artificially cheap prices.

Of course, this would greatly disrupt the entire value structure of both world currencies and assets, and cause severe short-term economic and political distortions. In fact, such events actually occurred. During the 1930s, an estimated $180 billion (present-day dollars) of gold were transferred from the rest of the world to the U.S. By 1939, gold was flowing into the U.S. at the rate of over $3.5 billion per year, and total U.S. gold reserves rose to over $16 billion.

By the end of World War II, the U.S. owned $25 billion in gold, over 60 percent of the world's gold reserves. This systematic destruction of the international gold standard and financial system, and the resulting subordination of Europe to the U.S., was by far the most blatant use of power exerted by the U.S. on foreign nations in its history. This was an act of selfishness and extreme desperation. It was symptomatic of the times and showed that during difficult conditions financial and economic "power plays" of this nature would be attempted. World War II, the rise of Hitler, and, to a significant degree, many of our present monetary problems can all be directly related to the aftermath of these policies.

As the depression progressed, the Federal Reserve gained even more extensive new powers. With the Banking Act of 1935, its basic function changed from a relatively passive and powerless central bank to an aggressive money manager affecting all financial aspects of the economy. The Board of Governors, which was formerly controlled by the large private banking institutions, was replaced by administrators appointed by the President for 14-year terms. It was created as a sovereign institution, under the *de facto* control of the President and Congress.

In addition, the Act gave the Federal Reserve extensive powers of intervention in the credit markets. The Fed now gained control over the level of the money supply by: 1) buying and selling U.S. government securities in the open market, 2) establishing reserve requirements for banks, and 3) raising and lowering the discount rate, thus "setting the tone" for other interest rates. More importantly, the Act retained the gold backing of the currency at its standard 40 percent, but with gold paper certificates now used in lieu of physical gold to fulfill "gold" requirements. At this point, gold bullion was officially replaced in the monetary system by a ledger entry called "gold certificate credit." With this Act, gold lost its last link to the dollar in the domestic markets and was effectively removed from the monetary base.

Throughout the rest of the 1930s and early 1940s, the dollar remained relatively undervalued, enabling our products to be competitive in world markets. Our recovery from the depression continued at the expense of our overseas trading partners. Recovery was further enhanced by our entry into World War II.

World War II was very costly for the U.S. From 1941 to 1943, war expenses exceeded $280 billion, compared with only $35 billion in World War I. However, with price controls in effect and because of the excess capacity in the nation's industrial base, the wholesale price level rose a paltry 30 percent during the war years. The war was financed primarily by increasing the amount of currency in circulation (from $6 billion to $27 billion), increased taxation, and the public sale of U.S. government securities. By 1944, so much currency was in circulation that the statutory gold certificate-backing requirement for the dollar was reduced to 25 percent.

In 1944, when it became apparent that the war would soon be over, the economic and financial leaders from most of the major countries gathered in Bretton Woods, N.H., to lay the foundation for a new monetary system to promote the postwar resumption of international trade and commerce. After long debate, it was decided that a system similar to that agreed upon in the Geneva Convention of 1922 would be employed. The major difference was that the U.S. dollar at a par value of $35 per ounce of gold would replace the British pound as the predominant reserve currency, and whenever possible dollars would be used to settle balance-of-trade differences between countries. These policies seemed logical, since the dollar was backed by over 60 percent of the world's known gold reserves, and the United States was by far the strongest and most stable country. Still greater U.S. stability was predicted due to the country's apparently high level of gold production. This, of course, was because of the artificially high, fixed price of gold. *Hence, by the stroke of a pen, the dollar became the premier currency of the world, and the gold-exchange standard changed into a dollar-exchange standard. The world had abandoned the gold standard, its currencies being backed only by the full faith and credit of the U.S. government.*

## THE U.S. REPLACES ENGLAND

The advantages of a dollar-based monetary system to the United States were obvious to all parties. This arrangement effectively allowed the dollar to be used as a reserve asset in both the Federal Reserve and foreign central banks alongside gold. Since these dollars could only accumulate in foreign central banks as a result of the United States consumer buying more goods from abroad than foreign consumers bought from America, the United States immediately replaced England as the only country in the world that could run balance-of-trade deficits and not experience a drain on gold bullion supplies.

Since most of these foreign central banks preferred to hold U.S. Treasury bills and Treasury bonds as reserve assets instead of dollars, since dollars do not pay interest, this arrangement had the added bonus of allowing foreign central banks to help pay for our domestic budget deficits and reduce the level of interest rates in the United States to much lower levels than they would be normally. In return, the United States pledged to maintain the value of the dollar by buying or selling unlimited quantities of gold to central banks at $35 per ounce.

This dollar-exchange system worked fairly well during most of the 1950s. There were some serious problems, however, as weaker European countries were forced to competitively devalue their currencies in order to accommodate the effects of widespread political and social unrest emerging throughout the world. Nevertheless, our trading partners conceded that the rapid reconstruction of war-torn Europe depended solely upon financial cooperation by the United States. During the initial stages of the dollar-exchange standard, little consideration was given to the idea that the United States would abuse these new monetary standards. It seemed that the best interests of all parties were served by keeping the dollar as good as gold. Unfortunately, this proved not to be the case.

During the late 1950s and 1960s, the United States began to run increasingly large balance-of-trade deficits. This was largely due to the still relatively cheap value of the dollar with respect to most other major currencies and the huge sums of foreign aid being transferred to Europe.

Since the foreign governments preferred to settle their balance-of-payments deficits in dollars instead of gold, the dollar-exchange system remained intact and international trade flourished. Foreign central banks particularly preferred to hold dollar-denominated assets that functioned as a base from which to expand their domestic money supplies and earn market interest simultaneously. From 1950 to 1957, the U.S. balance-of-trade deficit totaled over $12.5 billion, of which only $1.7 billion was demanded in gold. However, by the end of the decade, the system began to show instability.

By 1959, the purchasing power of gold declined to almost its lowest point in history. As a consequence, new gold-mining ventures virtually ceased, and existing mines closed in record numbers. Gold productivity dropped to a fraction of its former levels. With no new gold flowing into the Treasury, it soon became apparent that the amount of total gold assets backing our outstanding currency and credit was declining rapidly. It also became apparent that the political climate of the nation was turning more liberal in its monetary and fiscal policies. For the first time in U.S. history, the volume of dollars held overseas exceeded the Treasury's total gold reserves. These forces began to put downward pressure on the dollar.

By 1960, it became increasingly difficult to hold the value of the dollar at $35 per ounce of gold. On the London market, the price of gold now exceeded $40 per ounce. Our liabilities to foreign nations now exceeded $23 billion and were beginning to accelerate in volume. President Kennedy tried to prevent the depreciation of the dollar by instituting trade and currency regulations, but these had little effect. He eventually adopted the easiest solution and dropped the "mandatory" 25 percent gold-backing requirement and continued to print currency to finance his domestic social adventures and the early stages of the Vietnam War. The dollar immediately became more overvalued and our balance-of-payment problems worsened. By 1968, U.S. liabilities to foreigners exceeded $35 billion versus our $10.5 billion in gold bullion reserves. By 1971, liabilities exceeded reserves by $60 billion. At this point, gold traded in the free markets of the world at $60 per ounce.

In late 1971, President Nixon, realizing the futility of trying to stabilize the dollar in world markets at $35 per ounce, officially suspended all further gold payments to central banks at that price. Liberated from the forced constraints of the government, gold began to trend upward in price seeking its free-market value. Conversely, the dollar began to depreciate in value proportionally. As the dollar collapsed, the inflation rate soared to record levels.

From late 1971 to late 1974, the price of gold rose from $38 per ounce to almost $200 per ounce, an approximately 400 percent increase (Figure 15). Additional confirmation that gold was now officially demonetized was reflected by an act of Congress on January 1, 1975, that Americans could once again own gold assets.

When the nation was on a pure gold standard, the constraining forces that tended to terminate the growth stage of the Kondratieff Cycle were the fixed price and declining production of gold. When a country abandons the gold standard, the constraining force then becomes the level of outstanding credit in the economy. By 1973, total worldwide debt became too great for the financial system to absorb, and a contraction became imminent.

That year, the government was forced to begin orchestrating a postwar recession. The economy was visibly out of control as reflected by the flight from the dollar to real assets, particularly gold. So serious was the crisis that, near the peak, the price of gold exceeded its value as a pure commodity by a factor of 4:1. Historically, overextension of 2:1 or more in gold prices typically occurred only in times of excessive financial panic when the actual political and financial viability of the nation was questioned. Largely as a result of the postwar recession, the crisis soon abated, and gold fell to a more rational $100 per ounce.

## THE 1975 PLATEAU

As the nation entered the plateau in 1975, a loose monetary and credit posture became almost habitual. Too many sectors of the economy had a vested interest in both a continuation of inflation and relatively easy money. Although the trend to a more conservative financial posture, characteristic of the plateau, was beginning to surface, most of the liberal political leaders in Congress survived the election and were not yet motivated to modify their "stimulative" posture. Therefore, during the Carter Administration, the financial markets correctly perceived that a stimulative monetary and fiscal policy by the government would continue and in certain cases actually accelerate. Both inflationary expectations and the price of gold exploded to new highs. By 1980, the dollar was at its lowest valuation in history relative to most other currencies.

The world was in panic. OPEC raised the price of oil to $35 per barrel. The dollar became discredited in the international community,

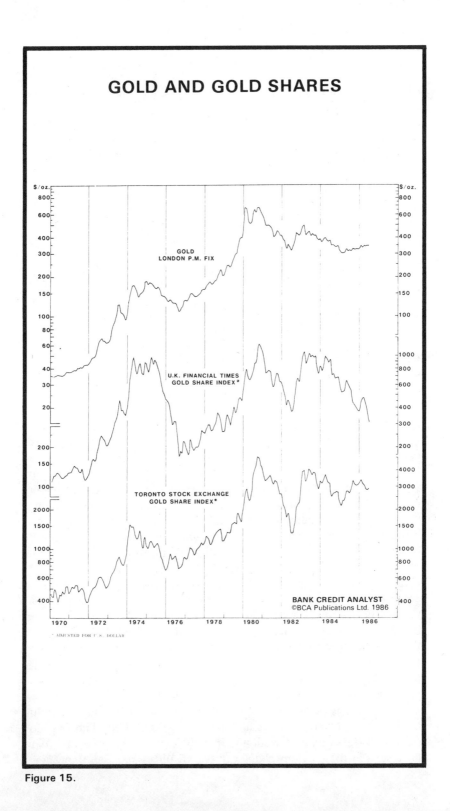

# GOLD AND GOLD SHARES

GOLD
LONDON P.M. FIX

U.K. FINANCIAL TIMES
GOLD SHARE INDEX*

TORONTO STOCK EXCHANGE
GOLD SHARE INDEX*

BANK CREDIT ANALYST
©BCA Publications Ltd. 1986

* ADJUSTED FOR U.S. DOLLAR

Figure 15.

and the nation's rate of inflation exceeded 20 percent. In this environment, gold exploded to $850 an ounce, greatly exceeding its "pure
commodity" value of about $200 an ounce. This was the greatest
overvaluation of gold in U.S. history, and it caused President Carter to
desperately sign the Monetary Control Act of 1980, giving the President
of the United States virtual dictatorial powers in the event that a financial
collapse occurred.

However, with the election of the ultraconservative Ronald Reagan
in 1981, the worldwide economy quickly began to stabilize. Inflation
dropped to less than 4 percent, and the dollar again became the premier
currency of the world. Gold fell to approximately $300 per ounce, near
its proper valuation as a commodity. By 1982, the world economy finally
began to exhibit the more conventional characteristics of the middle
stages of the plateau.

## CONCLUSION

Now that the United States has apparently completed a final transition
into the down phase of its fourth long-term gold cycle, a broad range
of diverging opinions have emerged regarding the future direction of
gold prices. As is typical of this stage of the cycle, the public is again
perplexed by the economic crosscurrents that determine this direction.
On one side, the hyperinflationists are predicting that the stage is being
set for another round of massive monetary and credit creation leading
to a rapid escalation of inflation and an accompanying depreciation of
the dollar. They argue that the resulting devaluation of the dollar, with
its accompanying federal spending deficits and loss of respect for the
government, will eventually justify flight from all paper currencies in
favor of real assets, including gold.

In contrast, a rapidly emerging conservative faction in the investment
community is predicting lower gold prices based upon evidence of a
worldwide credit contraction that will cause a downtrend in both
commodity prices, economic activity, and inflation. This, of course,
would cause a rebound in the value of the U.S. currency. Lower gold
prices would be an obvious result of this scenario. A correct resolution
of this disparity of opinion is vitally important to those investors who
presently own gold or plan to do so in the near future.

In an analysis of the future price trend of any commodity, including
gold, two important considerations must be evaluated. The first consideration is its relative position in its individual long-term cycle. As we
have seen in the previous chapter, it is difficult to make an unprofitable

commodity purchase when the long-term trend of the commodity cycle is turning up. Even a relatively poorly timed investment in a generally uptrending market eventually develops into a profit if the investor is patient. Conversely, in downtrending markets, even "bargain" purchases inevitably turn sour. *For most commodities, market timing employing this form of long-term cyclical analysis is by far the most important aspect in evaluating its investment appeal.*

The second consideration in making a determination of the investment potential of a commodity is the possibility of its relative overvaluation or undervaluation with respect to other competing commodities as a result of extraordinary events. There are a variety of reasons why a specific commodity becomes overvalued or undervalued with respect to other commodities in the market at any given time. Perhaps the most obvious form of market disequilibrium is produced by government interference, cartels, and monopolies in free markets. In the past, cartels and monopolies in commodities, such as salt, jade, silk, tea, and fur, have artificially distorted relationships. Cartels such as OPEC in oil, South Africa and Israel in diamonds, and the United States and Japan in a wide range of high-technology products, are a few of the most obvious artificial examples of price distortions in our modern industrial society.

Even more important than cartels is the interference of governments in free markets. Instances abound regarding the interference of governments in the commodity markets. Regulations, tariffs, and commodity price supports are a few of the most prominent examples.

Government interference in the financial market normally comes in times of economic stress. History is full of examples of governments overvaluing or undervaluing currencies, gold, and debt securities in order to promote "stability." Most often these interferences are usually of short duration, and are quickly resolved in the free markets by the discovery of new sources of products or by the breakup of the cartel either by financial or military means.

From a short-term investment viewpoint, it is vital that any distortion caused by extraordinary events be known and understood. History shows that most market losses are taken as a result of purchases made at the height of overextended markets using inadequate or erroneous information. Conversely, for those investors who are able to properly evaluate such relative price disequilibriums, significant rewards are possible. For example, in the case of undervalued commodities, purchases can be more confidently made in anticipation of the market's return to a more realistic level. In the case of an overvalued commodity, it can either be sold or sold short for an expected lower purchase price. There are a variety of methods to determine whether a particular commodity is artificially overvalued or undervalued. Perhaps the most straightforward is the concept of the relative differential in prices of a specific commodity to a broadly based composite price index.

It has been our observation that the long-term price trends of many commodities tend to most closely approximate those of the Producer Price Index. This is especially true of cyclical price trends in the nonprecious metals, such as copper, iron, and lead, and many of the grains, such as wheat and rice, and to a certain extent the precious metals, silver and gold. The common denominator underlying this phenomenon is that each of these commodities has a broadly based international production and distribution system largely free of government or institutional interference.

In each of these commodities, it is remarkable to observe how closely a percentage rise in the individual commodity almost exactly parallels the percentage rise in the Producer Price Index over long periods of time. Although in certain instances it is common to see as much as a 5 to 10 percent deviation in this relationship, natural market forces usually tend to quickly correct such deviations. Many commodities, such as cattle, hogs, sugar, diamonds, petroleum products, and many other commodities, which are continually subjected to significant market distortions and interference, tend not to readily lend themselves to this analysis.

As we attempt to apply this form of analysis to evaluate the present price level of gold, our historical studies from 1790 to the present in the U.S. indicate a relatively close harmony with the trend of commodity prices in general. Throughout most of the gold cycle, the rate of inflation is usually quite stable in that economic price appreciation remains in close equilibrium with the rate of inflation.

This orderly relationship is maintained until a major international war at the peak of the cycle causes a sharp currency and credit expansion and an accompanying rapid rise in the rate of inflation.

As the currency rapidly depreciates in value, the price of gold in the free markets of the world accelerates sharply upward. The resulting instability again causes a financial panic and the removal of deposited gold from the financial system by frightened depositors.

Eventually, the gold standard is broadly abandoned. The resulting financial dislocations often reach such a magnitude that the price of gold becomes significantly distorted and is often bid to much higher than justifiable levels in a relatively short period of time. At this point, gold may sell at a significant premium above the Producer Price Index unless government intervention in the market prohibits the overvaluation from occurring. However, this distortion is usually short-lived. Eventually, the peak war terminates, resulting in a major postwar recession and sharply lower economic activity. Gold, as well as most other commodities, is sharply reduced in price to reflect lower economic activity and the rapid abatement of inflation.

As the world economies settle into an extended period of general stagnation, the international financial system begins to experience significant stress as the debts built up during the war come due. In order to forestall a deepening crisis and potential depression, it is widely felt that a quick return to the stability of a gold-based monetary system is necessary. Within a few years following the remonetization of gold, world economies begin to enter the initial stages of a debt collapse leading eventually to a full-scale deflationary depression. Usually, near the point of remonetization, the price of gold has declined so that the relationship of the free-market price of gold and the Producer Price Indices are again in close alignment. This relationship usually continues for the duration of the depression stage.

If we trace the relationship of the free-market price of gold to the Producer Price Index from the late 1700s to the present, we can easily observe the repetitive nature of this phenomenon.

There were times in the history of the United States when the price of gold and the Producer Price Index were at general parity. An obvious point of parity was the year 1803. During that year, the price of gold in the United States was fixed at $19.36 per ounce, and the Producer Price Index stood at 97.

During the subsequent years leading up to the peak war of 1812, the price of gold and the Producer Price Index were in general harmony. However, by the start of the war, the relationship began to moderately destabilize. By the end of the war in 1815, the free-market price of gold in the London bullion market advanced to the equivalent of $28 per ounce or an approximate 50 percent gain. During that same period, the Producer Price Index advanced from 97 to 140 or an approximate gain of nearly 44 percent. It seems that even though a more significant premium price for gold might have been warranted in view of the major panic sweeping the banking system, and with a weak central government in apparent jeopardy, these factors were largely offset by the rapid influx of investment capital from abroad, mainly in the form of gold bullion.

In any event, the financial panic was extremely short-lived. By 1817 the gold standard was easily re-established, with the price again fixed at its prewar level of $19.39 per ounce. By 1819, the Producer Price Index declined to a level in perfect equilibrium with gold.

In the Civil War cycle, which lasted from 1843 to 1864, the free-market price of gold rose to nearly $60 per ounce at its peak in 1864, or a gain of nearly 116 percent. By comparison, the Producer Price

Index rose to a relatively modest value of 146.6 or a gain of only 56 percent.

As we described previously in this chapter, the primary cause of this relatively high 77 percent premium was the high level of uncertainty regarding the survivability of the government. Even as late as 1864, the victory of the Union over the Confederacy was still in doubt. It must be assumed that the markets continued to fear that, in the event of a Confederate victory, the nation's currency would become worthless. The historically large premium paid for gold was in part a hedge against this risk. Since the war eventually was resolved in a decisive Union victory, this disparity was quickly erased. By the end of the postwar plateau in the middle 1870s, the free-market price of gold declined rapidly enough relative to the Producer Price Index that there was again approximate parity. By 1879, gold was officially remonetized at $20.67 per ounce and remained at that level until 1932.

During the third Kondratieff upswing that lasted from 1896 to 1920, the free-market price of gold in the London international markets attained its highest level at the equivalence of $26 per ounce, or a price increase of approximately 33 percent from its official price in the United States. During this same period, the Producer Price Index advanced to a level of 178.7 or an increase of over 84 percent. This unexpectedly large 38 percent discount in the price of gold can in part be explained by several facts. Perhaps the most obvious explanation is that tremendous supplies of gold and foreign currency were flowing into the United States during World War I. This influx of capital greatly overvalued the dollar relative to gold and artificially forced its price to extraordinary levels. With the dollar artificially strong and interest rates high, there was simply no need to hold gold. Furthermore, due to the relatively low level of involvement of the U.S. in World War I, there was virtually no fear of significant political or economic disruptions as a result of the war. As it was in each of the past postwar plateau periods, the remarkably close parity between the price of gold and the Producer Price Index was again re-established.

By 1926, most of the world returned to the gold standard at the equivalence of $20.67 per ounce. By 1929, the price of gold in the market was again in almost exact parity with the Producer Price Index, with the price of gold at $20.67 per ounce and Producer Price Index at 100.

During the fourth Kondratieff Cycle, of which we are now a part, a virtually identical scenario to that described in the previous cycles is being repeated. As one might expect, throughout the 1945 to 1972 period, the price of gold maintained a close parity with the Producer Price Index. By 1972, both the Producer Price Index and the free-market price of gold were in almost exact parity with the price of gold close to its London price of $60 per ounce. However, with the massive credit-creating events of the Vietnam War and the social revolution beginning to greatly destabilize both the dollar and the international banking system, this harmonious relationship soon fell apart.

At the height of the Vietnam War, during the years 1972 through 1974, and the subsequent six years of the postwar recession and plateau, the Producer Price Index advanced over 200 percent. Through these same years, the price of gold advanced from $60 per ounce to its highest level of $850 per ounce in January 1980. This astounding 1,250 percent gain in the price of gold, and the accompanying premium of over 600 percent, was unprecedented in world history.

In subsequent years, the free-market price of gold has fallen to a much more realistic level of just over $400 per ounce. Even at this level, gold still remains grossly overvalued by all historical standards. This continued degree of disparity between the free-market price of gold and the Producer Price Index is hard to rationalize. One can only conjecture that unprecedented events such as the potentially explosive growth of the Eurodollar market, the exponentially increasing costs of both government and private debt in the United States, third world political instability, and the increasingly likely collapse of the international financial system, are apparently critical enough to justify this unprecedented premium. One thing is certain: The resolution of this disparity to more historically normal levels will no doubt greatly add to the risk of gold investments in the near future.

It is our contention, based on historical precedent, that this extraordinary high premium being paid by the market for gold will eventually be corrected. As we have seen in the United States, the correction in any disparity normally takes place either during the latter half of the plateau period or during the first few years of severe deflation. Although some consideration must be given to the possibility that the premiums will be dissolved by a rapid upsurge of inflation brought on by a massive increase in the money supply, we feel probabilities do not realistically favor this option. If the volume of dollars in the international markets is allowed to expand to sufficient levels to forestall a depression, historical precedent suggests that the value of the dollar in the international markets would collapse, interest rates would quickly climb to intolerable levels, and our democracy would be subjected to extreme stress.

Instead, probabilities favor instead an extended period of deflation in which the free-market price of gold declines to the point where parity is re-established with the Producer Price Index. This being the case, the question only remains as to how far the price of gold must decline to reach this parity.

At present, the Producer Price Index has risen nearly 200 percent from its last point of parity in 1972. During the same period, the free-market price of gold has risen from $60 per ounce to its present price of approximately $400 per ounce. To achieve parity, the price of gold should be approximately three times its 1972 price of $60 per ounce or around $180 per ounce. If this parity were to be achieved by the end of the plateau period and if the rate of inflation continues to advance at its present relatively nominal level of between 2 and 5 percent a year, an acceptable parity price of gold could be achieved at around $225 per ounce.

However, assuming that parity is not attained until well into the depression phase of the cycle, it is interesting to speculate on what price gold would attain.

As we have seen in previous chapters, the Producer Price Index declined at least 50 percent in each of the three prior depressions in the United States. Gold could then easily fall to the $75 to $125 per ounce level. Should the depression become even more severe, the price of gold would decline proportionately.

To accomplish this realignment, a general deflationary scenario, closely paralleling those of the three prior gold cycles and modified by the higher level of interaction of modern international financial institutions, would be most probable.

For the remainder of the plateau period, we expect this rate of inflation to continue to increase at a relatively moderate rate. Although we expect the money supply to continue to increase at its present relatively rapid pace, we do not expect it to significantly affect either the actual or expected rate of inflation. The accelerating deterioration of stability in the international financial system caused by the increasingly rapid transfer of assets to lower-risk currencies and gold will give modest upward pressure to the price of gold. If the world financial system appears more unstable than expected, gold could be in proportionately greater demand than dollars. Also supporting higher gold prices could be the increased desire to return gold to the world banking system.

In these troubled times, it will become increasingly obvious that the system is in desperate need of stability. Discussions regarding the possible remonetization of gold and the reimposition of the gold standard will become increasingly serious. It should be properly rationalized that because of the insufficient amount of gold in most government treasuries and its overvalued price in the market place, a return to a world gold standard will not be feasible immediately. However, both central banks and conservative investors should begin to accumulate gold during the plateau in anticipation of its eventual remonetization.

Conversely, casting the largest negative pall on the price of gold will be the realization that it is overvalued in world markets. This disparity will be highlighted when it becomes obvious that a new round of inflation is not forthcoming, and that both the dollar and real interest rates will continue to remain strong. On balance, we expect the price of gold to trade between $200 and $500 per ounce for the duration of the plateau.

However, with the advent of the depression phase of the long-term gold cycle, the role of gold in the world financial system should begin to rapidly expand in its scope. In the initial years of the depression, the price of gold should rapidly decline to approach approximate parity with the Producer Price Index. In prior depressionary periods, this realignment usually was accomplished within the first several years. At that point, the replacement of the dollar by gold in the world financial system could become a logical alternative.

Once it is perceived that probabilities favor a worldwide remonetization of gold, the governments will begin a determined effort to accumulate gold bullion as quickly as possible. The stakes will be high. History suggests that those countries able to attract the largest hoard of gold at the point of remonetization suffer the least relative economic and political trauma, and greatly enhance their power and prestige in the financial arena.

Historically, this accumulation of gold by the government was accomplished using several techniques. A popular one is to buy gold from the public markets at a price much higher than the free-market value. Usually a 50 percent premium is enough to dislodge most private gold hoards.

In the event that the financial panic is so severe that the public cannot be induced to give up their personal gold, stronger government measures may be necessary, such as confiscation of privately held gold coins and bullion, nationalization of gold and silver mines, and measures to enhance exploration for and production of gold.

Should these measures still not be sufficient to accumulate the desired level of monetary gold, even more stringent steps may be taken. One such radical program may be the sequesterization of other nations' gold. One possible source may be the gold bullion deposits of foreign central banks in the Treasury's gold depository in New York. It is thought that most of the world's monetary gold still resides within the physical boundaries of the United States. During the depressionary years of the 1930s through the World War II era, vast quantities of foreign gold were transferred to our shores by our allies to pay for war supplies.

As we have seen, the United States owned almost 60 percent of the world's monetary gold at the end of World War II. In subsequent years, as the U.S. continued to run increasingly large balance-of-trade deficits, most of this hoard was "officially" transferred back to the accounts of foreign governments. *We believe that this transfer might have been only a bookkeeping entry. The physical gold bullion may still reside in its original location at the Treasury. At present, the U.S. "officially" owns only one-quarter of the original hoard.*

It is quite possible that in times of crisis, the government of the United States may find it necessary to sequester this gold in the name of national interest. One easy method might be to confiscate the gold of foreign countries who default on their debts to our government. Another might be to retaliate for the nationalization of many of our private business interests abroad in the event of an overthrow of an existing government, or repayment of war debts.

In any event, at some point in the depression, the international economy will reach such a degree of instability that it will be deemed necessary to remonetize gold. When enough gold has been accumulated by the Treasury to comfortably back the dollar, and it has fallen to a low enough price to establish a close parity with the commodity markets, it will again be remonetized.

History shows that the remonetization of gold by itself does little to promote the desired stabilization of the international financial markets. The most obvious benefits lie in the ability of the gold standard to promote political and social stability since the public perceives it as an alternative to paper money should the destructive effects of the depression increase. In reality, it does little good to try to stem the progress of the international debt collapse. Historically, both prices and wages continued to fall for an additional 15 years after prior remonetizations.

At the bottom, with the dollar again fully backed by gold and the nation's financial and political systems in a basically cautious posture, we should again emerge from the next depression as the strongest nation in the world. As always, gold will continue to play an important role in international finance for many years afterward, just as it has done since the beginning of the capitalist system.

*"There is only one key that unlocks the door to big profits in the [stock] markets, and that key is knowledge."*

—W.D. Gann

# Chapter VI
# Common Stock

## POWER CYCLES AND WHY INVESTORS BUY COMMON STOCKS

Since the turn of the century, common stocks have proven to be one of the most successful investment vehicles in the United States. This is due to a number of factors. Perhaps the greatest advantages of common stocks lie in their diversity and liquidity. At present, there are over 15,000 listed stocks on the major exchanges and over-the-counter markets. Because of the tremendous diversity of their businesses, these stocks allow a wide range of investing strategies. These might range from a conservative strategy using a portfolio of utility stocks to a highly aggressive one using a host of volatile "penny" stocks in the over-the-counter market. In addition to liquidity and diversity, common-stock purchases are relatively inexpensive. Contrary to investment alternatives, such as real estate, collectibles, numismatic coins, and limited partnerships, where commission and management costs often range from 7 to 50 percent or more, listed common stocks can be purchased for a commission charge in the 1 to 2 percent range. No-load mutual funds can be purchased at no cost.

Additionally, common stocks and their related investments provide the opportunity to greatly enhance overall return through the use of a wide range of defensive strategies. One important strategy is the short-sale. Instead of buying a stock and attempting to sell it at a higher price, a short-sale allows a stock to be sold at its present price and bought back at a lower price. With the use of short-selling, an investor can make profitable trades in declining markets. In the past decade, the power of the short-sale has been enhanced by a host of new vehicles that allow the investor to short-sell on leverage using Put options on stocks, stock indices and stock index futures; these are investment vehicles where the degree of leverage can approach 40 times or more.

Since the purpose of this book is to outline a basic investment game plan for the conservative investor, *we recommend that most short-sales be limited to hedging on existing portfolios.* Defensive strategies such as "shorting-against-the-box" and writing call options can be acceptable conservative hedging strategies. More complex strategies are best left to professionals. We expect that during the coming years, stock market investments will rapidly grow in both size and scope as their advantages become more widely recognized by the public.

Of all investment mediums, more effort has been expended in trying to determine the direction of common-stock prices than all other investments combined. This is mainly due to the complex nature of the world economy. The equity markets are the summation of world economic variables. To complicate the situation, equities may or may not respond to purely economic forces. Unexpected political and social events may intervene to significantly affect the price that investors are willing to pay for a particular common stock. To make matters more complicated, not all stocks move in the same direction for the same reasons. *In fact, some stocks trend up for the same reasons that others trend down, making published market averages, such as the well-known Dow Jones industrial average, very difficult to interpret and utilize.*

*Perhaps the primary determinant of the future direction of stock prices is the actual and expected growth rate of the profits and dividends of a company.* All things being equal, a stock that is earning $5 per share is likely to sell for a much higher price than a stock that is earning only $1 per share. If we expect the lower-priced stock to earn $5 per share in the coming year, we are willing to pay considerably more for it than if we expect it to continually earn $1 per share. If we foresee declining earnings, we would expect the stock to fall in price.

This analogy also is true with dividends. For example, suppose that a business is currently earning $5 per share and paying an annual dividend of $4 per share. The expectations of the investor may be that the earnings will increase to $6 per share and dividends will be $5 per share.

If the investor pays $100 per share for the stock, the present dividend of $4 equals a 4 percent return on his investment. If the investor is expecting a $5 dividend next year, he might be willing to pay $125 for the stock because a dividend of $5 next year would equal a 4 percent return on the investment. In other words, if this investor expects a 4 percent return on his money both currently and as the company grows, he might be willing to pay 25 times the expected future dividends.

Some investors buy stock in a company that shows no promise of paying dividends, expecting to get the equivalent of a dividend in the form of capital appreciation as the company invests its profits internally to expand. However, the majority of conservative investors and institutions buy stock for investment income. It is surprising how closely most stocks remain within a price range governed by the income they produce or are likely to produce.

*A second important influence on stock prices is the present and expected rate of interest in world money markets.* This is the place where stock and bond markets are tied together. Suppose that the expectations for the growth of a stock's dividend are diminished. A 4 percent return may seem too low for investors since they can obtain a return of 5 percent or better in the bond market. In this case, they might refuse to pay more than $100 a share for stock about to pay a $5 dividend. Likewise, if the bond market is yielding only 3 percent, investors might be willing to pay more than $100 per share for a stock with a $5 dividend. Stocks often fluctuate in price for essentially the same reasons that bonds do—the change in the availability of money and its costs forces investors to accept a higher or lower rate of return for their investment dollars. The same analysis is true for all competing investments, such as real estate, mortgages, municipal debt, commercial paper, etc.

*A third major influence on the valuation of stock prices is the relative purchasing power of the dollar in both domestic and foreign markets.* The average American investor does not usually scrutinize the relative value of world currencies and products with the same intensity as his foreign counterpart. Throughout history, America has always remained primarily a self-contained entity, not overly dependent on our foreign trading partners for the necessities of life. The opposite is true of our foreign neighbors. They typically have smaller, less integrated social and economic structures and are thus more interested in foreign goods and investments.

For this reason, foreign investors periodically make sizable purchases of stocks in nondomestic markets, especially the United States. Hence the value of the dollar in the world's markets plays a primary role in influencing stock prices in America. Whenever the dollar is overvalued relative to other currencies, its purchasing power is high relative to the purchasing power of other currencies. Conversely, if the dollar is undervalued relative to other currencies, domestic rather than foreign purchases are encouraged.

*The final and, in our opinion, the most important influences on the stock market are the overall vitality and liquidity of the economic system.* A good financial and economic base is essential for a sustained expansion in stock prices. This is particularly important for the timing of purchases at major cyclical turning points.

This is where an in-depth analysis of long-term stock market cycles and the overall knowledge of the Kondratieff Wave are of particular importance. For example, at the bottom of the Kondratieff Cycle, consumer debt is low and corporate balance sheets are in a conservative and highly liquid position. The economy and the stock markets are set for long-term expansion. There is also plenty of room for credit expansion and monetary growth. Historically, as we shall see, this is the ideal time to purchase common stocks with low economic risk and at exceptionally cheap prices.

Conversely, at the top of the Kondratieff Cycle when the economy is basically illiquid and consumer and business debt extension is at its highest, long-term growth in stock prices becomes difficult. In this high-risk economic environment, it becomes appropriate for the knowledgeable investor to either take a defensive posture with his stock market portfolio or sell his positions altogether.

## THE IDEALIZED STOCK MARKET CYCLE

This chapter focuses on the development of an idealized long-term stock market cycle and then shows how this cycle has influenced the course of stock market behavior throughout the history of the United States. We conclude with a discussion of the future trend of stock prices in view of our findings.

At the start of the long-term cycle (at the bottom of the Kondratieff Wave) a 20- to 25-year period of world economic growth emerges (Figure 16). In general, the stock market and, in particular, specific stocks in key industries become poised to lead the economy out of depression. World governments provide support for stock prices by using various stimulative measures. The purpose of these programs is to reliquify the banking system in order to avert a deepening financial panic. These programs usually consist of a variety of money- and credit-creating schemes. Along with the direct injection of printed currency into the banking system, the governments use such powerful tools as open-market purchases of government or corporate debt by a central bank; the introduction of a second precious metal, such as silver, into the nation's monetary system; and an artificially low interest rate policy through government manipulation of the discount rate and reserve requirements.

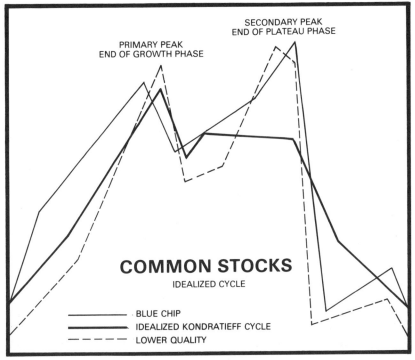

Figure 16.

The overall effect of these government stimulative policies on the panic-stricken equity markets is always very positive. Initially, the government's determination to reverse the downward slide of the economy is met with some skepticism by the average investor. The problem is seen as too pervasive. This attitude gradually changes as both the scope of programs and the heavy barrage of positive rhetoric begin to intensify. Eventually, the stock market begins to experience a robust rally. Since the market is often greatly depressed at this point, the magnitude of the rally is typically swift and powerful.

During the first few years of the growth phase, the major cause of higher stock prices is almost exclusively lower interest rates. Because the economy is still generally depressed and since there remains a tremendous amount of excess manufacturing capacity, the risks of investing in most business ventures appear very high from a future earnings viewpoint. All but the highest-grade common stocks are not expected to be profitable for many years. Because of this, most investable funds are initially placed in U.S. government Treasury bills and bonds, and high-grade commercial paper. This depresses interest rates and triggers a rise in bond prices. Higher bond prices aid liquidity in the banking system, and the level of excess reserves quickly reverses from historical lows to historical highs.

At the bottom of this rally, Treasury bills historically yield between 1 and 2 percent and Treasury bonds yield between 3 and 4 percent. Since lower interest rates on income securities tend to increase the relative attractiveness of common stocks, a major revaluation of stock prices is soon in progress. Especially popular are well-capitalized, dividend-paying stocks. It is common to see the average stock double and sometimes triple in the first three to four years of the growth stage. Those with bright earnings prospects do even better.

As the economy continues to improve through the first decade of the growth stage, the stock markets continue their cautious advance. Because of accelerating earnings expansion and the expectation of even higher profits, businesses begin to slowly expand the scope of their operations. Earnings are especially helped by an increase in business productivity as much of the idle plant capacity built up during the depression is returned to production. Productivity is also increased by the positive attitude of the labor force. During the depression, labor had most of its deadwood cleaned out, and remaining workers are eager to accept employment.

Business balance sheets and corporate cash reserves have also significantly reliquified, aided by the sharp drop in interest rates and increased earnings growth. Because of the decline in long-term interest rates, most long-term corporate bond debt has been called in and financed at much lower rates. Since short-term rates are also much lower, the cost of financing current inventories and the variable costs of most businesses are sharply reduced. Rents are also low, and new plants and equipment are relatively cheap and easily financed.

These and other factors lead to the rapid emergence of a wide variety of new and innovative industries. Aggressive entrepreneurs emerge, eager to seize the opportunity of a lifetime. To these astute businessmen and investors, risks appear low and profit potentials high. Venture capital for fledging enterprises begins to find its way into the stock market in increasing volume, especially since most other investments, such as real estate and bonds, are performing relatively poorly.

Also adding to this new pool of capital is a significant influx of foreign capital from less stable countries whose stock markets continue to perform badly. At this point in the cycle, most of the poorer countries are trying to recover from both the unsettling effects of the depression and the trough war. While their problems are being worked out, continued stagnation reduces domestic capital formation and forces investment in the strongest and most stable areas of the world. Historically, foreign investment capital is always one of the principal contributors to the rapid rise in stock prices in financially stable countries during the first 10 years of the growth stage.

By the end of the first decade of the growth phase, many equities have appreciated substantially in price. At the forefront are well-capitalized, high dividend-paying, investment grade stocks. Blue-chip issues with international markets are held in special favor by more aggressive investors. Interest rate-sensitive issues, such as banks, insurance companies, and utilities, are also very profitable. By this time, the banking and insurance industries have greatly expanded their earnings from profits generated by the huge capital gains on their bond and stock investments. Utilities benefit from lower borrowing requirements as old debt issues are recalled and refinanced at lower rates.

Also rising in attractiveness is a select group of well-established high-technology companies that has emerged to supply the expanding economy with a wide range of new and innovative products.

## THE BUILDUP TO AN EXPLOSION

By the middle years of the growth stage, prices of virtually all listed stocks are in a steady and rapid uptrend. Business profits are high, and there are expectations of them going higher. Confidence has returned, and most fears of depression are forgotten. Business activity and profits rise dramatically as consumers increase demand, while labor and business costs continue to remain moderate. An added boost to business profitability is a sharp reduction in federal and state tax rates to both consumers and corporations. The growth periods of the short-term business cycles remain characteristically long and the accompanying recessions mild and short-lived.

By this time, weaker countries have successfully stabilized their political and financial systems to the point that their economies are beginning to contribute to prosperity in the world economy. Especially noteworthy are the rapid decline in unemployment and the sharp increase in the level of foreign trade. International commerce is greatly aided by the increasing strength and stability of most foreign currencies. As a result, gold and investment capital begin to flow back into these formerly high-risk areas in increasing amounts. By the end of the first 10 to 15 years of the growth phase, world trade is approximately in balance, and there is general harmony among nations.

This is the era of greatest worldwide prosperity and stability during the Kondratieff Cycle. In this relatively risk-free environment, all stocks reach their peak valuations with respect to the anticipation of future profits as reflected by their price-earnings ratios.

At this point, most common stocks are participating in the general upswing of the market. Many of the lesser-quality growth stocks, especially those showing high growth rates and attractive future prospects, have replaced the more conservative, high-yield blue chips in market leadership. Especially spectacular are high-technology stocks that are at the forefront of a trend toward new products and business efficiency. Internationally oriented stocks taking advantage of the sharp increase in world trade are also market leaders. Industries, such as transportation, international banking, steel, and machine tools, accelerate in strength. Other stocks just beginning to strengthen are residential and commercial construction companies that have greatly benefited from a variety of government and private building projects and an accelerating residential real estate cycle.

As the growth phase of the cycle matures to a point just prior to the peak war period, the stock market becomes historically overvalued for the first time in many decades. Ironically, this is a time of maximum economic and financial euphoria when it seems virtually impossible to make a mistake in either business or investment decisions. In business, aggressiveness and daring are quickly rewarded with success. Wealth and luxury are both respected and glorified by the news media.

Since money and credit are plentiful and borrowing increasingly popular, the public goes on a sustained spending binge. Business profits soar to record levels, convincing most businessmen of continued prosperity. This causes a rapid expansion in capital expenditures.

Because most recessions continue to remain short-lived and mild, business recessions become increasingly viewed as an ideal opportunity to take advantage of lower material and labor costs to further expand capital investments. The euphoria eventually spills over into a larger segment of society, inducing an even greater number of people to participate in common-stock investments.

Because of this, stock prices are bid increasingly higher. Dividends also rise, keeping pace with business profits, and larger increases are expected. The average price-earnings ratio of stocks advances to historically high levels as the public becomes captivated by the huge profits being generated in the stock market. Creative investment products and the securities brokers to sell them materialize to meet the public's voracious appetite for equity investments. Because of the generally overvalued relationship of common stocks to bonds or commercial paper, most companies elect to issue new stock as opposed to raising debt capital. These new issues are quickly sold out. Stock underwriting firms make huge profits on commissions as trading volume reaches record highs. Brokers are unable to keep up with the trading volume as both institutional investors and the general public are caught up in the frenzy.

As volume builds, newly formed companies with no earnings or dividend histories and only a promise of future profits go public for the first time at absurdly high prices. After issuance, it is not unusual to see these new issues explode even higher in price.

The phenomenal rise in stock prices spreads worldwide, as the prosperity of strong nations spills over into the weaker and less developed ones. Since most of the manufacturing concerns of these countries are either partially or wholly owned subsidiaries of companies based in the industrialized countries, much of the profits generated are reparated back to their parent companies, further increasing earnings in the strong nations. At this point, the world has apparently found the correct formula for social and economic stability. The prevailing economic theory is touted as the final solution to the problems of high unemployment and poverty.

Then the world economy begins showing the first signs of internal breakdown. As this is perceived, the international equity markets begin the extended process of forming a major peak in price. The primary cause of the market's initial problems is the high and rising level of interest rates caused by excessive debt burdens. Near the top, most sectors, including the government, private individuals, and corporations, have run their levels of debt to the point that growth and profits are difficult to achieve. As debt reaches these historically unsustainable levels, the financial community recognizes the increased risk and reduced growth prospects by raising interest rates and more closely monitoring potential borrowers.

Along with rising interest rates, inflation also becomes a serious problem. As the euphoria of apparent long-term prosperity permeates the economies of the world, the demand for industrial commodities becomes intense. This is especially apparent in the government sector, where fears of impending war cause significant stockpiling. In response, world labor and material costs begin to soar.

Wage demands by a growing number of employee organizations and labor unions are especially harmful to many of the basic industries of the economy. At this stage of the cycle, wage increases usually do not keep pace with the rate of inflation. This induces organized labor to make unreasonable demands on companies already in serious financial trouble. Realizing, in many cases, that a prolonged strike would be economically crippling, management gives in to these exorbitant demands with only token resistance. This postpones the crisis but does little to stabilize increasingly violent labor unrest. In this environment of higher wage costs and reduced labor productivity, business profits begin to suffer, especially in those industries where labor unions comprise a major portion of the work force.

Government interference in the economy also becomes a severe retardant to business profits. As the economy becomes unbalanced due to inefficient expansion during the latter portion of the growth phase, the government usually attempts to stabilize the economy with a variety of incursions. Wage and price controls, additional taxation at the federal and state levels (which tends to be increasingly progressive in nature), interest rate ceilings, usury laws, and hidden taxes caused by the protection of politically sensitive industries are some examples.

Perhaps the most pressing problem for the stock market in this economic environment is the relative lack of competitiveness of common stocks versus most alternative investments. As the first peak in the long-term stock market cycle approaches, most stocks are greatly overvalued relative to bonds, real estate, and mortgages. During most of the growth stage, there is a general preference for equity investments relative to bonds and mortgages due to their overall higher return. But as inflation begins to accelerate at the top of the growth stage, bond and mortgage yields rise to the point that they become significantly more attractive than common stocks. This historically high overvaluation leaves most stocks vulnerable to profit taking. In response to this, private and institutional investors steadily shift their emphasis away from equities toward fixed-income securities.

Eventually, as these factors combine to stall the economy and growth estimates fail to attain their high expectations, price-earnings ratios decline and common stocks peak, beginning the agonizingly slow process of a major downward revaluation to reflect a slower-growth economic environment. This subtle peak in the stock market historically precedes the actual peak in the Kondratieff growth phase by three to five years.

However, not all companies and industries experience difficulties during this period. Those that continue to remain profitable include many raw materials-producing and manufacturing businesses. As the natural demands of an inflating economy combine with the labor and material demands of the peak war, the prices of raw materials on the open market begin to rise sharply. Huge profits are made by these companies, not only because of a sharp increase in sales volume, but also because of windfall inventory profits made between the time the goods are held in inventory and actual delivery.

Other sectors of the economy also experience sharp increases in profits. Especially noteworthy are financial industries, such as mortgage banking, securities underwriting, and commercial banking and insurance, with the most rapid advance in profits obtained by large commercial banks and insurance companies. These businesses become highly profitable because of their characteristically strong and stable earnings. Although in inflationary times they lose some money in depressed security prices as a result of advancing interest rates, profits explode as these institutions get increasingly higher interest rates on deposits in addition to increased business transaction activity and administration fees.

## AN ECONOMY OUT OF CONTROL

By the time the end of the growth stage is reached, inflation is out of control. In response to the growing levels of public disenchantment brought on by the resulting high interest rates and accelerating inflation, the government reluctantly attempts to halt inflation by contracting the volume of currency and credit in the financial system and imposing an even wider variety of wage, price, and business controls. *The results of these policies are virulent and persistent fiscal deficits and a severe financial crisis.* Interest rates move to historical highs as credit becomes scarce and in many cases nonexistent, then plunge to extremely low levels as the deflationary effect of the resulting recession is inevitably felt in the money markets. The government may put the economy through several of these minibooms and busts.

In each resulting recession, as government is forced to step in and subsidize faltering business enterprises in such vulnerable sectors as housing and steel production, inflation becomes increasingly embedded in the economy, and interest rates surge to even higher levels. Such actions are merely short-term expedients that blunt and delay the imposition of normal disciplines. The apparent ability of government to minimize economic corrections by the use of artificial rescue techniques provides the business community with further encouragement for even greater debt extensions.

*Each time the central banks retreat, they validate the entire inflationary process and create sufficient additional new bank currency and credit to sponsor an even faster rate of inflation while leaving its basic causes untouched. Thus, each new wave of inflation forces greater rundowns in liquidity, guaranteeing that each new round of credit squeezes will have an even more dramatic impact on interest rates. This creates more frightening prospects for the depletion of liquidity.*

Inflation finally becomes so severe that it is politically expedient to initiate a postwar recession to cool the economy down. The resulting credit-tightening monetary policy of the government causes high rates of unemployment, high business and personal bankruptcy, and a crashing stock market.

Although the common stocks of many companies have already been in obvious downtrends for many years, their previous price declines are small compared with those experienced in the postwar recession. In its aftermath, the average blue-chip stock will have lost over half the appreciation generated during the growth phase. Many lesser-quality issues decline much further. Manufacturing output slows perceptibly, and unemployment rises to extremely high levels as business failures are numerous and widespread. Major industries that cannot liquidate their inventories quickly are the most seriously injured. Especially hurt are those corporations that had boosted their earnings with inventory profits and asset appreciation. Usual examples of these industries are mining, farming, coal production, and real estate.

The vast majority of high-technology stocks, especially those that had excessively high earnings and dividend projections, are usually the greatest market casualties in postwar recessions. Also hard-hit are stocks associated with international trade, as both demand and price for their products drop sharply in response to the severity of the worldwide recession.

Those few stocks that are least subject to severe price erosion are usually involved in supplying basic necessities, such as personal-care products, drugs, and food. Also left relatively untouched are companies granted monopoly powers by the government, such as electrical utilities, telephone companies, and public transportation.

Devastating as they are, postwar recessions usually last only one to two years and, in the long run, prove extremely beneficial to the economy. By their conclusion, they accomplish the intended function of significantly reducing the rates of inflation and interest to more acceptable levels and allow the emergence of a relatively solid political and financial base in which a period of stable and prolonged economic expansion can once again occur.

As the postwar recession moves into the plateau phase, most investments are in general equilibrium. On a value basis, the average common stock has fallen in price to the point that its investment value approximately equals that of the average bond, real estate property, or comparable foreign common stock. However, this seeming stability is deceptive. Most investors soberly realize that their previous optimistic concepts of extended, long-term, worldwide growth and prosperity have been irrevocably shattered by the near collapse of the international financial system. The investors have again replaced expectations of unlimited riches in a riskless society with caution and prudence.

The public tries to reduce its discomfort by returning to a more traditional and conservative life-style. The first step is to blame those government officials in power for creating their difficulties and replacing them with new leaders who promise economic tranquility and a quick return to better times. True to their word, these newly elected leaders quickly stabilize the economy by implementing large personal and corporate tax cuts.

Also during this period, the government takes the first tentative steps toward promoting a speedy recovery. It encourages the injection of both currency and credit into the banking system to relieve the liquidity problems of distressed financial interests. The new money is quickly absorbed by the general slack in the economy and is not inflationary. This further reduces interest rates and inflation to levels not seen since the early stages of the growth phase and tends to help promote stability.


## ENTERING THE PLATEAU STAGE

The first years of the plateau stock market boom are usually characterized by a general revaluation of oversold equity prices to historically more normal levels. This usually involves a gradual rise in the average price-earnings ratio. Significant earnings and dividend increases are usually not fully reflected in stock prices because of the tentative and cautious nature of the recovery. Most common stocks, however, do participate strongly in this upswing.

As in most prior periods of uncertainty, the first stocks to recover are usually the strongest and most stable blue-chip and financial issues. These companies' earnings benefit most from the sharply lower interest rates brought on by the depth and severity of the recession. As stability and recovery become more visible, most other stocks join the upswing. By the end of the first year of the rally, price gains of over 100 percent are common.

As the plateau progresses, a tentative stock market boom continues to develop. Balance sheet-liquidity rises to levels that allow corporations to regain confidence in the survivability of their companies. Corporate earnings begin to improve and in some cases move strongly higher. There are still many shaky and near-bankrupt companies struggling to survive, but most have retrenched to the point that survivability is highly probable. Especially favoring the future outlook for most common stocks is the low and continued stable rate of inflation. By this point, the rate of inflation has declined to less than half of its wartime high and appears surprisingly stable. With the Federal Reserve Board's monetary and fiscal policies in a conservative stance, and with businesses and consumers too cautious to rekindle a new period of indiscriminate spending and credit extension, a return to another period of hyperinflation is not expected. Reinforcing this notion are the strongly conservative free-market policies of the newly elected government leaders.

By the middle stages of the plateau, stock prices continue to improve steadily. These new gains are now largely caused by earnings and dividend growth as the average price-earnings ratios of stocks begin to stabilize at an historically average level. Interest rates have increased moderately to reflect the increase in consumer and business credit demands but not enough to seriously threaten the bull market. At this point, the average stock continues to remain fairly valued with respect to most other investments (with the possible exception of the real estate market, which is greatly benefiting from a postwar housing shortage).

The strong value of the dollar relative to most of the major world currencies is of surprising benefit to the stock market and fixed-income debt securities during the middle years of the plateau. As world economies slowly recover from the effects of the peak war, most come under severe pressure to repay their war-induced debts. This also becomes a problem in countries not involved in the war since they have had to support their economies with greatly overpriced imports during the inflationary war years. As the war comes to a close and these debts are exposed, it becomes obvious to world financial institutions that most loans extended to both business interests and foreign governments probably will never be repaid.

Additional lending to these high-risk countries is sharply curtailed, causing intense financial pressure as their economies begin to stagnate. As unemployment rises, the resulting unstable political environment precipitates a huge outflow of capital into nations whose economy and political situations appear more stable.

Since most of this transferred capital is earmarked for relatively low-risk, highly liquid investments, the vast majority of it is invested in the government securities and common-stock markets of the few remaining financially and politically strong countries. By the beginning of the latter half of the plateau, this influx of capital has helped set the stage for a surge in general business activity in these countries.

The resulting, apparently positive, financial climate tends to give the average investor a false sense of prosperity and induces additional stock market commitments. Investment decisions are greatly influenced by the upbeat rhetoric of the conservative political leadership, which increasingly takes credit for the improving economy. Little consideration is given to the slow but steady financial deterioration in weak countries where the business climate remains stagnant and unemployment stubbornly high. In fact, during the last half of the plateau, inflationary and deflationary forces are in a constant state of disequilibrium. Periodically, it seems that the recovery will prove sufficiently powerful to perpetuate a continuation of the long-term economic expansion experienced in the prewar growth phase.

Since this is in the best interests of both the government and business communities, attempts are periodically made to aid the recovery with a series of monetary and financial policies that pump money and credit into the economy. *However, these policies are largely negated by the deflationary effects of an increasingly precarious international debt crisis casting a pall on the world financial structure.*


## A SPECULATIVE FRENZY

During the final years of the plateau, the forces of deflation are becoming more pervasive, especially in the weaker sectors of the world economy. Commodity prices and economic activity begin to trend downward as the twin burdens of high debt and slow growth finally cause a decline in consumer demand. One by one world bourses turn down in response to the accelerating flight of capital from the weaker economies. At this point, risk capital avoids all but the strongest and most stable markets.

In response, the few remaining "stable" stock markets around the world explode in a huge, speculative frenzy. Stocks especially favored in these markets are the more speculative issues that have not yet fully participated in the boom. In these frantic times, it is common to see certain "hot" issues rise over 100 percent in price within a few months. The long-term stock cycle usually reaches its second and normally higher peak at this time as the stream of money becomes a torrent, putting extreme upward pressure on the stronger countries' currencies. Eventually, these currencies become excessively overvalued, causing their export industries to lose their ability to compete in international trade.

Especially affected are the basic industry stocks, such as mining, chemicals, steel manufacturing, domestically produced petroleum, automobiles, and manufactured products of all kinds. As unemployment accelerates in these industries, severe political pressure is placed on government leaders to correct the problem or be voted out of office. At first, the government puts financial pressure on those foreign countries whose currencies hold the greatest degree of undervaluation. Initially, policies, including bilateral trade agreements, currency controls, and minor trade barriers, are attempted but with little success. These weaker countries are in too poor a financial condition to restrict their export industries in any meaningful way. Even if able to do so, government leaders would probably refuse. Restricting exports would only raise unemployment to even higher levels and jeopardize their own jobs.

International tensions quickly escalate in this environment as further selective trade barriers are imposed by both sides. At some point, the problem becomes too much of a burden, and an international trade war results. The world slips into depression.

## THE PATTERN OF DEPRESSIONS

Depressions usually follow a fairly predictable pattern. The first phase usually includes a sharp but relatively short-lived period of price and credit contraction in which a large portion of the economic inefficiencies built up during the growth and plateau stages are purged from the economy. The second phase might be characterized as a sustained period of generally stagnant economic conditions as the world tries to recover from the first phase. In this phase, select industries prosper while others continue to decline toward future absorption or bankruptcy. Depending on the nature of the depression, this period of stagnation with selective prosperity can last over a decade.

Eventually, as business conditions fail to improve, a second and usually more violent wave of price deflation and credit collapse occurs. The world then spirals into a final contraction.

The first few months of the depression are usually the most dramatic for stock prices. The sudden change from euphoria to despair in such a short time is very unsettling. The shock to the business and investment interests of the nation is almost indescribable. Paper fortunes in common stock disappear as investors are forced to sell holdings for a fraction of their former worth. Most stocks immediately decline to less than half their former values. Especially hard hit are the lesser-quality, high price-earnings ratio stocks, which were stellar performers in the latter years of the plateau.

The shares of those companies that do not go bankrupt almost immediately decline to small fractions of their former prices.

## THE QUIET FALL

*Ironically, the profits of most companies are not seriously affected during the first year of depression.* Most of the initial losses in stock prices are caused by declines in price-earnings ratios rather than declines in earnings and dividends as the markets begin to discount the declining growth prospects of the world economy. As a result, in the initial years of the depression, a wide range of differing opinions develops regarding the future direction of stock prices.

Many investors feel that most of the speculative excesses have been washed out of the economy and that the stock market is poised for recovery. Most economic and investment advisors still consider the steady runoff in economic activity a normal corrective recession resulting from the financial excesses of the latter stages of the plateau. They rationalize that not only have most stocks become extremely oversold with respect to present dividends and earnings, but also that they are relatively cheap compared to most investment alternatives. This is especially true of short-term interest rate investments such as Treasury bills and high-quality commercial paper where yields are now only a fraction of most stocks dividends.

Eventually, however, it becomes broadly apparent that a pickup in economic activity is not forthcoming and the stock market again plummets into a severe decline. As the financial markets begin to experience an intense liquidity crisis, money becomes scarce and many businesses are prohibited from obtaining credit. Especially hurt are the foreign borrowers who have been on the verge of loan defaults for several years. Only steady and frequent injections of new money have enabled them to repay their obligations. When new money is not forthcoming, they begin to default, at first selectively and then *en masse*. The international financial system quickly collapses, sharply reducing world trade and international cooperation. Political and social instabilities often hasten the final decision to default.

Additional protective trade barriers are demanded by the domestic industries of most countries, because prices of products have simply fallen too low to make an acceptable profit. Many of the weaker countries of the world are in the initial stages of full-scale revolutions as the populace seeks a new answer to its problems. Most of the stronger countries are able to retain their political identities unless they selectively opt to destroy their currencies by excessive monetary inflation.

As the end of the first down-leg of the depression approaches and the panic becomes more severe, government leaders are forced to intervene with a variety of fiscal and monetary measures. The scope of these policies is usually proportional to the seriousness of the situation. Emphasis is initially placed on restoring the volume of currency and credit in the monetary system. In effect, these policies attempt to increase the value of money in circulation by raising prices and relieving the debt loads of the private sector.

Governments may also resort to the socialization of distressed businesses if the continuation of their operations constitutes an essential component of society. This may occur directly through the outright purchase of the existing stock of the companies or indirectly by selectively overtaxing financially strong and successful businesses still making profits, while granting subsidies to industries facing imminent bankruptcy. In time, the combination of government intervention and naturally corrective market action halts the decline and sets the stage for an extended period of reduced economic growth.

By the end of the first down-leg of the depression, which usually lasts three to five years, a significant portion of world debt has been liquidated by actual default or has been rescheduled in *de facto* default. The average common stock has lost between 50 percent and 60 percent of its value in relatively mild depressions and up to 85 percent in severe depressions. Most businesses still in existence are in a serious if not critical financial condition. Declining earnings, in addition to high debts, have seriously reduced balance sheet liquidity to the point that most companies are not able to borrow money to maintain operations. Most dividends either have been eliminated or sharply reduced. Banks are in similar illiquid conditions, and in many instances are unwilling to make loans except to the most credit-worthy. Internationally, trade between nations has almost ceased.

## THE PURGING EFFECT

At the same time, the economic chaos brought about by a deflationary depression also benefits world economies by cleaning out a large portion of the inefficiencies and excess capacity that previously existed. In addition, powerful deflationary forces usually push the economy and stock prices into a significantly oversold condition, so that most businesses and investments are greatly underpriced by historical standards. This sets the stage for stabilization and an eventual strengthening in both the economy and most investments, including common stocks.

Having been stabilized, the economy enters the stagnant phase of the depression—a protracted period of stable but reduced economic growth—as the world attempts to adjust to its more complex and precarious financial environment. Through the average 10-year duration of the stagnant phase, unemployment continues to remain high and business activity subdued. Although much of the debt and business inefficiencies have been cleansed from the economy, the depression has not been sufficiently long or severe enough to complete the cleansing process. The stagnation period might be characterized as a protracted bridging period between deflationary panics where the economy gets a chance to catch its breath. Most businesses that remain viable during this period survive by increasing their productivity and eliminating inefficiencies in their work forces.

There are some industries that actually prosper. Especially noteworthy are money center banks and financial institutions that have become flush with deposits from government and private sources, and have used these funds to make huge speculative profits trading in the bond markets. Select-quality industrial and high-technology stocks also prove relatively strong. High premiums are paid for stocks of companies that seem likely to survive a return to depression. Lesser-quality growth stocks continue to be largely avoided.

As the end of the stagnation period approaches, it is widely assumed by most investors that the worst of the depression is over. This is usually not the case. Many of the remaining excesses built up during the "positive" side of the cycle have not been completely purged from the economy. Debts and excess plant capacity are still substantial. Especially noticeable is the continuing burden of large-scale foreign debt still overhanging the market.

Throughout the depression years, many of the weaker countries of the world have made desperate efforts to restore confidence and political stability to their economies. Perhaps the most popular technique is the artificial maintenance of an undervalued state in their currencies, called competitive devaluation. To achieve this result, they usually force the amount of their currency in circulation to extraordinary levels, far exceeding their needs. This currency inflation produces a short-term decline in interest rates, a boost in consumer prices, and a decrease in its value. In the initial stages of the stagnation period, this policy is often successful since, with increased trade through lower-valued exports, economic and social problems are partially transferable.

The positive effects of these policies are negated by the markets as investors soon avoid a country whose currency depreciation is slowly eroding the value of their investments.

With the removal of capital, social and economic discord soon follows. This leads to the eventual rise of dictators, revolutions, and, in many instances, contributes greatly to the trough war phenomenon. The immediate effect is a rash of further foreign debt defaults, since these countries are eventually faced with an inability to pay their bills.

*The specter of these foreign debt defaults on the international credit markets is usually the prime contributor to the final and often most devastating phase of the depression.* The new wave of overseas defaults by weaker and more unstable countries quickly translates into bankruptcies in stronger nations. Prices again fall and the demand for goods drops, causing unemployment to climb to historically high levels. The effects on the already weakened economy are severe. This is a period of large-scale bank failures and business embarrassments.

In this final phase of the depression, virtually all common stocks suffer severe price erosion, the only exception being gold-mining companies that are operating at record capacity. This, of course, assumes that the nation is on a gold standard with gold being fixed in price at an artificially overvalued level (See Chapter V).

Eventually, after an average of five years of serious depression, most inefficiencies have been purged from the system, and the economy once again begins to stabilize. The prices of most items are at historically low levels. Labor is again plentiful and cheap. Interest rates are at a long-term cyclical low since credit demand is almost nonexistent. Corporate profits are at rock bottom and have no place to go but up, and gold is increasingly plentiful, making the banking system liquid and financially solid. In this environment, most stocks reach their lowest price levels. After several years of further consolidation, the cycle again emerges into the growth stage of the next Kondratieff Wave.

## THE KONDRATIEFF CYCLE IN STOCK PRICES

Throughout the history of stock prices in the United States from the Revolutionary War period to the present, it is interesting to note how closely this idealized stock market scenario is paralleled through each of the long-term Kondratieff Cycles.

Contrary to most other forms of investment, very little is known about the trend of common-stock prices in the United States prior to the early 1800s. The most apparent explanation may be the fact that the Colonies during the 1700s were primarily agrarian with a limited financial infrastructure. Public ownership of business interests was primarily confined to farm-related real estate investments and, to a lesser extent, participation in local and essentially family-owned shipping and fishing enterprises located in the New England States. In this environment, most trade was conducted by barter.

Our financial industry was considered extremely primitive by world standards. The few large banks in operation were all located in the more populated urban centers of New York, Philadelphia, and Boston, and were restrictively provincial, not broadly serving the financial needs of the nation. The relatively unprogressive economic development in the prerevolution Colonies was a direct consequence of the self-serving economic and political policies of the English Parliament.

During the early Colonial era, Parliament concluded that it was to England's advantage to keep the Colonies in a position of subservience. It was decided that if the Colonies ever became financially or economically independent of England, the economic harmony of the Commonwealth would be severely threatened. To implement this philosophy, Parliament systematically established a wide range of restrictions and regulations in the Colonies. The most visible were directed at financial interests. The major central banks were either directly or indirectly controlled by English authorities in every facet of their operations. Severe restrictions were imposed that selectively controlled the allocation and purpose of business loans.

If it was in the best interest of the British Empire that one among several competing companies was favored for a loan, it was usually granted to that interest that demonstrated the greatest loyalty to the Crown. This control was easily accomplished since most major central banks were either directly owned by British citizens, or the majority of their deposit accounts and financial interests were dominated in some way by English trading partners. The monopoly was strengthened further by Parliamentary dicta that absolutely forbade the printing of currency by any bank or financial institution located in the Colonies. These regulations created a primitive and highly inefficient economic and business climate. More importantly, they also created a hostile political atmosphere that would eventually trigger the Revolutionary War.

In addition to financial control, England's systematic repression of domestic manufacturing companies was of particular concern to the Colonies. Since it was deemed to England's advantage that our manufactured goods be barred from competing with English goods in world markets, Parliament instituted a series of regulations and taxes to stifle colonial manufacturing. Widely employed tactics included prohibitive taxes and bounties imposed on all exports.

During this period, most business interests were concentrated in a few industries, such as lumber, fishing, and ocean transport. With the exception of a few large companies, ownership was largely restricted to small associations and family partnerships. Common-stock ownership was rare. Of the few stock transactions that did occur, most were private purchases. The few recorded trades that transpired in public forums probably did not represent an accurate indication of economic activity levels essential to a proper evaluation of the direction of stock prices. However, some assumptions about stock trends can be inferred from scattered records of other indicators of economic activity during this period.

During the 20-year period preceding the Revolutionary War, it is generally known that economic activity rose modestly. The prices of most commodities sold in the major urban centers of New York and Philadelphia rose over 50 percent. It is also known that practically all banks and financial institutions prospered greatly from the tremendous increase in shipping. This shipping included the transportation of a huge influx of immigrants into the Colonies from Europe and a great expansion of international commerce. It is also known that during the Revolutionary War, many businesses experienced great economic hardship due to the continental currency fiasco and the blockage of the main ports by the British Navy.

After the war ended, the nation experienced a series of financial panics as a severe deflationary depression enveloped the country. Institutions especially hard hit by the depression included those involved in the financing of various real estate ventures in farming and construction. Farmers were particularly devastated by depressed crop prices and reduced demand for farm products. Many lost everything when the majority of farm mortgages defaulted. Urban center banks fared much better than rural banks because the values of their bond portfolios appreciated greatly as interest rates fell in tandem with the rate of inflation.

Ocean freight companies were one of the few industries not significantly affected by the depression due to continued migration from Europe after the war. As the depression in Europe intensified, the promise of a new and more prosperous life in America, free from the repressive social structure of ruling monarchs, accelerated migration.

By 1791, the United States had largely liberated itself from the economic inefficiencies imposed upon it by the English Parliament and had begun to restructure its economic and financial system in preparation for an emergence into world commerce. By the middle 1790s, the present-day Constitution was ratified, giving the government full taxing authority to support business, and allowing it to issue a currency fully backed by gold to standardize monetary transactions. The eventual outcome of these policies was a reduction in both interest rates and debt to historically low levels. The young nation was now prepared to embark on its first period of long-term economic growth and prosperity.

In the early years of this growth phase, most businesses cautiously expanded their activities. With some significant exceptions, profits were generally modest. By the early 1800s an unprecedented number of new settlers poured into the "West," which then constituted the Mississippi Valley and the Great Lakes region. Companies that supplied goods and services necessary to facilitate the westward migration benefited greatly. These included road-building and wagon-making companies, residential and commercial construction, and real estate sales.

The West was not the only source of new business activity in America. The Napoleonic Wars stimulated the emergence of a host of new industries on the Eastern seaboard. Because most European armies were involved in the war, there was significant demand for war materiel and supplies. New companies grew to meet these needs. These primarily included the ship-building, munitions, and food-processing industries along with clothing manufacturers in the Middle Atlantic States. The basic technology for this rapidly expanding industrial base came from the machinery designs and techniques of our European competitors, who were participating in the industrial revolution in Europe.

This new-found prosperity proved to be somewhat ephemeral. By 1807, a significant financial crisis enveloped the nation. England block-aded European ports from northern Germany to France, severely curtailing the American export trading industry. After several years of blatant harassment, Congress finally declared war on Great Britain.

The costs of the War of 1812 had a profound effect on business interests. As war expenses began to escalate, state-chartered banks were forced to issue additional currency and credit at sharply increased rates. During the war period from 1812 through 1817, total state bank notes in circulation increased dramatically, causing wholesale prices to increase over 50 percent and the yield on U.S. government bonds to rise from less than 6 to over 8 percent. With interest rates at these heights, banks and other lending institutions profited spectacularly.

Conversely, in the manufacturing sector, productivity and profitability fell sharply due to labor unrest primarily caused by the inability of wages to keep pace with inflation. Many interest-sensitive industries with large bond and mortgage debts saw the value of their companies steadily depreciate. During the worst part of the inflation, from 1812 to 1815, the average bank and insurance stock lost over 50 percent of its value. Real asset oriented stocks, however, continued to perform well due to the general inflation.

## THE POSTWAR SYNDROME

By 1816, a year after the war, the greatly overextended economy entered a typical postwar recession. As loans to a growing number of companies began to default, money became scarce, forcing interest rates to extremely high levels. With lower earnings and higher borrowing costs, most common stocks collapsed in a major financial panic and recession. Many prominent companies declared immediate bankruptcy. Prisons overflowed with debtors who were unable to make loan payments. Formerly stable industries experienced severe drops in employment and earnings. Many had to devalue their stagnant inventories or liquidate products at prices far below production costs. However, the recession succeeded in partially reducing most of the speculative excesses built up during the growth period and set the stage for the emergence of the postwar plateau.

During the 10-year duration of the plateau, the value of currency in circulation increased only gradually, and prices remained remarkably stable. Domestically, the economy was primed for expansion. Internationally, severe economic sanctions were imposed on our export industries while competing products from Europe were dumped on our economy at below-production costs. In New England, cotton mills became unprofitable through foreign dumping of competing products. In Pittsburgh, iron refineries were subjected to protective import tariffs raised in England, France, and Germany. Several European governments prohibited the importing of our grain products altogether. The United States retaliated by implementing its own import sanctions. When these moves failed to stabilize international trade, the United States began to expand internally, concentrating its resources on the movement to the West.

The first years of the plateau were characterized by a revaluation of oversold common-stock prices to more historically normal levels. Since the mood of both the business community and the consumer was cautious due to the severity of the recession, business activity and earnings growth remained sluggish. The strongest stocks in the early stages of the plateau included a handful of manufacturing companies located in the urban cities of New England that produced processed food and clothing. Also strong were the road- and canal-construction companies of the Western frontier. By late 1818, the first road connecting the Eastern seaboard with the Ohio Valley was completed. Altogether, 1500 miles of roadway were laid in the United States during this plateau period.

As we learned earlier, the New York Legislature authorized construction of the Erie and Champlain canals in the 1820s. The great success of the project soon became apparent. Even before their completion in 1825, "road and canal fever" seized the fancy of investors. Promoters and speculators in canal- and road-building stocks bid share prices to unprecedented heights. At the climax of the building boom that followed, canals and roads were constructed linking most areas of the Ohio Valley and the Great Lakes region in the Northern frontier with the Mississippi Valley and Middle Atlantic States.

Interstate commerce prospered as never before. All areas of the nation expanded rapidly. Particularly profitable were the banking and insurance companies located along the Atlantic seaboard that supplied capital for expansion. From 1816 to 1825, the average, major, financial stock, as represented by the Bank and Insurance Company Index, rose from $2.50 to over $12 per share. Most of the gains were derived from the appreciation of their bond and mortgage portfolios through the continued steady decline of inflation and interest rates.

By the middle 1820s, most stock prices had significantly risen as a result of rapid earnings increases from the steady gains in business activity. However, much of these profits were artificial in nature, being derived from debts incurred by both European investors and U.S. financial institutions. These debts, added to the huge government debts incurred during the War of 1812, that had only been partially repaid, eventually resulted in a greatly overextended financial system. By 1825, the aggregate national debt was so massive that economic activity became seriously retarded.

By early 1826, the stock market boom was abruptly terminated as the nation began to experience a 17-year depression involving steadily dropping stock prices and widespread financial embarrassments. By 1840, most companies had either declared bankruptcy or had sharply reduced or omitted dividend payments. The vast majority of banks were bankrupt.

The situation became so severe that President Andrew Jackson recommended to Congress that the federal government assume the debts of a select group of the most prestigious companies in order to preserve the financial integrity of the nation. Many bankrupt companies forced their creditors to accept pennies on the dollar for their stock. Railroads ceased all transportation construction projects and sharply curtailed operations in order to remain solvent and to protect their credit ratings. Most foreign loans to the railroads were repudiated. Railroad stocks during the years 1836 to 1843 dropped an average of 80 percent, and their bonds fell over 50 percent.

This represented one of the worst periods of deflation and destruction of wealth the nation ever experienced. Eventually, the excess debt and inefficient businesses built up during the growth phase were washed out, allowing the nation to once again be poised to participate in the next upswing in the Kondratieff stock market cycle.

By 1846, the nation was eager to embark on a new period of long-term prosperity. The trough war with Mexico instilled pride in the military strength of our nation. Economic and financial conditions stabilized, and most stock prices appeared to halt their plunge.

## CAPITAL FLOWS IN

Since interest rates were low and the currency was regaining its strength, businesses soon began to experience a significant inflow of risk capital from both domestic and foreign sources. Initially, most of this risk capital was placed in the construction and railroad industries, which were again aggressively participating in the colonization of the West. The popularity of this area of investment was reflected in the high premiums paid for railroad stocks. Some rose over 70 percent from their lows at the beginning of 1846 to the end of 1852. Europe quickly became the largest foreign market for our industrial products. This enabled many international trading companies and their associated industries to operate profitably for the first time in over two decades.

By the middle 1850s, common stocks were at the cyclical height of their popularity. Because the financial system liberally accommodated loans for new business ventures, capital spending reached its highest level in history. Corporate earnings and dividends rose dramatically, giving the public added incentive to invest in well-established companies and speculate in a variety of newly emerging ones. Railroad stocks were again especially attractive since they were favored by the government via a series of financial incentives aimed at building additional routes westward. Farming and shipping interests were also favorably treated.

This was also the dawning of America's high-technology industries. The 1850s and early 1860s saw the perfection of such innovations as the steam-driven sewing and fiber-weaving machines and the Bessemer process, which mass-produced high-quality steel. Since the markets were booming, the most expedient means of obtaining investment capital for these emerging industries was by offering shares to the public. The major New York stock markets first came of age during this period. Increased activity was particularly pronounced on the New York Stock Exchange. It was transformed from an auction house to a major financial industry in just a few years.

By the late 1850s, after almost 20 years of virtually uninterrupted economic growth, the economy began to overheat. At the height of this euphoria, banks seemed oblivious to risk, expanding both the size and volume of their lending activities to dangerously high levels not seen since the War of 1812. Borrowing to initiate new business ventures of all kinds became popular, and the use of a leverage was strongly encouraged.

In early 1858, the credit demands of the government, led by a need to finance many newly initiated building projects, began to clash with those of business. This forced the cost of money to extraordinarily high levels. By late 1858, interest rates on commercial paper in most of the large money center banks rose to between 24 and 28 percent, with inflation a significant problem. By the start of the Civil War in early

1862, the cost and availability of money were the primary concerns of most business managers.

During the Civil War, the Wholesale Price Index more than tripled. Industries that were not allowed to raise their prices due to lack of consumer demand or government regulation suffered severely reduced earnings. Many were forced out of business. Only a few select industries thrived. Especially profitable were the railroads, where average stock prices almost tripled during the war years; and raw material and munitions manufacturers, such as the Du Pont Company, that made fortunes during the war. Banks, which were directly involved in lending money to the government in return for special concessions, were also especially profitable.

## CONFIDENCE RETURNS

In 1865, when the war ended, the government decided to reduce the rate of inflation to prewar levels by effecting a sharp contraction of credit in an attempt to subdue growing public dissatisfaction. As the liquidity squeeze intensified, many prominent businesses, especially those generating most of their profits from war-related sales, slid into bankruptcy. Huge losses resulted in the stock and bond markets as corporate earnings plummeted. In the two-year postwar recession, the average common stock lost over 65 percent of its value. However, similar to all postwar recessions, this one proved to be typically sharp but short-lived, eventually depressing both the rate of inflation and interest rates to more historically normal levels. Public confidence was quickly restored, allowing the stock market to move into the reconstruction plateau.

In this plateau, our industrial and financial infrastructure experienced widespread recovery. As is typical, economic activity progressed slowly at first but gradually gained strength, allowing the basic conditions for a major stock market boom to soon become visible to the investing public. Both business productivity and earnings enjoyed a spectacular rebound, especially in the transportation and financial industries, that had been severely hurt by the recession. Common-stock prices moved rapidly upward, due largely to an infusion of over $2 billion in European capital into our stock market. These foreign investments in the U.S. were spurred by the replacement of President Andrew Johnson, who was liberal and antibusiness, with the conservative, probusiness Ulysses S. Grant. Much of this capital found its way into the still burgeoning railroad industry.

During the reconstruction period, the economic impact of the railroad industry reached its zenith. By 1870, it accounted for over 20 percent of the gross national product. Because of the high cost of materials and labor, the capital requirements of the railroad industry were immense. By far, the bulk of the necessary capital was generated from private and foreign sources, primarily as a result of solicitation by securities brokers and investment promoters. *These individuals were so successful in Europe, that by 1870, the majority of all railroads in America were owned by foreign interests.* Many prominent Wall Street underwriting firms existing today were born during this reconstruction period.


## GOVERNMENT KILLS TRADE

Although most sectors of the U.S. economy were making significant progress during the postwar plateau, our export industries were again suffering a severe postwar recession. Just as after the War of 1812 plateau, the government decided that the national interests were best served by barring foreign imports from our domestic markets. Government leaders and members of the business community strongly believed that this action was appropriate in order to properly rebuild the basic industries of our economy during the postwar plateau.

It was rationalized that foreign companies could make identical products much more cheaply than their American competitors because of higher U.S. wages and material costs built into the economy as a result of Civil War inflation.

As a result, from the Civil War through the early 1870s, the United States government systematically eliminated most imports. In 1861, the maximum tariff was raised from 20 to 24 percent, and by 1864, to almost 50 percent. By 1873, the remnants of world trade had collapsed to the point that a major banking panic and depression were soon in progress.

During the first few years of the depression, the prices of the vast majority of common stocks fell sharply. Railroad stocks declined over 50 percent while the average industrial common stock, as represented by the Clement-Burgess Composite Index, declined over 45 percent. Foreign demand for U.S. goods plummeted, causing severe financial problems for all companies involved in international trade. Raw material-manufacturing industries also experienced severe difficulties. Production levels of pig iron and nonprecious metals declined over 30 percent. Unemployment was widespread in all regions of the country. The only moderately successful industries were the money center banks that were profiting tremendously on their rapidly appreciating bond portfolios.

This initial depressionary stage of declining stock prices lasted nearly four years until late 1877.

The downtrend then moderated, and the economy entered a relatively prolonged period of widespread stagnation, characteristic of the middle stages of a Kondratieff depression.

During this period of general stagnation, some stocks continued to experience significant weakness, while others performed spectacularly. The prices of the strongest railroad stocks exploded, increasing an average of over 300 percent from late 1877 to 1881. Some financial stocks advanced even more rapidly. The Standard & Poor's Composite 500 Stock Index (S&P 500) increased over 100 percent, from $2.73 to $6.58. In sharp contrast to these impressive gains, an equal number of industry groups continued to experience severe profit erosion. These included agricultural and mining companies, metal and basic commodity manufacturing companies, and all real estate and construction companies.

This extended period of economic lethargy continued throughout the 1880s and well into the early 1890s without a significant change in the overall economic health of the nation. Few industries experienced any significant stock price appreciation. Between 1881 and 1892, the Standard & Poor's Industrial Index fluctuated between $6.58 and $5.60. Late in 1892, this broad trading range was abruptly halted as the economy proceeded into the final and most severe stage of the depression.

This second and by far the most virulent period of deflationary depression was largely propelled by a series of major loan defaults in both the United States and Europe. Unlike the previous rapid depression period in the late 1870s, this phase was characterized by significant political and social unrest. During the panic of 1893, the increasingly severe economic crisis in America began to create doubt in the international financial community concerning the survivability of our country. As a result, during the next several years, large quantities of investment capital were transferred from America to more stable political climates in Europe. As a result, by 1894, over 180 railroad companies and over half of our basic industry, went bankrupt. Stock prices plummeted. Unemployment, strikes and workers' riots were widespread. By the end of the depression in 1896, most of the great industrial fortunes built up during the previous cycle were either significantly dissipated or completely wiped out. In August of 1896, the stock market, as represented by the S & P 500, hit bottom at $3.81, the second lowest trough price on record (the lowest being a $2.73 reading recorded at the bottom of the first down-leg of the depression in January 1877). This was the last time in stock market history that the S & P 500 would fall below $4. By comparison, during this same period, the Dow Jones Industrial (DOW) Average fell from $39.10 to $20.90, the low point of this long-term stock market cycle.

By the late 1890s, as the country emerged into the growth stage of the next cycle, the economy was beginning to improve. Debt levels were once again low and political stability largely restored. As the nation faced a new century, few realized that the next 30 years would represent the greatest period of industrial expansion in its history.


## THE FINEST HOUR

During the first 10 years of the expansion, growth was moderately strong. Businessmen who had been devastated by the recent depression were replaced by a new generation of more conservative entrepreneurs. Business taxes were so moderate as to be of almost no consequence. Labor unions were peaceful and inoffensive, since most of the current labor laws had not been written. The government was many years away from strangling the markets with a barrage of regulations and controls. This represented laissez-faire capitalism in its finest hour, and the captains of industry made the most of it.

Such household names as Rockefeller of Standard Oil, Edison of General Electric, Carnegie of U.S. Steel, du Pont of the Du Pont Company, and many others made the great bulk of their fortunes during this period. Perhaps the greatest technological contribution came from the invention and mass production of the automobile. By the early 1900s, at the time of steel railroad electrification, the automobile was still a curiosity and widely considered to be only an experimental gadget. Due largely to the innovative production-line techniques of Henry Ford, fairly reliable cars became common. Like the railroad in its day, the automobile spawned a wide variety of peripheral industries, such as road construction, car repairs and service, fuel production, and others.

This period showed the greatest advance in overall stock prices since the founding of the exchanges. From 1896 to 1906, the Dow average rose over 270 percent, from $20.09 to $76.57. The broader S&P Index climbed to a record $10.03, an almost 200 percent gain. These gains were relatively steady with few exaggerated fluctuations in either direction.

Some common stocks greatly outperformed the market averages. The most noteworthy of these included the transportation stocks led by the railroads. During this initial decade of the growth phase, the Dow Jones Railroad Averages advanced 350 percent. High-technology stocks, such as automobiles, performed even better. Ford Motor Company, although not yet at the pinnacle of its popularity, was a top performer.

By the end of the second decade of the growth phase, the nation was in the midst of a euphoric stock market boom, characteristic of a terminal stage of the plateau. The Dow average had risen to over $110, and most business sectors had positive, even euphoric, expectations for the future. However, at the height of this euphoria, in 1916, stock prices began to experience an extended period of deterioration.

As was the case in both past cycles, just prior to the top, businesses had been increasing their spending on new plants and equipment in anticipation of continued prosperity. This put a tremendous strain on the financial system, causing interest rates to move higher. With the involvement of the United States in World War I, the economic stability of the business community began to noticeably weaken. As the money supply was increased to finance the war, both inflation and interest rates quickly moved to substantially higher levels in a very short time.

Most businesses could not adapt rapidly enough to these new economic burdens. Labor unions demanded higher wages, and the government instituted price regulations and quotas. The labor force was disrupted as men were displaced from industry to fight the war. Earnings suffered as productivity slowly declined.

During the principal war years from 1915 through 1918, the Dow average lost over 40 percent of its value, while the average price of commodities almost tripled. Not all common stocks declined. As in each past cycle, those companies that dealt in raw commodities and those not regulated by price controls fared quite well. Other industries with high-earnings growth and strong stock patterns included real estate development companies, farming enterprises, and a select group of emerging high-technology companies with tight patent protection.

As the war effort intensified and the inflation rate reached what seemed almost uncontrollable limits, the public was conscious of the loss of the purchasing power of the dollar and began to buy real items including common stocks. Many were purchased on the most leveraged credit terms possible with the intent of later selling these items at highly inflated prices. This strategy accelerated the already euphoric credit expansion and forced interest rates to even higher levels.

The stock markets began to experience a brisk business as the public became an increasingly active participant. It became more profitable to hedge against inflation in the highly liquid equity markets than to risk capital on long-term business ventures. Investors began to speculate with increasingly higher levels of margin. Money that was formerly used to finance capital formation was now being used to finance speculation in light of the inflationary scenario.

During 1918 and 1919, the Dow average nearly doubled, advancing from $66 to $120. By late 1919, the President and Congress became concerned about the high level of speculation in the equity markets. On May 17, 1920, the Senate adopted a resolution requiring the Federal

Reserve to advise them of the steps necessary to stabilize the problem. Almost immediately, the Federal Reserve raised the discount rate to a record 7 percent. This policy had an immediate negative impact on the stock markets. The nation rapidly plunged into a severe financial panic accompanied by a sharp drop in the stock market.

## APPROACHING CLOUDS

During the subsequent postwar recession, economic activity fell over 30 percent and business failures increased over 100 percent. The stock markets dropped sharply. From the start of the decline in November 1919, until August 1921, the Dow average lost over 37 percent of its value. The more stable indexes, including the Dow Jones Transportation and Utility Averages, lost less than 20 percent each. Speculative issues on average lost over 50 percent of their values. Unemployment rose to historically high levels, and business failures were widespread. Industries that were unable to promptly liquidate their inventories were especially affected. The huge quantities of inflation-hedge goods on hand made liquidations even more difficult. Many conservative corporations skipped paying their dividends for the first time. By the end of 1922, the severe recession and credit liquidation ceased, and a gradual stabilization in stock prices emerged.

During the early 1920s, the nation experienced a mild shock from the effects of the recession. Businesses were very hesitant to expand. The Federal Reserve proceeded to increase the money supply at a modest level of 5 percent per year for the remainder of the decade. This allowed short-term interest debt (U.S. Treasury bills) to fall from yields of over 6.5 percent to less than 3 percent. Moreover, long-term U.S. Treasury bonds fell from a yield of 5.75 percent to just over 3 percent. Correspondingly, the wholesale price index fell over 55 percent.

*With both the rate of inflation and interest rates at such low levels, and with economic and financial stability a reality, the economy contained the perfect ingredients for a stock market boom of once-in-a-lifetime proportions.*

By the end of 1924, the economic recovery was again in full progress. The Dow average advanced from 50 to slightly over 100, and the rate of inflation and interest rates continued to remain stable at historically low levels. The federal budget was balanced, and the dollar was strong on international currency markets. As a result, credit once again became easily available. This induced expansion of businesses producing a variety of new and innovative products to satisfy the appetites of an increasingly consumption-oriented populace.

As the decade of the 1920s progressed, the public became wealthier and spent a greater portion of their income on investments. By 1925, responding to a host of favorable economic indicators, the stock market broke out of long-term trading range and began a strong and sustained rally. Since the real estate market was in the process of completing its midplateau peak and beginning a trend downward, the stock market represented the only visible opportunity for spectacular gains. By 1927, the stock market had caught the fancy of the public and institutional investors such that by the end of the year, the Dow average exceeded 200 for the first time, a 50 percent advance for the year. Many stocks significantly outperformed the market averages. Particularly noteworthy were high-technology stocks. These included synthetic fibers, up 275 percent; radio manufacturers, up 100 percent, and drugs, up 70 percent. Financial institutions, whose corporate portfolios included bond and common stocks, also performed well. Insurance companies and investment companies were up 90 percent, and bank stocks advanced 70 percent.

By the end of 1927, according to most historical standards, the average common stock was modestly overvalued. However, there were many extraordinary forces that perpetuated the rally for another two years. Among these forces were the widespread social and economic dislocations in Europe, which was having significant problems recovering from the war. Attempting to stabilize their currencies and returning to the gold standard were two of the most prominent of these difficulties. Other major problems included widespread unemployment and the lack of sufficient funds to rebuild their war-torn industrial base. Strikes became common as most European countries incurred political shifts to the left, some moving toward Socialism and others toward Communism. This caused many of the financially weaker countries to experience severe financial difficulties to the point that they were on the verge of defaulting on their international debts.

Africa, South America, and Asia were particularly shaky areas whose economies depended on high levels of world trade. Minor European countries, including Belgium, Luxemburg, Austria, and many of the present-day Warsaw Pact countries, were also in serious financial trouble. As a result, investment capital in the form of gold and currency began to be increasingly transferred to the few remaining stable countries, including the U.S. By late 1927, most of the world's stock exchanges showed decreasing prices, while exchanges in the few remaining stable countries continued to experience new highs.

*By 1928, this relationship split the world economy in two, with the U.S. on one side and everyone else on the other.* Conditions were so bad that most countries were either at or near bankruptcy, while the

U.S. had accumulated a large portion of the world's capital. This, of course, led to a greatly overvalued dollar, artificially low interest rates, and a rise in world trade barriers. While there was no apparent economic deterioration in the United States, several key sectors were in deep trouble. Farmers were suffering a severe financial crisis as low crop prices and high real rates of interest were slowly eroding their assets. Real estate markets, including undeveloped land and residential and commercial properties, had been in a severe depression since 1925 and showed few signs of stabilization or recovery. Basic industries led by autos, steel, chemicals, and mining were being suffocated by highly competitive international markets.

In the spring of 1928, the Federal Reserve first attempted to forestall an international crisis and stabilize the steadily deteriorating international financial system by employing a series of monetary and fiscal measures. After several abortive attempts to use manipulative measures, such as import/export controls, trade restrictions, and tax differentials, the Federal Reserve was finally forced to use its currency- and credit-creating powers to artificially lower U.S. interest rates and thus take pressure off the dollar. During the months after this policy was implemented, large sums of money were pumped into the banking system.

Although this policy did succeed in temporarily lowering interest rates, the positive results proved short-lived. As the public perceived a continuing easy-money policy, greater amounts of capital were withdrawn from short-term debt instruments and transferred to the stock market. As a result, by June of 1928, both the stock markets and interest rates were advancing to new highs. The Dow Industrials exceeded 250 and was showing few signs of weakness.

For the remainder of 1928 and through the first half of 1929, the stock markets soared to new highs. During this period, the Dow Industrials advanced to over 380. The Dow Jones Utility Average performed even better by moving from 25 to 82, representing an outstanding 228 percent gain in an historically conservative investment. Specific industries performed even better. The big gainers were in high technology, with radio-manufacturing stocks advancing over 500 percent, and electronic stocks over 200 percent. Financial stocks also rose sharply. The Standard & Poor's Bank Index rose 145 percent, the Financial Company Index advanced 215 percent, and closed-end investment companies' shares moved up over 160 percent. Speculation became a major feature of these advances. During this period, total public participation in the market rose from 7 percent to over 11 percent, and net odd-lot purchases more than doubled.

Credit buying of securities rose exponentially (Figure 17). The average price of common stocks relative to the bond/stock ratio, which measures

# BROKERS' LOANS BY GROUP OF LENDER

QUARTERLY 1918-32, CALL DATES 1933-35

BILLIONS OF DOLLARS

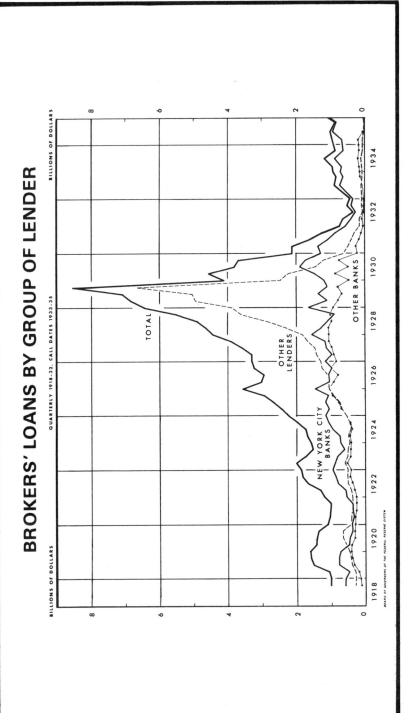

BOARD OF GOVERNORS OF THE FEDERAL RESERVE SYSTEM

Figure 17.

the overvaluation of stock yields, rose to an historically high level. Millionaire stock speculators were becoming common. Brokerage houses were manned by salespeople with little or no knowledge of the stock market. All that was necessary to sell securities to the greedy public was a positive attitude and a good story.

Throughout 1929, interest rates continued to soar to new highs primarily due to increased market speculation. As the quality of bank loans continued to deteriorate, the Federal Reserve began to decrease the money supply. By mid-1929, it had dropped an astounding 20 percent. Housing-related securities immediately declined over 50 percent. Most lower-grade common stocks began their cyclical declines at the same time.

## FALL OF THE HOUSE OF CARDS

The general stock market stubbornly continued to make new highs, and credit continued to remain readily available. In late 1929, the discount rate was raised in several abrupt steps to 6 percent, a sufficiently high level to finally break the credit markets. In October, the stock market collapsed on Black Tuesday, when the average stock lost over 30 percent of its value in one day. The market crash had begun (Figure 18).

When the break in the economy came, paper fortunes in the stock market disappeared rapidly as investors were forced to sell their stocks to meet margin calls.

During the next three years, the United States was to experience the most rapid collapse of its stock markets in history. Many former highly rated common stocks either stopped paying dividends or sharply reduced them.

Most nations, especially those with high debt structures and weak leadership, repudiated their debts and fell into revolution. By 1930, virtually all the world's currencies were off the gold standard and international trade had ground to a halt. As the decline in prices of raw materials and finished goods began to adversely affect the profits of businesses associated with international trade, extreme pressure was placed on Congress to raise tariffs on imports. In 1930, the Smoot-Hawley Act increased the average duties on most imports to 40 percent. Many foreign nations soon retaliated with even higher duties and import quotas that eventually precipitated an international trade war and even lower stock prices.

At the end of 1930, contrary to present-day popular opinion, most economists and financial experts did not believe that the nation was

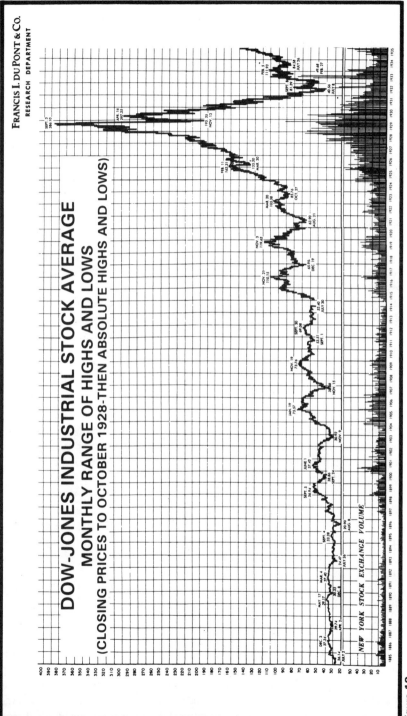

Figure 18.

falling into a depression. The economy had contracted but not to an excessive degree. Business activity had diminished modestly as both corporate profits and consumer spending remained relatively stable. Housing starts and automobile sales were sharply depressed in relation to their highs but still remained within historical norms. The only truly obvious casuality was the stock market.

Many financial advisors rationalized that the markets had simply washed out the speculative excesses of the 1928/1929 period and that stocks were now fairly priced. Since most stocks were at or near their preblow-off levels of 1927, and the price-earnings ratio of the Dow Industrials stabilized at the historically normal 15 times earnings these relatively optimistic predictions were eagerly accepted by the investment community. Because of this, government intervention was deemed unnecessary. Both Congress and the Federal Reserve decided against any overt action. In fact, since the loose monetary policies of the Federal Reserve were considered largely responsible for the speculative fever during the 1928/1929 period, they thought it prudent to reduce its exposure in the free markets to the largest degree possible.

Had it not been for the continued economic and financial deterioration in the rest of the world, the rapid spiral into depression in the United States might not have occurred. It would probably have been milder, similar to those spirals experienced during the War of 1812 and the Civil War periods.

Starting in early 1931, the severe economic problems of other nations began to seriously affect the United States stock markets. Many countries had either defaulted on most of their foreign loans or were on the verge of insolvency. As these defaults spread to our financial markets, banks became overly cautious and money became increasingly scarce. The unavailability of credit severely crippled business interests. From 1931 through the spring of 1932, the stock market experienced its worst crash in history. The Dow Industrials declined over 80 percent, falling from 200 to 40 in a little over a year. There were few rallies in the Dow of over 5 percent. The huge loss of wealth in so short a period was unprecedented.

From its high in 1929 until the final bottom in early 1932, the Dow Industrials lost over 90 percent of its value. The more conservative Dow Jones Utility Index lost 85 percent, and the Dow Jones Transportation Average 95 percent. Speculative issues fared worse. Stocks of major industries that lost over 90 percent of their value included airline manufacturers, agricultural machinery, automobiles, copper mining, fertilizer, metal fabricating, and retail department stores. Stocks losing over 95 percent of their value included closed-end investment companies, motion pictures, and radio manufacturers. Those industries that performed the best were tobacco, down 40 percent; soft drink bottlers, down 55 percent; soap, down 80 percent; food retailers down 75 percent; and oil and drugs, down 75 percent.

By late 1932, the national unemployment rate exceeded 25 percent. Many banks and respected corporations had gone out of business (Figure 19). This wholesale collapse of the nation's largest industries reinforced to the public the severity of the depression, as individuals who had been trying to sustain their former standard of living finally began to panic. On March 6, 1933, President Roosevelt, in attempting to stabilize the markets, ordered all securities exchanges closed. Simultaneously, the Securities and Exchange Commission was created to diminish fears of a further round of brokerage house bankruptcies.

These programs had an immediate effect on financial institutions. In order to ease the international dislocations brought on by the high tariffs of the Smoot-Hawley Act, Congress passed the Recovery Trade Agreement Act of 1934. This gave the president a period of three years to implement substantial tariff concessions of up to 50 percent of the currently existing rates. By 1937, world trade had been restored to a moderate level of activity.

Roosevelt also implemented a wide range of innovative industrial programs during the early 1930s. To support distressed companies, in 1933, Congress passed the National Industrial Recovery Act and the Reconstruction Finance Corporation, which made inexpensive loans available to industries that were incapable of obtaining financing from commercial banks.

## THE TURNAROUND

These federal programs slowly began to have a positive effect on the national economy. By 1937, the economy and the financial markets were showing evidence of health and stability due to increased business activity and renewed confidence (Figure 20). The Dow average rebounded to the 200 level, regaining over half of its former losses.

Unfortunately, this optimism proved premature. By 1937, after over four years of steady recovery, the fragile world economy again began to tumble. Much of the excess capacity built up from the turn of the century still had not been completely liquidated during the depression. The strain of newly instituted, high government tax rates on business interests, coupled with a new wave of central bank defaults in Europe, precipitated the panic of 1937. While this final down-leg in the depression was not as severe as the 1929 to 1933 period, it did cause significant

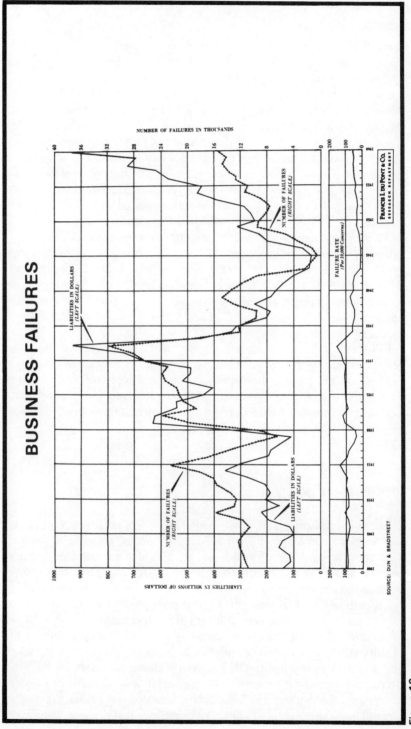

Figure 19.

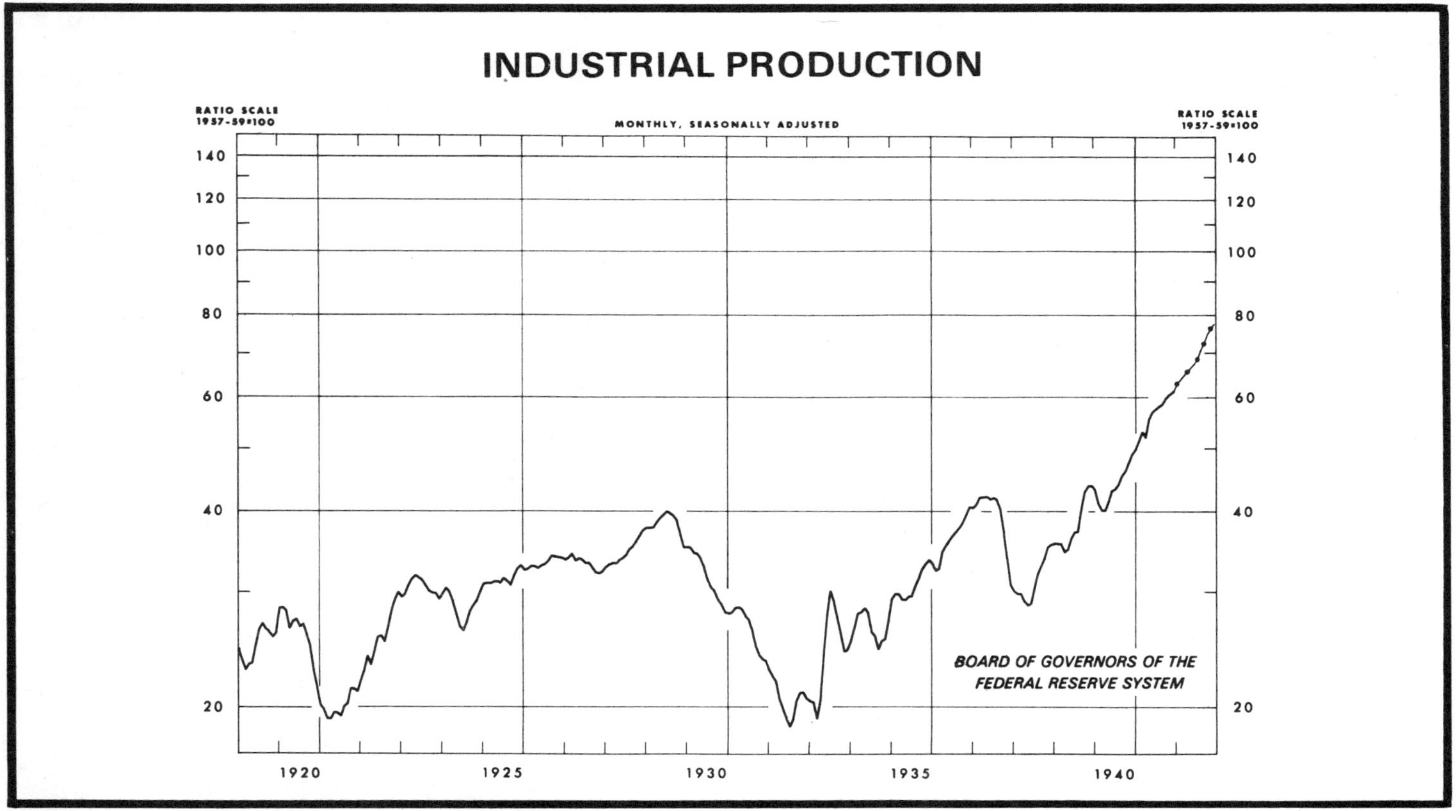

INDUSTRIAL PRODUCTION
RATIO SCALE
1957-59=100
MONTHLY, SEASONALLY ADJUSTED
RATIO SCALE
1957-59=100
140
120
100
80
60
40
20
1920
1925
1930
1935
1940
BOARD OF GOVERNORS OF THE
FEDERAL RESERVE SYSTEM


Figure 20.

labor unrest in many of the distressed basic industries. As a result, in the midst of the panic, labor movements began to gather strength and collectively demand government protection from increasing unemployment. However, this final down-leg of the depression proved to be temporary as the government began to prepare for World War II.

The 1940s was a particularly lackluster period for the securities markets. Between 1940 and 1950, the Dow Industrials advanced only 50 points, an average gain of only 2.5 percent per year. Gold-mining stocks were among the few profitable investments, increasing over 250 percent during this period. Unfortunately, profitable business opportunities were virtually nonexistent due to the wide range of war-induced economic controls and regulations. Especially constraining for business were federally-imposed wage and price controls, rations, and quotas. The most noteworthy effect of the war was the dumping of huge quantities of currency and debt into the nation's banking system. Since the bulk of this money could not be spent for consumption, it was put into savings. Interest rates subsequently plunged to artificially low levels. Treasury bond rates fell to 2.5 percent and 90-day Treasury bill rates to less than 1 percent.

As the war came to a close, the United States emerged as the most powerful country in the world. Its powerful and growing industrial base was unaffected by the war in contrast to the economies of Europe and the Far East. America was cognizant of this leadership status and exploited it to the fullest during the postwar years.

By the early 1950s, America's big businesses were beginning to emerge in the world economic arena. The decade of the 1950s could be characterized as a period of cautious but sustained growth in a wide range of business areas. Interest rates remained at historically low levels and the rate of inflation rarely exceeded 1 percent during any one year. Long-term bond rates averaged less than 3 percent. Corporate and investor liquidity was near cyclical highs, giving the consumers and businessmen an opportunity to expand their levels of debt.

Typical of all the first decades of the growth stage, investors responded to these strong fundamentals by bidding up stock prices to spectacular levels.

During the decade of the 1950s, the stock market, as exemplified by the Dow Industrials, rose from 200 to nearly 700, a 250 percent gain. The more broadly based Standard & Poor's Index advanced over 300 percent. Certain groups performed significantly better. High-technology issues were spectacular. The drug stocks were up 400 percent, electrical equipment 600 percent, and electronics and computer-oriented business machine stocks were up 1,000 and 1,100 percent, respectively. By the end of the decade, the average stock had a price-earnings ratio of over

20. Since most companies' earnings during the decade averaged less than 10 percent per year, much of the spectacular increase in stock prices was due principally to higher expectations of future profits.

Due largely to the conservative monetary policies of the Federal Reserve, growth in production averaged only 4 percent per year during the 1950s. In response, throughout the 1960s, business interests demanded a more expansionary policy by the government. John Kennedy based his election platform on more active government participation in the economic affairs of the nation. Immediately upon winning the election in 1960, Kennedy instructed the Federal Reserve to significantly increase the money supply. These measures, in addition to substantial corporate and personal tax cuts, gave the economy a spectacular boost that was to continue almost unchecked throughout the decade of the 1960s.

This represented the greatest economic boom era in American history. Corporate profits more than doubled in response to pent-up demand for goods and services. The Federal Reserve insured that money and credit were available to make these purchases. Banks were strongly encouraged to become increasingly active lenders to individuals and businesses. Total automobile purchases soared over 120 percent, and residential home purchases increased over 150 percent. Municipal debts more than tripled. Because the inflation rate averaged only about 4 percent during the decade and interest rates remained moderate through 1966, real incomes were high, greatly exceeding the depreciation of the consumer's purchasing power through inflation.

During the 1960s, the stock market, as indicated by the Dow Industrials, nearly doubled in price.

The computer emerged as the technical marvel of this cycle. The U.S. was at the forefront with a host of supporting industries, such as transistors, data communicators, and microprocessors, providing new and exciting avenues for entrepreneurs. Other highly profitable industries included aircraft manufacturing, advanced electronics, electric and nonelectric machinery, and consumer durables. Internationally oriented stocks were also attractive as worldwide trade barriers were generally relaxed. Principal stocks in this category included multinational banks. The attractiveness of these stocks is attributable to the fact that they were greatly aided by the creation of the Eurodollar markets, developed as a result of the dollar replacing gold as the primary store of wealth.

The economy was in a huge economic and speculative boom. The stock market surpassed all-time highs almost monthly. Brokerage firms could not keep pace with the heavy volume of trading as institutional and public investors bought securities in record volume. Many newly formed, high-technology companies went public for the first time at ridiculously high prices, making their founders millionaires almost overnight. Businesses greatly increased their capital expenditures in anticipation of continued future growth and prosperity. In 1968, the stock market, in real terms, reached its highest valuation in history and proceeded to form a major top in anticipation of the inability of the economy to sustain its growth rate.

## INFLATION HEATS UP

Toward the end of the 1960s, the growth phase began to show subtle signs of destabilization. The most apparent indications of deterioration included a sharp rise in both interest rates and inflation. By 1968, the combination of huge government borrowing and the demands of business began to steadily overheat the economy. Treasury bill rates exceeded 8 percent, and the rate of inflation approached double-digit levels.

Because the stock markets proceeded to trend sideways from 1968 to 1973, the economy was rocked by a series of severe recessions immediately followed by sharp recoveries. These oscillations were caused by measures adopted by the Federal Reserve in an attempt to perpetuate economic growth while keeping both inflation and the cost of money at reasonable levels. As a result, most stocks stagnated, the exception being companies whose earnings were based upon underlying real assets such as real estate; raw materials production, such as farming and mining; and companies exempt from wage and price controls and excessive government regulation.

The rest of industry did its best to cope with rising prices and shortages. Some corporations proceeded to purchase their raw materials in far greater amounts than required, the idea being that there would be greater shortages later as goods became more scarce. This induced an artificially strong, capital-spending boom worldwide, further increasing the costs of labor and materials. This caused labor unions to demand and receive huge wage increases and automatic, inflation-adjustment clauses in their contracts.

Some companies resorted to financial means such as leverage to overcome the destructive effects of inflation and stabilize earnings. Banks that were the source of their funds made huge profits and, in many instances, encouraged further speculation. This widespread credit expansion greatly exaggerated the already overextended financial markets and forced the cost of money to the highest levels in American history.

Beginning in the spring of 1973, the Federal Reserve initiated a program to withdraw funds from the banking system in an attempt to arrest inflation. By the summer of 1974, these tight credit policies finally broke the markets and forced the economy to enter its most severe economic crisis since the final years of the depression. Unemployment levels reached over 8 percent, the worst in over 20 years.

## THE GREAT CRASH OF 1973

The stock market crashed with startling speed, immediately losing over 50 percent of its value as represented by the Dow Industrials, and over 70 percent as represented by the more broadly based New York Stock Exchange Industrial Index.

Major corporate bankruptcies were numerous, and dividend payments were sharply curtailed. Companies especially hurt by the postwar recession included highly leveraged industries, such as real estate development, banking, finance, conglomerates, and industries involved in farming, mining, and manufacturing, and concerns caught with huge inventory stockpiles. However, as is characteristic of all postwar recessions, this one also succeeded in bringing both interest and inflation rates to more historically normal levels. Unfortunately, before the full benefits were reaped from the natural purging of most of the economic excesses accumulated prior to the entrance into the plateau, the recession was prematurely halted as the Federal Reserve responded aggressively to the growing panic with a series of uncharacteristically large monetary injections.

Throughout 1975 and 1976, confidence slowly returned. As a result, the stock markets progressed steadily upward in response to declining interest rates.

Since business interests were initially too frightened to exploit this huge injection of currency and credit by engaging in long-term projects, much of the money was directed to fueling a bond and stock market rally. From late 1974 to the end of 1976, the Dow Industrials increased nearly 85 percent, and the more broadly based New York Composite Index increased nearly 100 percent. Many deeply depressed high-technology stocks, which were on the verge of bankruptcy at the bottom of the postwar recession, increased up to 10 times in price. Bonds gained an average of 40 percent. The 1974 to 1976 rebound in stock prices is generally considered one of the most explosive bull markets in modern history.

However, by 1977, the excessive monetary and fiscal stimulation of the 1974/1975 period had again translated into inflation, and the stock market once again began to falter. By 1980, the rate of inflation exceeded 17 percent, and the prime rate hit 20 percent. The U.S. dollar reached historical lows against most foreign currencies. Because the purchasing power of the dollar fell so rapidly, common stocks lost half their value in real terms, although their actual prices remained relatively constant. At the height of the panic, President Carter signed a bill that gave the President exclusive power to shut down the securities markets in the event of a financial panic. This law is still in effect today.

In 1980, Ronald Reagan replaced the discredited Jimmy Carter and quickly restored economic and financial stability by orchestrating a significant midplateau recession. Once the recession succeeded in reducing the prime rate to half of its former value and cutting the rate of inflation to almost zero, Reagan proceeded to implement a series of fiscal policies historically consistent with each of the former plateau periods. The most important of these included a series of personal and corporate tax cuts, measures to balance the federal budget, and a tight monetary policy.

By mid 1983, the positive effects of these programs were reflected in a tremendous upsurge of stock prices. The New York Composite Index almost doubled in price, and the less broadly based Dow Industrials gained over 60 percent. Economic fundamentals suggest that the stock markets are again poised to complete their final up-leg so typical of the last half of the plateau in each of the previous Kondratieff Cycles in the United States.

## CONCLUSION

### EXPANDING POTENTIAL

It is becoming increasingly apparent that we are rapidly approaching the final stages of the long-term stock market cycle. As we can see in Figure 21, in real terms the stock market, as represented by the S & P 400 Index, achieved its last major peak in 1968. From that point, the stock markets proceeded to complete their expected postwar recession bottoms in late 1974, and have since been in decided uptrends. If the classic Kondratieff long-term stock market cycle continues to hold true, we can expect to see one last explosion and overextension of the equity capital markets culminated by the depression phase of the cycle. Currently, we see most of the ingredients for this classical final advance falling rapidly into place.

Perhaps the most positive indication that we are well into the plateau period of the long-term stock market cycle is the rapid decline in the rate of inflation (Figure 22). As we have seen, inflation, as presented by the Producer (wholesale) Price Index, peaked near the 25 percent

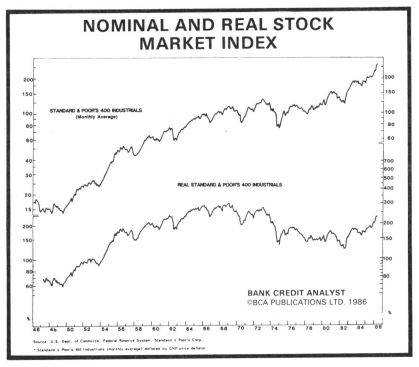

**Figure 21.**

per year range, and by late 1986 was actually negative. Many of the major commodities, such as raw and refined petroleum products, sugar, soybeans, wheat, cattle, and copper, have as of this writing actually fallen below their long-term trend lines and are presently showing negative rates of inflation. Historically, this abatement of inflation through the steady decline in raw material costs during the plateau has always given a significant boost to common-stock prices.

During peak war periods of rapid inflation, the profitability of most businesses tend to come under extreme pressure. In addition to domestic disruptions caused by high cost and scarce raw materials, interference in the markets through excessive trade rules and regulations also causes severe business problems to occur.

Perhaps the most obvious cause of unstable profits in times of intense inflation is the inability of companies to successfully finance expansion. Most corporations are forced out of the equity markets and are required to seek much needed capital in the debt markets (bonds and short-

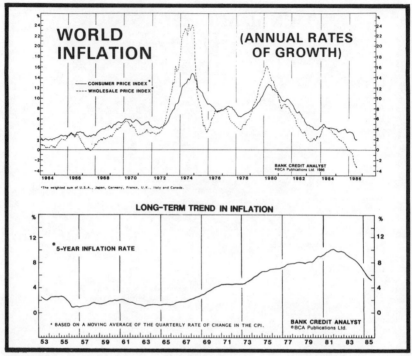

Figure 22.

term commercial paper). This causes balance sheets to deteriorate to the point that the risk of bankruptcy seriously retards growth.

During the inflationary decade of the 1970s, corporate liquidity reached its lowest level in history as total business debt more than doubled to $1.2 trillion. Unfortunately, most of this was the dangerous short-term variety. Only in the best of economic times could the average business hope to operate effectively with such an overextended debt structure. Typically, at the first hint of recession, most companies began to experience cash flow problems, inventory and cost control disruptions, labor difficulties, and severe liquidity squeezes. Profits quickly dropped to the point that many businesses were on the edge of bankruptcy. To compensate for this added risk, the share prices of most companies were bid to lower levels.

As the rate of inflation steadily declined throughout the postwar plateau, these inefficiencies quickly began to unwind. Investment capital proceeded to steadily shift out of the inflation-hedge investments, so popular in the inflation years, and into the stock markets, to take advantage of undervalued securities whose earnings potentials again appear bright. This can be especially seen through the tremendous volume of investment capital flowing into high quality companies in recent years.

This inflow of capital has significantly enhanced the capital structure of many companies, greatly abating the risks of potential bankruptcy. Significant changes have also been initiated to pare down debt in many corporations. This includes selling off unprofitable subsidiaries, issuing secondary stock, and paying off outstanding long- and short-term debt. If the Kondratieff Wave holds true to form, we would expect even further improvements in the average company's balance sheet over the next few years. This could greatly enhance profitability, further reduce risk, and give the average stock a significant boost in market valuation.

The second major cause of advancing stock prices during the plateau is the decline and stabilization of interest rates. Throughout the plateau period, both long- and short-term interest rates tend to fall rapidly in concert with the general rate of inflation.

Short-term interest rates, as might be represented by the prime rate, has fallen from a peak level of 22 percent (Figure 23). Presently, the prime rate has stabilized in the 8 percent range. As a result, the profits of most companies have significantly benefited from the reduced costs of inventory, short-term loans, and bank debt.

For the remainder of the plateau, we expect short-term rates to remain near their present levels with the upper range being near 13 to 17 percent and the lower range around 7 to 8 percent. Should this happen, we do not foresee the need for the initiation of a major recession in the remainder of the plateau period. Without significant recessions, the economy should continue to expand at a modest rate. This should continue to produce the strong financial base so necessary for the development of an extended bull market.

Declining long-term interest rates affect profitability in much the same way that short-term interest rates do, but with the added bonus of greatly enhancing the attractiveness of common-stock dividends. The relative attractiveness of any investment is primarily its percentage return. Common stocks generate their return on investment by both dividend yield and earnings growth, which can vary from one year to the next, depending on the fortunes of the company. In alternative investments, such as bonds, yields are usually fixed in value. Thus when either dividend yields are increased, or long-term interest rates decline, the relative attractiveness of common stocks as investments is greatly enhanced.

Since October 1981, yields on AAA long-term bonds have fallen from nearly 16 percent to a low of 8.0 percent (Figure 24) or at an over 50

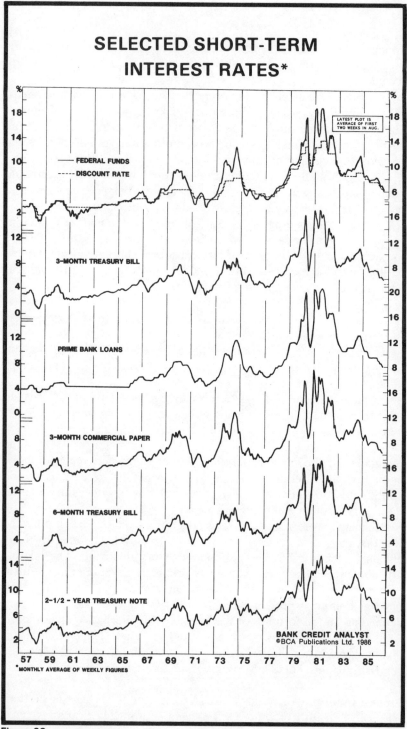

Figure 23.

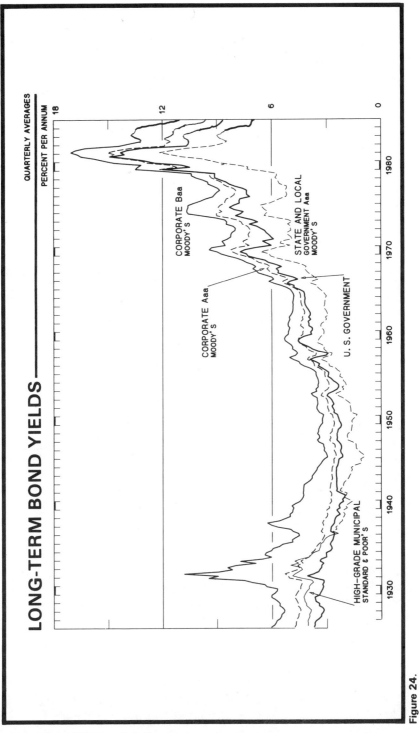

Figure 24.

percent gain in total return. During this same period, the dividend yield of the average common stock has only declined modestly, while earnings growth has increased steadily. As a result, common stocks have become relatively more attractive than bonds.

Because we expect that long-term interest rates will generally stabilize at or near their present levels for the remainder of the plateau and could actually decline in yield if the federal budget deficit were brought under control, fixed-income securities should continue to present a steady lower relative return on investment.

Conversely, because we expect both dividend and earnings growth to advance at their present rate of around 7 or 8 percent for the remainder of the plateau, the relative attractiveness of common stocks over bonds should continue. Only toward the end, when corporate profits begin to falter and the dividend yield of the Dow Industrials approaches the historically critical yield of 3.5 percent, should stocks again begin to experience a competitive disadvantage with bonds.

In addition to these financial factors, governments have historically played a strongly supportive role for the stock market in all past plateau periods of the Kondratieff Cycle. Typically, as the plateau begins, governments assume a more conservative probusiness posture and set about unwinding most of the liberal fiscal excesses built up during the growth stage.

This has been especially apparent since the election of Ronald Reagan in 1980. Since then we have seen a definite shift in the political and social climate of the United States to the more conservative, probusiness posture so characteristic of the plateau period in American economic history.

## INCREASED GOVERNMENT INTERVENTION

During the peak periods of the growth phase, the government tends to champion the concepts of a strong central government and enhanced social spending. This is often at the expense of business interests. As tensions mount, an international war usually breaks out that further magnifies the social and financial ills of the nation. Eventually, as increased deficit spending with resulting inflation eats up the bulk of the gains made during the growth stage, tensions are heightened even further.

At the conclusion of the war, the nation is further shaken by the severity of the postwar recession. As the plateau is entered, the public blames liberal leaders for its discomfort and overwhelmingly replaces them with ultraconservatives. This faction usually remains in power for the duration of the depression and proceeds to unwind the bulk of the social and economic programs implemented during the growth phase.

In our present cycle, the liberal factions of government have proven more difficult to dislodge. It was not until the midplateau election year of 1980 that the conservative faction was allowed to gain control over most of the decision-making apparatus' of government. However, once in place, the conservatives acted quickly.

Since the election, President Reagan has enacted a broadly based cut in taxes through the Tax Reform Act of 1981 and 1986, lowering the maximum tax bracket down to 28%. He has also cut government spending in all areas but defense; made great strides toward the future reform of the Social Security System and Medicare; and initiated the deregulation of a host of government agencies, such as transportation, communication, and finance. Although many liberal and other powerful interest groups have continued to display significant residual strength, the public has increasingly become more receptive to this conservative viewpoint.

The conservative thrust is, of course, not limited to the United States. The overwhelming victory of Margaret Thatcher in England, Helmut Kohl in Germany, and Brian Mulroney in Canada, and their subsequent successes in conservative economics have now firmly established the conservative trend of world leadership. Those countries that have remained liberal, such as France, have suffered deep economic and social trouble, and the political party in power has been put under great stress to shift their economic policies to the right.

## CONSERVATIVE TREND TO CONTINUE

For the duration of the plateau, historical precedent suggests that this conservative trend will become more pervasive. This is a time for nations to make great efforts to balance their budgets and get their finances in order. Although it appears to be an unlikely prospect in view of the $200 billion deficit now being projected for 1987, we strongly feel that in the next few years, spending cuts combined with economic growth will significantly reduce this figure. If necessary, additional and possibly more stringent steps, such as a further revision of our tax codes, could be implemented. One way or the other, it is important for the orderly completion of the plateau that the deficit problem be resolved.

The continued implementation of the present conservative economic philosophy should continue to give the stock market an upward momentum. The realignment and corresponding reduction in the cost of government should have the important benefit of freeing capital from such relatively nonproductive sectors as public housing, health care, welfare, and defense, and transferring it into growth- and productivity-enhancing areas, such as factory construction, scientific research, technological modernization, and capital formation for newly emerging companies.

From a fundamental point of view, the realization that the government is again actively promoting industrial growth will give the business community the added confidence to make the long-term spending decisions necessary to effect this transition.

In addition to these important factors, the foreign capital inflow into the United States from abroad is expected to contribute significantly to the advance of stock prices for the remainder of the plateau. Since many countries are beginning to experience major political and financial disturbances characteristic of all plateau periods, an accelerating shift of foreign capital to lower-risk investments in the United States will increase.

When a foreign investor decides to purchase a U.S. investment, he must purchase U.S. dollars by selling his own country's currency. This, of course, puts upward pressure on the dollar and downward pressure on the foreign currency. From late 1982 to 1985, the dollar has soared in international markets due to an accelerating rate of transfer of capital from abroad. Although the dollar has dropped recently, we expect this trend to continue for the duration of the plateau.

As is typical in the plateau, safety and reduction of risk are of prime importance to professional investors. With many foreign loans either near or at the point of default, and unemployment and political unrest remaining at crisis levels in many parts of Europe, Africa, Asia, and South America—and projected to get worse—there is little doubt but that the flood of foreign capital into the relative safety of the United States will increase. Another concern is the rising tide of protectionism accompanying the record strength of the dollar.

As the dollar continues to become overvalued, many American-based companies, hurt by this artificial disparity, will seek, and in many cases obtain, government protection from overseas competition. The auto, steel, and farm industries are a few notable examples. As our foreign trading partners begin to retaliate, Kondratieff predicts that an international trade war will emerge.

At the first signs of a global trade war, capital flows into the U.S. should accelerate. We expect foreign ownership of U.S. companies to expand for the remainder of the plateau and greatly contribute to the bidding of stock prices to higher than expected levels. As we view the major stock markets of the world, all indications suggest that we are already well into the expected plateau stock market boom for our present Kondratieff Cycle. From its low of 577 made in late 1974 at the lowest point of the postwar recession, the Dow average has advanced steadily to a high near the 1900 level (Figure 25A), a gain of over 229 percent.

Broadly based indexes, such as the Standard & Poor's 500, have risen at an even faster pace. Low-priced stocks of newly emerging high technology companies have advanced an average of over 1,000 percent during the same period.

This stock market boom has not just been isolated to the United States. As expected, the rise in stock prices has become a worldwide phenomenon. Virtually all the stock markets of the major countries have been trending upward since 1974. At the end of 1986, virtually all of the major stock markets, including New York, London, Holland, Japan, France, and Germany, were within a few percent of their all-time highs (Figure 25B).

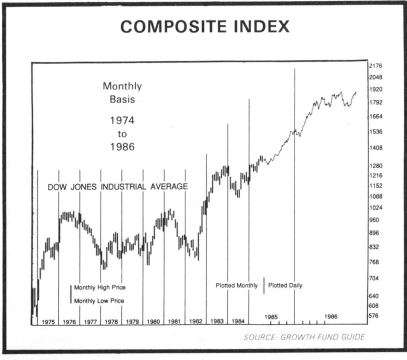

Figure 25A.

## STOCK PRICE INDICES

| | Mar 18 | 1985/86 high | low | % Change on one week | one year | record high | 31/12/84 in local currency | in $ terms |
|---|---|---|---|---|---|---|---|---|
| Australia | 1124.6 | 1124.6 | 715.3 | + 5.8 | + 41.7 | nil | + 54.9 | + 33.9 |
| Belgium | 3382.7 | 3382.7 | 2090.7 | + 2.2 | + 46.9 | nil | + 55.6 | +114.1 |
| Canada | 2984.2 | 2993.9 | 2348.5 | + 0.4 | + 13.8 | − 0.3 | + 24.3 | + 18.2 |
| France | 325.6 | 325.6 | 180.9 | + 4.5 | + 58.2 | nil | + 79.5 | +150.4 |
| W. Germany | 2073.3 | 2161.8 | 1111.8 | + 0.5 | + 70.3 | − 4.1 | + 87.1 | +162.4 |
| Holland | 261.0 | 267.0 | 185.8 | + 1.8 | + 27.3 | − 2.2 | + 43.4 | +101.0 |
| Hongkong | 1561.7 | 1826.8 | 1220.7 | − 4.7 | + 20.0 | −14.5 | + 30.1 | + 30.3 |
| Italy | 654.5 | 658.0 | 228.6 | + 8.5 | +139.3 | − 0.5 | +184.5 | +260.5 |
| Japan | 14639.3 | 14664.5 | 11545.2 | + 4.1 | + 17.3 | − 0.2 | + 26.8 | + 82.3 |
| Singapore | 570.3 | 852.7 | 570.3 | − 5.8 | − 30.9 | −46.8 | − 29.8 | − 29.3 |
| South Africa | 1180.1 | 1180.1 | 767.1 | + 2.7 | + 50.5 | nil | + 39.4 | + 38.6 |
| Spain | 149.0 | 154.4 | 74.7 | + 6.7 | + 80.8 | − 1.1 | +102.3 | +147.9 |
| Sweden | 1956.1 | 1960.7 | 1285.3 | + 1.8 | + 36.8 | − 0.2 | + 44.4 | + 80.3 |
| Switzerland | 578.0 | 625.5 | 388.7 | − 0.5 | + 34.1 | − 7.6 | + 49.9 | +107.1 |
| UK | 1374.6 | 1374.6 | 911.0 | + 3.6 | + 37.8 | nil | + 44.3 | + 84.0 |
| USA | 1789.9 | 1792.7 | 1185.0 | + 2.5 | + 40.8 | − 0.2 | + 47.7 | + 47.7 |

SOURCE: THE ECONOMIST

Figure 25 B.

We expect this general rise in equity prices in the U.S. to continue and even accelerate as the terminal stages of the plateau approach. Immediately prior to the depression, foreign stock markets will begin to selectively falter as increasing worldwide economic distortions begin to disrupt their stability. Already in apparent trouble are the stock markets of Hong Kong and Singapore, having declined between 15 and 50 percent from their all-time highs.

We feel most of these declines are primarily the results of isolated political events and are not as yet actual indications of present or expected world financial problems. In fact, the relative strength of most of the markets in these relatively weaker countries seems to suggest that the plateau period has some time to go. For example, although the U.S. stock market (as represented by the Standard & Poor's 500 Index) rose over 47 percent in 1985 in dollar-adjusted terms, the German market rose 162 percent, the French 150 percent, the Italian 260 percent, and the Belgian almost 114 percent.

During the remaining years of the plateau, we expect the U.S. stock market to outperform all of its foreign counterparts by a wide margin.

If the historical Kondratieff scenario continues, the stocks in the U.S. should overextend in the same manner and to the same general degree as the gold and real estate markets did previously.

Within the context of this projected advance in U.S. equities, we expect a distinct divergence of performance among individual industry groups and between common stocks in those industries.

For the next several years, as the world economic system goes through the agonizing process of restructuring itself to accept the reality that the high growth rates of the past are over, investment capital should begin to increasingly concentrate on less risky issues. Common stocks that should outperform the market are the well-capitalized, financially solid, blue-chip companies with little or no debt or a strong debt-to-equity ratio. Other highly attractive qualities to consider are stocks in aggressive industries with high profit margins, low raw material costs, and creative product innovation. These companies can more easily expand their level of production and at the same time control overhead in difficult economic environments. High-quality companies, such as IBM, Minnesota Mining, Motorola, General Motors, and General Electric, all fit into this general category.

## COMPANIES IN DANGER

Those stocks that should begin to underperform the equities market are undercapitalized, financially troubled companies unable to make the necessary adjustments to effect the transition from an inflationary to a deflationary economy. Especially unattractive will be natural resource companies, such as the oil, mineral, metal, and farm commodity industries, or those companies that have borrowed money to buy inflation-hedge-oriented companies as subsidiaries. In the upcoming years, these companies will be continually faced with high real rates of interest, uncompetitive positions in international markets, and declining asset prices. Recent examples of these types of "leveraged buyouts" are Du Pont's purchase of Continental Oil, Standard Oil of Ohio's purchase of Kennicott, Atlantic Richfield's takeover of Anaconda, and the acquisition of St. Joseph's Minerals by Fluor Corp.

Other prominent industries expected to be hurt by a change in the economy will be residential and commercial construction; highly leveraged industries that are now uncompetitive, such as trucking and railroads, where fare structures have been based on government supports; heavily unionized industries with intractable wage structures; and import/export companies with strong foreign competition.

As we approach the final year of the plateau, virtually all common stocks, including the underperformers just mentioned, should begin to experience a euphoric surge as the public begins to aggressively participate in the upswing. In this increasingly speculative environment, we expect the best performance to be displayed by the less-than-highest-quality secondary companies in such aggressive areas as high technology, drugs, medical supplies, and bioengineering. The market should be aided additionally by a strong increase in the levels of margin buying as public speculation increases.

This combination of factors should allow the stock market to achieve a typical final burst of overextension prior to the depression. If history repeats itself, the level of overextension would probably allow such indexes as the S&P 500 to attain price-earnings ratios near the 20:1 level. If corporate profits continue to expand near our projected levels of 7 to 8 percent per year through 1987, it is logical to expect the S&P 500 could advance to the 350 to 370 level. If the recently proposed rules allowing banks to own and sell mutual fund shares directly to depositors and the dissolution by the Federal Reserve of all margin requirements on securities purchases are put into effect, aggressive speculation by the public could easily carry the market to even higher levels of overextension.

This does not suggest that an investor should immediately go out and indiscriminantly load up on high-grade stocks in anticipation of assured profits. Plateau periods for stock prices are notoriously risky and often unpredictable. This could be especially true of the present plateau. At the present unprecedented levels of overextension of debt and prices, the world could collapse into depression at any time. It can also be easily rationalized that the final orgy of speculation experienced in the recent stock market explosion ending in 1983 was the final speculative blow-off just discussed.

During this market boom, it was not uncommon to see high-technology stocks rise 300 to 400 percent and achieve price-earnings ratios of over 40 at the culmination of the advance. If you consider that the average speculative stock had advanced over 1,000 percent since the lows achieved at the end of the postwar recession in 1974, a strong case can be made that the nadir of the final long-term stock market cycle has already been reached. During that same period in the 1920s plateau, the average low-priced stock from the 1922 low to the 1929 peak advanced almost exactly the same percentage (Figure 26).

*All things considered, we feel that probabilities still favor our predicted advances in the stock market. Eventually, at some point probably between now and the end of the decade, the stock market should reach a high enough level of overextension that it will be extremely vulnerable*

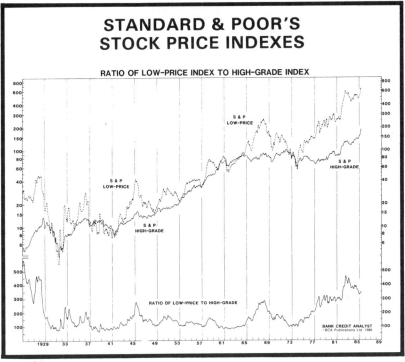

**STANDARD & POOR'S STOCK PRICE INDEXES**

RATIO OF LOW-PRICE INDEX TO HIGH-GRADE INDEX

Figure 26.

*to a major international financial shock, which historically initiates the depression phase.*

During the first and usually most dramatic phase of the depression, the best advice for the conservative investor is to completely shun the ownership of common stocks. Virtually no companies are profitable during this period of the cycle. In addition, faulty business practices and the high probabilities of hidden criminal activity, such as embezzlement and fraudulent balance sheets, make these periods highly risky even for prudent and knowledgeable investors. Such workable defensive strategies as selling-short common stocks and stock index futures represent above-average risk even for professional investors.

Throughout the initial decline, most companies will either sharply reduce or stop paying dividends altogether, forcing many income-oriented investors to sell their stocks in favor of bonds or short-term debt instruments. Those companies associated with foreign trade will be especially affected. As foreign nations begin to repudiate their debts and experience political discomfort, the threat or implementation of protectionism and the nationalization of businesses will accelerate the collapse of international business relations. Domestically, as in all prior depressions, those industries suffering the most will be inflation-hedge-oriented corporations or highly leveraged companies, such as transportation, agricultural machinery, mining, department stores, and financial companies associated with investments and banking. Most mortgage companies and others associated with commercial and residential real estate probably will not survive without massive government assistance.

In a typical first phase of a deflationary depression, the average high-quality common stock usually loses between 50 and 60 percent of its value. During the Great Depression, the loss was in the 85 to 90 percent range. Without assistance by the government, a figure somewhere between the two should be reasonable for this depression.

Eventually, the shares will reach such a low level of valuation that the markets will begin to stabilize. The exact bottom will probably be created when the government feels compelled to implement a massive program of currency and credit expansion in the banking system in an attempt to forestall an acceleration of the financial panic. Depending on the severity of the depression, we expect the decline of the first leg to last somewhere between two and five years. Most stocks should make their lows at this time.

For an extended period of perhaps an additional 10 to 15 years, we expect the market to languish in a broad trading range. During this period, the offsetting crosscurrents of continuing heavy inflows of capital into the United States from abroad and extensive monetary and fiscal stimulation by the government should approximately balance the continuing debt collapse and deflation in the world economy. Although, we expect a second period of extreme anxiety to envelop the world economy toward the end of the depression, we feel confident that the problems associated with this second depression will be adequately handled and that a decline to a much lower level of economic activity will again be manageable.

Most businesses will suffer greatly. Those companies that are able to adapt to a business environment of lower economic growth and reduced profits should be able to again attract investment capital once the long-term stock market cycle begins to revive. At this point, with the costs of conducting business again low, and with significant slack in the economy, the stock market will again be favorably considered for its long-term investment potential within the context of the overall Kondratieff Cycle.

*"I place economy among the first and most important virtues, and public debt as the greatest of dangers. . . ."*
— Thomas Jefferson

# Chapter VII
# Power Cycles and Debt

## ESSENCE OF THE WAVE THEORY

Among the long-term investment cycles we have analyzed, including the stock market cycle, the monetary cycle, and the real estate cycle, none seems to capture the essence of the Kondratieff Wave Theory as does the debt cycle. In fact, the accumulation and destruction of debt along with the emotions of fear and greed, should probably be considered the primary driving forces of all long-term investment cycles. In its broadest sense, the long-term bond rate chart shown in Figure 27 becomes a proxy for the aggregate debt level of the nation.

Whenever a country assumes a position of overextension or underextension relative to its equilibrium level of debt, the natural forces inherent in the free market react to reinstate a more stable level. *Although government or other financially powerful institutions can temporarily postpone or skew the magnitude and the duration of the debt cycle, the natural corrective process of the free markets always prevails, and economic balance is eventually restored.*

In a typical debt cycle, as the peak of the debt overextension approaches, investments begin to lose viability. The financing of most

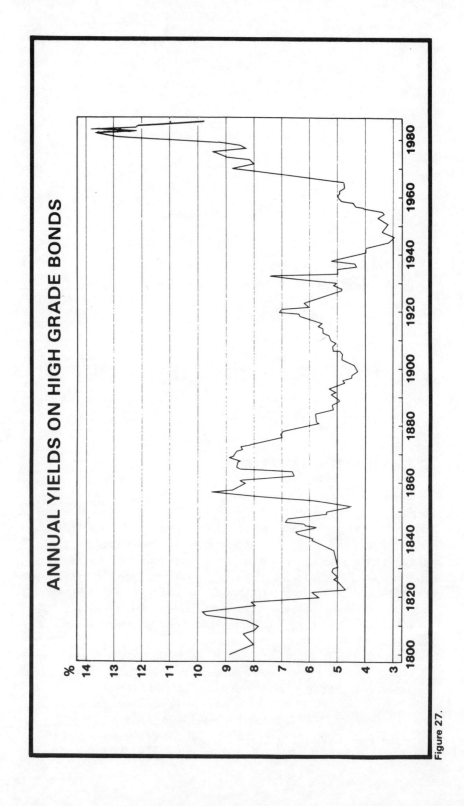

Figure 27.

business projects simply becomes too expensive as interest rates rise to prohibitive levels. Lenders require greater returns on their money to compensate for the rising risk of loan defaults and loss of purchasing power by the currency due to inflation. Inflation also causes most investments to become overvalued in proportion to the level of excess credit in the economy. This makes them vulnerable to the slightest degree of financial instability. Eventually, natural market forces recognize these general levels of overvaluation in the economy, and produce the appropriate corrections to restore economic health. These corrections always entail a sharp reduction in debt levels through the processes of loan default and bankruptcy.

Conversely, at the bottom of the cycle in a period of low aggregate debt, many investments offer opportunities to earn potentially high real rates of return. Here, lenders consider it prudent to maintain higher than normal levels of liquidity to accommodate another round of deposit withdrawals, and borrowers remain reluctant to make long-term commitments. As a result, the financial system becomes flush with money, and interest rates fall to historically low levels. At these levels of extreme undervaluation, most investments respond favorably to even the slightest economic upturn. Natural market forces finally recognize this imbalance and effect a rapid revaluation of prices to higher levels. The rapidity of the recovery is often aided by military adventures, new gold discoveries, and direct government stimulation in the form of currency and credit injections into the financial system.

The Kondratieff Wave phenomenon already outlined is simply a graphic representation of this swing in the levels of debt from one extreme to another. Through this mechanism, the world economy oscillates around a general point of equilibrium from one cycle to the next, each cycle being altered only by changes in the institutional composition of the world economy. The magnitude of these oscillations is in direct proportion to the relative level of debt that is allowed to be generated in each specific cycle.

In our research, we have carefully analyzed a wide range of factors that apparently tend to cause significant changes in this relative level of debt. From our analysis of long-term debt cycles throughout the modern history of a number of countries, we have reached the surprising conclusion that the magnitude of a country's debt extension or over-extension can be attributed primarily to two factors: 1) the magnitude and breadth of its participation in the peak and trough wars, and 2) its relative financial strength in the world economy.

We have found that whenever a nation significantly participates in a peak or trough war, incurring heavy costs in terms of both men and materiel, its basic financial stability is proportionately altered. As we have shown in our historical studies in previous chapters, peak wars invariably occur at some point near the terminal stage of the growth phase. The economy has already experienced a long period of growth and prosperity, and business activity and consumer spending are at historically high levels.

When the extra costs of the peak war are imposed on the already overburdened economy, a massive and unsustainable overextension of debt inevitably occurs. Peak wars typically cause an exponential burst of inflation and debt extension in a relatively short period of time. These are largely brought on by a sharp reduction in the labor force and a rise in the demand for war materiel. This sharp increase in demand always leads to an escalation in the need for money. Since it is politically expedient to pay for war expenditures by the creation of currency and credit in lieu of tax increases, inflation and currency depreciation inevitably follow.

As a consequence, government debt always expands to extremely high levels during the peak war period. This is also true of both industry and consumers. Due to government wage and price controls and a host of new regulations and production quotas, the free market becomes greatly distorted and inefficient. Some businesses and industries prosper at the expense of others from favorable government contracts and preferential financing. But the profitability of most business diminishes.

As balance sheets and profitability deteriorate, businesses are forced to borrow money to support dividends and skyrocketing operating costs. As the cost of money accelerates sharply higher near the peak of the cycle, businesses are often forced into additional borrowing to cover interest payments on their previously borrowed funds. By the peak of the cycle, virtually all businesses are in a precarious financial position.

## CONSUMERS BURDEN THEMSELVES

For many of the same reasons, the public also becomes excessively burdened with debt at the peak of the debt cycle. As wages fail to keep up with inflation, consumers typically try to maintain their standard of living by borrowing money. This is often greatly aided by a general relaxation in lending standards by financial institutions. As the inflation frenzy becomes even more intense, the public copes by becoming heavily involved with the leveraging of investments. By the peak of the cycle, it is not unusual to find the average consumer in debt up to 10 times the level of the previous cycle bottom. The more widespread and destructive the war, the more pervasive the problem.

During the immediate postwar years of the primary recession and plateau, the world community attempts to unwind these social and economic excesses and stabilize its economies at the prevailing high and unsustainable price and debt levels. By the end of the plateau, severe financial and economic dislocations develop, forcing the world into a prolonged period of deflationary depression. The depression continues until the bulk of its total debt has been removed and prices have fallen to historically low levels. Only when these two constraints have been largely eliminated can real long-term growth begin anew.

From our studies, we have concluded that when debt levels during peak wars only moderately overextend, the corresponding depressions tend to also be moderate, allowing the political structure of the country to remain relatively intact. This occurs because the collapse of both prices and debt is orderly and imposes a steady but not severe hardship on the economy. Occasionally, however, the peak war is extremely expensive, and the resulting depression phase begins from an unusually high debt level. In these instances, the resulting depressions prove extremely severe, especially during the first few years when the nation experiences the greatest economic shock. In these cases, the world political, economic, and military balance is often greatly affected for an extended period of time.

During these traumatic depressions, a single country usually emerges as the leading financial and military world power. Ironically, this is not necessarily the victor of the peak war, but rather the country that has preserved significant portions of its labor force and manufacturing base. As these traumatic depressions proceed to their conclusions, severe financial and political discord grows. Because risk avoidance is of paramount importance to the average investor, capital assets from around the world tend to flow out of the weak countries and into the countries that are least likely to suffer significant internal discord or a radical change in their basic judicial systems. Historically, the vehicles of this wealth transfer were easily transportable assets, such as gold, jewelry, and foreign currency. Once the bulk of the world's capital has been transferred to the most stable country, it is inevitable that that country then assumes the position of financial capital of the world and its currency or gold coins the principal unit of world trade. In earlier times, Greece, Babylon, Rome, and Great Britain in the 17th through the 19th centuries all assumed this role. In the 20th century, the U.S. replaced Great Britain as the financial capital of the world, and the dollar replaced the pound as the preferred currency of world trade.

The role of financial leadership of the world is a mixed blessing. On one hand, the nation reaps immense economic benefits as its business interests are allowed to expand into a host of foreign markets. In addition, the leading country is often able to coerce its trading partners into accepting favorable trade concessions. This often occurs under the guise of "protection" or military and financial threats. Invariably, the strong country continues to prosper greatly at the expense of competitor nations so long as it is able to maintain their respect.

In earlier times, maintaining respect was primarily a function of military strength. Whenever a weaker country rebelled, the insurrection was quickly squelched through force. In modern history, control is primarily exerted financially. Whenever subjected countries show dissatisfaction with the prevailing system, curtailment of credit by financial center banks is quickly imposed. Without credit, the subjected country soon experiences severe economic and political problems.

## WHEN CURRENCIES FAIL

The stable functioning of this international economic order works only as long as the dominant country is able to maintain control of its currency. Babylon, Rome, and England all maintained this stability with the use of a gold-backed currency. As long as a gold standard was maintained, they were able to perpetuate this "master-servant" relationship. When they were eventually forced to discontinue a gold standard-based monetary system, this vital aspect was lost, and the countries were forced to relinquish their world leadership role.

As might be expected, this divergence of financial power leads to a distinct contrast in long-term debt cycles between the weak and strong countries. As a rule, weaker countries have shorter growth phases, shorter plateau phases, and somewhat longer and deeper depressions than stronger ones. Because of the relatively high risk of their economies, capital is always cautiously invested there until the growth phase is firmly established. At the first hint of instability, especially during the latter years of the plateau, investment capital rapidly vanishes, forcing relatively premature and prolonged depressions.

Conversely, the growth and plateau phases are relatively longer and more broadly based in financially stronger countries. Capital flows quickly into a wide range of investments during the growth phase of the cycle and is removed only reluctantly as the termination of the plateau phase approaches. Even during the depression phase, investment capital continues to be transferred from abroad, artificially buoying up the economies.

Ironically, the depth and duration of depressions in the financially strong countries are often comparable to those of the weaker countries.

This is primarily the result of a much greater magnitude of debt that tends to accumulate in the stronger countries prior to a depression. Since both the growth and the plateau phases are much more extended in strong countries, a higher level of confidence usually encourages the overextension of the aggregate debt levels to much higher than expected levels. These higher levels of debt increase the severity of the credit collapse during the first few years of the depression, and tend to lengthen the time necessary to fully liquidate it. Thus, no country, despite its strength, escapes the natural corrective forces of the free markets during the depression phase of the Kondratieff Cycle.

*In our studies of past levels of debt in the economy of the United States, we have observed that the average level that accumulates during each phase of the debt cycle can be approximately quantified. Perhaps the most sensitive indicator we have found is the ratio of total money supply in the banking system divided by the Treasury's available monetary gold.*

In its simplest terms, the money supply (more commonly known by its Federal Reserve designation M-1), might be considered a proxy for the aggregate short-term debt of the nation. Within the money supply, the government's short-term debt is represented by a combination of the aggregate volume of minted coins and Federal Reserve notes outstanding in the banking system. The private short-term debt of both consumers and businesses is represented by the level of demand deposits in the banking system. For example, each time a loan is made, demand deposits expand. When a loan is repaid, demand deposits contract. The combination of a nation's coins, currency, and demand deposits represents an approximate measure of its aggregate short-term debt level. The ultimate form of money backing this short-term debt, should the government lose its ability to support the currency, are the gold holdings of the Treasury. When the money supply is divided by Treasury gold stocks, the relative level of short-term debt in the economy is obtained. We have chosen to call this level the "debt ratio."

We have found this debt ratio to be extremely useful in determining the historical relative over- or underextension of the levels of economic activity in the United States. As the economy expands during the growth phase of the cycle, the debt ratio tends to expand in proportion to the level of economic activity. The government prints currency to pay for its spending programs. Business and the consuming public increasingly expand their credit purchases.

Historically, we have found that if the debt ratio stays below 10:1, the nation is able to easily repay its debts, allowing economic growth and prosperity to continue. When the debt ratio begins to exceed 10:1, the ability of a nation to grow becomes severely hindered. At the terminal stages of both the growth and plateau phases, the debt ratio approaches the critical level of 15:1. At that point, the debt burdens of society are so great that economic growth slows. A severe economic contraction inevitably results. Apparently, there is a limit to the volume of debt an economy can accumulate before serious economic distortions appear and force the economy to contract to more manageable levels.

In those cases where the economy ends its plateau phase and enters a depression, the debt ratio tends to contract to much lower levels. By the depression trough, the debt ratio usually approaches 5:1. At this level, the volume of business and consumer lending is at a cylical low, and the banking system is accumulating monetary gold at a record rate to help forestall massive withdrawals. From this level, robust economic growth is once again able to resume since banking liquidity is high and most of the debt excesses have been removed from the financial system.

Obviously, this debt ratio does not take into account other types of debt obligations, including government debt instruments such as Treasury bonds, Treasury bills, and other government-issued debt; business-oriented mortgages; debentures; commercial paper; consumer mortgages; international loans; and a wide assortment of private financing. Such inclusions, of course, would greatly expand the scope and depth of our research. Unfortunately, the long-term statistical records that are necessary to include these elements in our results are incomplete. But we are quite certain that the overall accumulation of these forms of debt would generally parallel those included in the debt ratio and thus would not significantly distort the usefulness of our analysis.

It is instructive to monitor this debt ratio as it oscillates in tandem with the business activity of the United States through its almost four complete Kondratieff Cycles. In the first two cycles, characterized by the War of 1812 and the Civil War periods, the U.S. was considered a second-class world power, somewhat similar to the current positions of Brazil and Canada. During both of these Kondratieff Cycles, the growth phase and the plateau phase were relatively short-lived affairs. At the conclusion of the growth phase of each cycle, the aggregate debt levels in the economy were not excessive, and both phases culminated in a relatively moderate peak war inflation. In each instance, the governments in power were relatively weak and thus unable to significantly distort the free markets.

During each of their respective postwar recessions, the economy quickly removed excesses without a severe distortion of the social or political apparatus. Following the postwar recessions, each of their plateau periods was relatively orderly, lasting less than 10 years, and typically produced a conservative political outlook that greatly reduced both the rates of inflation and interest. Likewise, the subsequent depression periods were also relatively mild.

In both cases, the political and financial systems were not in serious jeopardy. Conservative presidents, who steadfastly advocated that free markets be allowed to work out the economic problems of the nation free of government influence, were largely retained in office for the full duration of each depression.

## THE RATIO OF GOLD AND DEBT

In the War of 1812 debt cycle, we are unable to completely quantify our debt ratio due to a lack of accurate financial statistics. The banking system was too primitive and fragmented to give an accurate picture of the nation's short-term debt levels. In fact, it was not until the National Bank Act of 1861 was passed that the government was able to establish a comprehensive financial record-keeping system with sufficient information available to give a reasonably accurate picture of the short-term debt levels of the economy.

For example, these statistics indicate that in the midplateau year of 1867—the Civil War plateau—the amount of gold held in the federal Treasury and state-chartered banks totaled $140 million, while the money supply of the banking system, including currency and demand deposits, was estimated at $1.32 billion. The resulting debt ratio of 9.4:1 represents an historically average midplateau value for the debt cycle. As the plateau progressed to its conclusion in 1873, the demand deposit component of the money supply rapidly expanded to eventually exceed $300 million, allowing the aggregate money supply of the banking system to increase to $1.622 billion.

During this same period, the monetary gold supply remained virtually constant. At this crucial point of the cycle, the debt ratio reached its highest cyclical level of a relatively modest 12:1. As a result, the subsequent post-Civil War depression proved relatively orderly, characterized by both a moderate but steady decline in economic growth and remarkable political and social stability. During the next 20 years the ratio slowly contracted to a level of approximately 7:1, the highest depression debt ratio in modern history.

Because the amount of coin and currency in circulation remained fairly constant throughout the depression years, the decline in the debt ratio was largely attributable to a substantial decline in its demand deposit or business loan component, and less importantly to a modest increase in the Treasury's monetary gold balances. The result of this modest reversal of the debt ratio proved extremely beneficial to society as a whole. The post-Civil War depression, although traumatic to many, was a remarkably orderly affair in which the economic excesses of the growth stage were slowly but efficiently purged from the system. At no time was the basic structure of the political or financial system in serious jeopardy.

Despite intense pressure by special-interest groups that were especially hurt by the deflationary effects of the depression, our gold-based monetary system remained intact and the concept of free-market Capitalism was respected. Similar to the peak war, the trough war was also mild and served to stabilize the economy after the debt-cleansing process had largely run its course.

At the turn of the century, the fundamental structure of the debt cycle in the United States began to subtly change. America was beginning to emerge into a first-class world power. Almost immediately following the end of the depression in 1897, the U.S. economy began to quickly strengthen. Increased foreign investment and significant gold discoveries in Alaska and Colorado were the primary catalysts for the rebound. In the resulting growth phase, U.S. military strength and a greatly expanding industrial base propelled our economy to its highest levels of activity in history. By 1920, at the peak of the growth phase, the debt ratio for the first time exceeded the critical level of 15:1, primarily as a result of debt accumulation accruing from the unexpectedly high costs of World War I.

In its initial stages, the war was expected to be a relatively modest skirmish fought exclusively on European soil, but it quickly expanded into a large-scale international conflict. Because much of the extremely high costs of the war had to be financed on credit, the debt levels of the major participants expanded to exceptionally high levels. This was especially true in France, England, and Germany, which suffered the major burden of the fighting, and the United States, who was eventually forced to provide the bulk of war materiel for the Allies.

During the most costly years of the war era—1917 to 1920—short-term debt level of the United States exploded from a comfortable 9:1 to the exceptionally overextended level of 15:1. Since the banking system's monetary gold supply remained virtually constant during these years, the sharp increase in the debt ratio was primarily a result of the printing of large amounts of currency and the sharply increased borrowing measured by demand deposits. Primarily as a result of these historically high debt levels, the postwar recession proved especially traumatic for most world economies. Commodity prices plunged more rapidly and deeply than at any other time in modern history, sending a financial shock wave throughout most nonindustrialized countries.

In Europe, as unemployment soared to record highs, only the strongest and most stable countries and businesses were allowed to borrow money. In these desperate economic times, the new-found concepts of Socialism and Communism became positively considered as viable alternatives to Capitalism.

In the United States, the severity of this recession was evidenced by a rapid decline in the debt ratio. By 1922, the ratio had again fallen to less than 11:1 and, by early 1924, it reached the lowest level of the plateau at 10:1. Since both the amount of gold in the banking system and the currency component of the money supply remained relatively constant throughout the recession, most of the decline in the ratio was attributed to the reduction of short-term business and consumer debt as reflected by demand deposits.

The extreme social and political traumas of this postwar recession began to radically affect the basic structure of the plateau period in the weaker countries of Europe. As capital began to flow out of Europe in increasing amounts, the plateau period in the weaker European nations proved relatively short-lived and unstable. By 1925, most of these countries along with the rest of the world began to drift into depression.

Ironically, the financially stronger countries, principally the United States and England, were the recipients of the weaker countries' investment capital and enjoyed great prosperity throughout most of the remainder of the decade. As we have seen virtually all of this capital was invested in building projects, short-term money market instruments, and consumer products. This artificial stimulation of the economy in turn greatly expanded corporate earnings while depressing interest rates, setting the stage for the greatest stock market boom in American history.

As the economy of the United States began to rapidly expand out of the postwar recession, so did the level of credit extended by the financial system. From 1921 to 1928, demand deposits outstanding in the banking system increased over 60 percent, although the amount of currency in circulation and the Treasury's monetary gold stock remained virtually constant.

By 1929, as the boom was approaching its highest level of activity, the huge increase in consumer installment purchases, a widespread business capital spending boom, and excessive credit borrowing for common stocks further expanded the volume of demand deposits.

Just prior to the beginning of the depression in late 1929, the debt ratio once again rose to the critical 15:1 level. When it became apparent to financial institutions that the economy was grossly overextended, they sharply reduced their volume of lending and forced our economy into its most traumatic depression in history.

As the depression increased in intensity, the nation experienced an unexpectedly rapid decline in its debt levels. By early 1932, after just two years of depression, the debt ratio fell to a more historically acceptable level of 10:1. This induced many economists and financial experts into believing that the depression was about to stabilize and allow the economy to enter another period of expanded growth similar to the postwar plateau. Upon closer examination of the financial basis for each of these two panics, it is apparent the panic of the 1930s was much more severe. In the 1920 recession, the reduction in the debt ratio was primarily a result of a 30 percent decline in demand deposits.

By comparison, in the 1930 panic, demand deposits declined an astounding 45 percent during its first few years. It is estimated that during the period from October 1929 to March 1933, the level of bank loans in the U.S. declined from $24.4 billion to $13.5 billion. Were it not for a 50 percent expansion in the volume of currency in the banking system by the Federal Reserve, the collapse of both the level of demand deposits and the debt ratio would no doubt have been much greater. As it was, consumer prices fell over 60 percent during this period to largely reflect the rapid decline of the money supply.

When the United States entered World War II in 1941, the debt ratio had fallen to an astounding 2:1, particularly reflecting the huge monetary gold inflows into the United States from abroad and a tendency by financial institutions to remain ultraconservative in their lending practices.

By the end of the 1940s, the U.S. Treasury owned over 60 percent of the world's monetary gold and the amount of debt outstanding was at cyclical lows. This incredible realignment of the nation's liquidity posture— from 15:1 to 2:1—was unprecedented in U.S. financial history. Not only did it reflect the devastating nature of an economic and financial credit collapse from a high debt level, but it also illustrated how quickly financial assets seek safety in the event of a severe panic. Although the debt ratio of the U.S. was at its most liquid level in history, the debt ratios of most of the rest of the world remained historically high. This mainly reflected the low level of monetary gold in their treasuries.

## ANOTHER TIMELY WAR

In the late 1930s, a potentially more severe stage of the depression apparently was averted by the entrance of the United States into World War II. The exceptional size and scope of this trough war tended to truncate the normal depth and duration of the typical Kondratieff Wave depression and elongate the subsequent growth and plateau phases of our present cycle.

World War II was a tremendously expensive war. Not only were great amounts of money and credit used by the government, but the stagnant industrial base of the nation was also completely refurbished to produce war materiel. By the end of the war, the nation enjoyed full employment and an historically high level of liquidity necessary to start the next growth phase.

Since the economies of the rest of the world were in shambles as a direct result of World War II and the legacy of the depression, the U.S. naturally assumed the role of undisputed financial and military leader of the free world. This leadership role was greatly enhanced by the strength and stability of the U.S. dollar, which was backed by more gold bullion than at any other time in history. It soon became the principal medium of exchange in world trade and the principal reserve currency held by central banks. During the ensuing years, the United States was to use and then abuse this privileged situation.

As discussed in Chapter V, the primary advantage that accrued to the dollar as the exclusive international reserve currency was that foreign interests paid for our federal budget deficits with recycled dollars received from our international balance-of-trade deficits. This occurred because many central banks and foreign financial institutions holding excess dollars that did not pay interest preferred to exchange them for U.S. government securities that did pay interest. All parties were happy with this arrangement as long as the dollar remained stable in value and foreign export industries were allowed free access to our domestic markets.

Throughout the 1950s and 1960s, the United States took full advantage of this arrangement by continuing to run increasingly large budget deficits to pay for ambitious government-sponsored social and military programs. There was simply no need or desire to balance our budgets. This caused a significant distortion in the normal course of the idealized Kondratieff growth phase in the United States. The most readily apparent distortions were the exceptionally rapid accumulation of debt and general prolongation of the growth phase from an average of 20 to 25 years to well over 30. *These two factors gave liberal influences (always present in the growth phase) additional time and resources to become more solidly entrenched and exert a much more extensive influence on the size and scope of the government's support programs.* Their influence acted to greatly overextend the debt structure of the nation.

By the peak of the growth phase in 1974, the government constituted over 30 percent of the gross national product as opposed to less than

10 percent at the peak of World War I and less than 2 percent at the peak following the Civil War. Long-term debt in real dollars was more than double that of the previous cycle peak.

By 1974, the huge pool of liquidity available to the financial system at the end of the depression had been consumed by economic growth and debt accumulation. At the peak of the growth phase, the debt ratio had climbed to well over 12:1. This included Treasury gold of $96 billion (valued at $200 per ounce), currency and credit (M-I) of $400 billion, and the Eurodollar market (U.S. demand deposits held overseas) of nearly $400 billion. Interest rates had risen to the point that the cost of financing most business projects became prohibitive in view of the high risks of loan defaults in the domestic and international markets. As a result, the post-Vietnam War recession was one of the most severe in the history of the United States.

Unfortunately, unlike each prior postwar recession, the 1974/1975 recession failed to materially reduce the size of the debt ratio as additional government borrowings in the financial markets largely negated the sharp reductions of borrowings by both consumers and business.

It seems that just as this unprecedented overextension of government interference tended to distort the growth phase of the cycle, so also did it tend to distort the plateau phase. Once high levels of public spending become integrated into the social structure of a society, it becomes extremely difficult if not politically impossible to reverse these programs. Too many special interest groups have a large stake in their maintenance. This was the problem faced by Presidents Nixon, Ford, and Carter. Each fought with these established interests represented by Congress and were soundly rebuffed. Nixon and Ford adapted a conservative stance and were removed from office. Carter made a weak attempt at government reform and balanced budgets but was also easily defeated by Congress. In a desperate attempt to show economic progress, he even resorted to additional fiscal and monetary stimulation prior to the 1980 election. This only led to a severe decline in the dollar and an unexpectedly large midplateau spurt of inflation. More importantly, it led to a massive increase in the nation's long- and short-term debt structure and caused the public to borrow even more to play the inflation game.

By late 1980, with the world financial system in disarray, and the U.S. economy in a severe economic malaise, the public became disenchanted with the liberal leadership of the country and voted Jimmy Carter out of office. The Kondratieff Wave suggested that a change to a more conservative form of leadership was long overdue.

The election of Ronald Reagan in 1980 greatly solidified the rapidly growing conservative power in the country. These conservative elements were already in place but remained latent as long as Carter was in office. Typically, plateaus are a time of balanced budgets, decentralized governments, reduced personal and corporate taxes, probusiness politics, and a general unwinding of the social excesses generated during the growth phase. Uniquely, these policies are only now being addressed at this late stage of the plateau. Before Reagan could implement conservative programs, interest rates had to decline to much lower levels, and inflationary expectations had to be eliminated.

The 1981/1982 midplateau recession largely accomplished this goal. The country now appears well on its way to a more typical plateau phase, which should progress toward an inevitable climax some time before the end of the decade. However, the extreme damage to the financial system has already been done, as the massive debts generated during the present plateau period have caused national debt of unprecedented levels. With the money supply now exceeding $700 billion, the Eurodollar market approaching $3 trillion, and a gold supply of only $120 billion (at $400 per ounce), the debt ratio now exceeds the astounding figure of 30:1! If the debt of financial institutions other than banks is considered, including insurance companies, mortgage institutions, government agencies, and corporate loans to both domestic and foreign sources, the ratio would be much greater.

## OVERLENDING TO FOREIGN GOVERNMENTS

At present, as we assess the damage that has been done to the debt markets, perhaps the most glaring problems are found internationally. By the end of 1986, the volume of loans to foreign nations exceeded the $1 trillion mark (Table 1). Approximately half of this total originated in the international banking system and with private lenders with the remainder from government-sponsored export credit agencies and direct government loans. It is apparent that most of the principal and interest payments due on these loans will never be repaid.

By far the best-documented and widely publicized examples of debt crises in the making are in the countries of Brazil, Argentina, and Mexico. It is estimated that Brazil has accumulated debts of over $115 billion, Mexico over $106 billion, and Argentina over $41 billion. The total public and private debts of these countries alone comprise over $265

| CENTRAL AMERICA, THE CARIBBEAN AND CANADA | BILLIONS |
|---|---|
| Canada | $ 53.5 |
| Cuba | 3.5 |
| Dominican Republic | 1.7 |
| El Salvador | 0.6 |
| Costa Rica | 3.5 |
| Guatemala | 1.0 |
| Honduras | 1.0 |
| Jamaica | 2.4 |
| Mexico | 106.0 |
| Nicaragua | 2.4 |
| Panama | 2.6 |
| Trinidad-Tobago | 1.0 |
| | $179.2 |

| SOUTH AMERICA | BILLIONS |
|---|---|
| Argentina | $ 41.8 |
| Bolivia | 6.0 |
| Brazil | 115.0 |
| Columbia | 9.9 |
| Chile | 7.5 |
| Ecuador | 6.6 |
| Guyana | 1.3 |
| Paraguay | 1.1 |
| Peru | 15.0 |
| Uruguay | 3.3 |
| Venezuela | 32.0 |
| | $239.5 |

| SOVIET UNION | BILLIONS |
|---|---|
| Afghanistan | $ 2.0 |
| Albania | 0.0 |
| Bulgaria | 1.9 |
| Czechoslavakia | 3.7 |
| G.D.R. | 13.0 |
| Hungary | 9.0 |
| Poland | 28.2 |
| Romania | 10.0 |
| USSR | 20.0 |
| | $87.8 |

| EUROPE | BILLIONS |
|---|---|
| Austria | $ 14.0 |
| Belgium | 13.8 |
| Cyprus | 0.6 |
| Denmark | 15.5 |
| Finland | 10.0 |
| France | 70.0 |
| Greece | 6.0 |
| Iceland | 1.1 |
| Ireland | 7.3 |
| Italy | 51.0 |
| Netherlands | 9.0 |
| Norway | 11.2 |
| Portugal | 14.2 |
| Spain | 30.0 |
| Sweden | 27.4 |
| Turkey | 19.0 |
| Yugoslavia | 18.5 |
| United Kingdom | 7.8 |
| | $326.4 |

| MIDDLE EAST | BILLIONS |
|---|---|
| Bahrain | $ 0.1 |
| Egypt | 21.0 |
| Iran | 15.0 |
| Iraq | 75.0 |
| Israel | 20.1 |
| Jordan | 1.7 |
| Lebanon | 1.5 |
| Oman | 1.0 |
| Syria | 3.8 |
| United Arab Emirates | 1.5 |
| Yehem | 1.0 |
| | $141.7 |

| FAR EAST AND AUSTRAL ASIA | BILLIONS |
|---|---|
| Bangladesh | $ 4.0 |
| Burma | 2.0 |
| China | 3.4 |
| India | 17.9 |
| Indonesia | 23.0 |
| Nepal | 0.2 |
| New Zealand | 4.9 |
| Malaysia | 5.7 |
| Pakistan | 13.0 |
| Phillipines | 22.5 |
| South Korea | 40.7 |
| Sri Lanka | 3.0 |
| Thailand | 7.9 |
| Tiawan | 6.9 |
| | $155.1 |

| AFRICA | BILLIONS |
|---|---|
| Algeria | $16.0 |
| Botswana | 0.3 |
| Cameroon | 2.3 |
| Congo | 1.6 |
| Ghana | 1.3 |
| Ivory Coast | 6.8 |
| Kenya | 3.1 |
| Libya | 6.7 |
| Malawi | 0.8 |
| Mauritania | 0.1 |
| Mauritius | 0.5 |
| Morocco | 7.0 |
| Nigeria | 11.8 |
| Sudan | 7.0 |
| Tanzania | 2.0 |
| Tunisia | 4.6 |
| Uganda | 1.0 |
| Zaire | 5.0 |
| Zambia | 3.3 |
| Zimbabwe | 1.2 |
| | $82.4 |

SOURCE: INTERNATIONAL MONETARY FUND 1983

Table 1.

billion, or more than one-half of the total outstanding debts to the so-called less developed countries of the world.

In recent testimony before Congress, it was revealed by international bankers that as of July, 1986, the nine largest international banks based in the United States had $32.2 billion, or 130 percent, of their combined capital in loans to these three countries alone. Of course, this percentage does not include the remaining $100 billion that these banks have lent to other equally depressed nations of the world. They further estimated that industrialized nations will collectively need to grow at a 7 percent annual rate for the next 10 consecutive years, and generate an average inflation rate of approximately 5 percent, in order for these countries to earn enough foreign exchange to repay this debt. If, as we expect, the volume of their exports continues to diminish in response to further massive cutbacks in foreign trade, periodic global recessions, and growing protectionist measures, the prospect of massive defaults should eventually be almost assured.

Actually, each of these countries has already declared *de facto* bankruptcy since they have failed to make payments of either principal or interest on outstanding loans. Instead they have rescheduled their debt or acquired fresh currency through additional loans from the creditor banks. Privately, it is realized that no creditor banks ever expect to see their money returned. Contingency steps are rapidly being implemented to reflect this reality.

The financial plight of Brazil is perhaps the best example. For the past several years, this country has grappled with the problems of growing debts and slow economic growth that at this point seem to have no workable solution. In 1986 alone, it was estimated that Brazil would have to pay over $20.0 billion in interest on its debt. Because Brazil now has a net negative balance of trade and negligible foreign reserves, the only way it has been able to make payments is by acquiring fresh loans. Western bankers are taking a hard line on new credits by publicly stating that Brazil can expect no more than $7 billion in fresh loans in 1987. In fact, Brazil is in actual default and can be declared legally bankrupt.

In June 1986, the Brazilian government, in desperation, submitted a detailed debt-reduction plan to the international financial community. The plan demanded a much longer grace period for paying the debt, including an immediate five-year moratorium on the payment of principal, and beyond that a 15- to 20-year repayment-of-principal schedule. In addition, the country demanded a sharp reduction in the level of interest on the loans, and elimination of all fees and concessions paid to creditor banks.

Additionally, lender banks were asked to restructure interest rates to "more properly" reflect the bank's true cost of funds, say, at rates approximately 0 percent over the rate of inflation. At present, with the rate of inflation in the United States at approximately 3 percent, this suggested interest rate on the loans would decline from its present average of around 13 percent to 3 percent. Brazil has also asked that the International Monetary Fund (IMF) radically diminish its present austerity program to allow for more economic growth and for additional credits.

These seemingly outrageous demands were largely brought on by the low economic growth and political problems facing the government of Brazil. The present politically moderate group in power is growing increasingly fearful that unless Brazil is granted some form of relief by bankers, a more radical populist or Communist leader may be swept into power on a "repudiate the debt" platform. It is assumed that continued economic hardship for the estimated 125 million citizens of Brazil, who have seen their living standards cut back to the levels of six years ago, cannot go on much longer. It has been reported that from 1984 through 1986, violent crime in Rio de Janeiro rose well above the previous 3 year period.

Because the bankers are not likely to submit to these proposals, repudiation is becoming an increasingly likely alternative to the present interminable rounds of negotiations to reschedule the over $100 billion in debt. In reality, the present government has publicly stated that it no longer believes that repudiation will cause financial ruin to their foreign creditors. They suggest that if the U.S. government was willing to bail out the depositors of the Continental Illinois Bank in order to prevent the spread of financial panic, there is no reason to believe they would not perform the same function for those international banks holding Brazilian paper.

In response to these harsh demands, the involved commercial banks of the United States, in conjunction with the Federal Reserve, are counterproposing two methods of reducing the financial pressures being faced by Brazil. One proposal suggests that the outstanding debt be converted to fixed-rate securities and financed in the international bond market. It is assumed that these bonds would require some form of government or IMF guarantee in order to make them acceptable to investors. So far, this proposal is being warmly embraced by the bankers as an acceptable method of shifting the risk of its debt holdings to the American public.

A second popular proposal is the use of variable maturity loans much like the variable-rate mortgages so popular in the real estate markets. In this proposal, the interest rate of the security is fixed so that as market rates trend higher, the duration of the loan is simply extended. Again, this would probably require significant government guarantees since, theoretically, the loan could be potentially extended indefinitely, and the owner of the security does not have the comfort of possessing title to the underlying property. Added features to enhance these proposals could include balloon payments and floating-rate loans with both maximum- and minimum-rate provisions. When market rates exceed the maximum, the difference is accounted for in a separate fund. This allows the borrower to make payments at a constant maximum rate, not subject to the vagaries of interest rate fluctuations, and still derive the benefits of lower-interest payments should they decline to lower levels.

Of course, these proposals are only stopgap measures. In order to prepare for the worst possible scenario, commercial banks are beginning to take drastic action. As a loan-loss provision, many of the largest banks have begun to set aside sizable reserve funds directly out of their profits and retained earnings. In addition, these banks have sharply curtailed new lending to troubled countries. In 1986, the nation's 10 largest international banks received more money in interest and principal from Third World countries than they lent. Furthermore, the legal departments of all of the participating banks have made punitive contingency plans to be implemented in the event of repudiation.

The necessary legal documents are already prepared to garnish the revenues from confiscated export products and other assets of the defaulting country that can be used to offset failed payments. However, the sequestering of assets would no doubt prove to be a pitifully small measure compared to the overwhelming size of the outstanding loans. It is estimated that should a 1 percent loan loss be incurred, it would reduce both the Bank of America's and Manufacturers Hanover's pretax profits by more than 10 percent. Thus, even a small actual default could have serious complications for all the capital structures of the financial markets, including the stock market.

With commercial banks no longer willing or able to continue to extend credit in the amounts necessary to prevent an international financial panic, it is becoming increasingly obvious that much of the burden of this international debt crisis is shifting toward the IMF. Both central banks and international commercial banks have tacitly informed the debtor nations that in the future, international agencies, such as the IMF, World Bank, and the Bank of International Settlements, will assume the bulk of additional lending until the situation stabilizes.

The IMF is a relatively simple organization. Tax revenues of the governments of the participating nations are lent directly to the IMF, which then relends these funds to needy creditor nations. Interest on the loans is then recycled back to the central banks and certain participating private banks of the international financial community. In recent years, the IMF has been instrumental in keeping many of the international banks solvent by the use of this transfer mechanism. However, this form of government subsidy to the international banks will go on only as long as the domestic taxpayers are willing to continue to support the bailout.

Already, we are beginning to see the first signs of revolt in the United States. In early 1986, Congress experienced great difficulty in passing the latest contribution of $4.1 billion to the IMF. This does not bode well for the expected $15 billion in promised contributions that must be raised over the next two years. It is becoming increasingly apparent to the public that tax revenues can be put to better use for domestic purposes than squandered in supporting unsolvable international debt problems.

In realization of this potential problem, the IMF is presently contemplating contingency plans to raise the necessary funds. One of the most popular schemes that has been devised is the purchase of a portion of foreign debt from the international banks. In exchange for this debt, the IMF would issue its own bonds to the banks for the face value of the debt. In this way, the banks would not write off the loans on their books and face potential bankruptcy. The bonds would then be issued at market rates with maturities more suitably adjusted to the abilities of the debtor countries to repay. Interest and principal payments would be paid to the banks, which would in turn use the funds to retire its bonds.

By acquiring the IMF's bonds, banks could substantially reduce their exposure to the foreign debt. In addition, as part of the arrangement, banks would be asked to extend new loans to those troubled foreign countries in amounts sufficient not only to make current interest payments, but also to support projects to stimulate their recovery. This plan, of course, would only work for countries that have a realistic potential of repaying their debts. The banks would still have to write off their loans to those countries that prove to be hopeless cases.

We feel that such stopgap measures as these most likely will not be implemented in time, in view of the expected reduction in the degree of international cooperation in the near future. Only when the crisis is clearly evident can such esoteric concepts be implemented. At that point, it will probably be too late. Plateau periods are historically periods of isolationism and nationalism, connoting a loss of cooperation.

## GOVERNMENT DEBT

Almost equal to the size and scope of the international debt situation is the accelerating financial crisis over the growing domestic debt of the United States. By far the most obvious and vexing problems are the unprecedented size and scope of the debts of the federal government. *At present, the "official" funded federal debt significantly exceeds $2.1 trillion and is growing at a rate of over $200 billion per year. This amount does not include "off-budget" debts of almost $400 billion in federal loans for public and private housing, over $200 billion in debt securities issued by government-sponsored agencies, over $100 billion in loans to farmers, and over $200 billion of securities backed by mortgage pools, including the Federal National Mortgage Association and Government National Mortgage Association. These debts now exceed a total of $2 trillion or well over half of the nation's Gross National Product. The yearly interest alone is estimated to cost the government well over $150 billion dollars—almost equal to the federal deficit for 1986.*

As we look at Figure 28, it becomes apparent that most of this debt has been incurred since the start of the plateau period in 1974 as a direct result of the government's decision to artificially stimulate economic growth. Unfortunately, this huge injection of credit into the economy failed to promote growth and succeeded only in causing a sharp rise in inflation, a destabilized dollar in the foreign currency markets, and an unprecedented explosion of debt levels in the world financial system. Many of the world's economic and political problems seen today are direct results of the implementation of these policies.

Only now, in the latter years of the plateau, are the nation and the world starting to come to grips with the sheer size and influence of their governments. The realization that governments cannot promote economic prosperity for long periods of time by fiscal and monetary policy is a phenomenon experienced in each of the past Kondratieff Cycles in the United States.

In all of these prior cycles, the nation quickly shifted emphasis from the monetary expansion attitudes of the growth phase to a more conservative financial policy with relative ease and efficiency. Immediately subsequent to the postwar recession, the public demanded the government rapidly reduce prolific military and social spending habits and balance the federal budget. These mandates were always quickly put into effect. Lower government spending quickly reduced both the rate of inflation and interest rates to the point that real and substantial economic growth could again resume. In response, the business climate

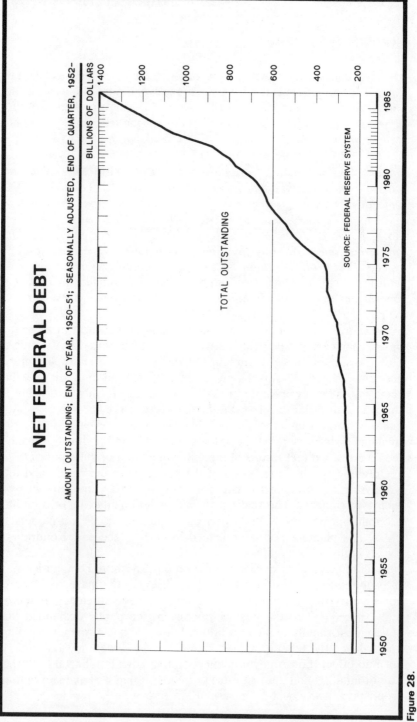

# NET FEDERAL DEBT

AMOUNT OUTSTANDING; END OF YEAR, 1950–51; SEASONALLY ADJUSTED, END OF QUARTER, 1952–

BILLIONS OF DOLLARS

TOTAL OUTSTANDING

SOURCE: FEDERAL RESERVE SYSTEM

Figure 28.

began to expand with unexpected strength. Tax revenues began to flow into the Treasury, allowing budget surpluses to accumulate.

This surplus of funds induced the government to sharply reduce both personal and corporate taxes to much lower levels, resulting in an even more rapid business expansion and greater consumer spending. By the end of the plateau, the economy was in an economic boom. However, the boom also produced an even more overextended debt level in the world economy so that by the end of the plateau, the financial system was poised for the initial financial shock that heralded the onset of depression.

President James Madison was the last of the highly liberal Presidents to hold office during the growth stage of the War of 1812 cycle. After the war in 1815, Madison startled the nation by calling for a sharp escalation in the already extensive government-spending programs to greatly expand the nation's military forces. The proposed methods of paying for these programs were by direct internal taxation and additional borrowing from the Bank of the United States. Because his party was given full blame for the costs and deaths associated with the war, the public was in no mood for further inflation or government interference in the economy.

In the next election the archconservative James Monroe was overwhelmingly elected to the presidency. Domestically, he immediately balanced the federal budget by sharply slashing federal spending and significantly reducing the role of government in the economy. During the remainder of the plateau, the country experienced seven years of substantial government budget surpluses and only three years of minor budget deficits. Business enjoyed immense prosperity throughout this first plateau period.

During the Civil War cycle, Abraham Lincoln was the most prominent of a long line of ultraliberal growth-phase Presidents who strongly promoted social fairness and advocated strong government intervention in the economy. During his tenure, he was able to officially abolish slavery in the states and its territories, allocate a quarter-section of government land to Western settlers, and establish government grants to support the state college systems.

By the end of the Civil War, the government was deeply in debt to the point that the survivability of the nation was in question. Lincoln had to assume virtual dictatorial powers to control social and financial instability. After his assassination at the beginning of the plateau period, his successor Andrew Johnson noted the growing strength of the conservative factions and proceeded to unwind much of the policies imposed on the nation by Lincoln. In his final days in office, Johnson vetoed the Civil Rights Act of 1866, and set about restructuring the monetary system to relieve the economic and social tensions caused by wartime inflation. By 1866, government spending was reduced to the point that the federal budget was again in surplus. This surplus was to be easily maintained for the duration of the plateau period through 1875.

The next President, Ulysses S. Grant, was considered even more conservative than Johnson. Grant and his extremely conservative successors were largely concerned with the re-establishment of credibility in the banking system. In his inaugural speech, Grant committed himself to a resumption of the gold standard and the repayment of all the government's outstanding debts in gold. In addition, he sought the enhancement of the nation's international trade interests by promoting protectionist legislation. These exceptionally restrictive tariff programs were solidly supported by a series of five successive conservative Presidents and remained in effect until repealed by the McKinley Tariff Act of 1890.

In the third peakwar period ending in 1920, Woodrow Wilson was the last of a series of increasingly liberal Presidents who promoted a strong central government and federal regulation of business. By the end of the war, the nation had become disillusioned by rising inflation and the growth of government debt. In 1920, the ultraconservative Warren Harding was overwhelmingly elected on a pledge to return the nation to "normalcy." Harding and his two even more conservative successors ran on a strong law-and-order ticket that particularly appealed to rural American citizens who felt deeply threatened by government influence in the social and economic fabric of the nation.

These presidents proceeded to sharply diminish federal spending for both defense and social interests, cut business and personal taxes, and reduce bureaucratic red tape. For the duration of the plateau from 1921 to 1929, the federal budget was in surplus. At no time in our history did the nation experience such a rapid growth in personal wealth. Only with the onset of depression did the federal budget again revert to deficit.

In our present cycle, we are beginning to see much of the same scenario develop. During the growth phase of this cycle, the increasingly liberal leadership greatly expanded the influence of the government in all areas of the economy. Following the Vietnam War, the nation began rebelling against these economic and social policies. With the election of President Reagan in 1980, the growing conservative mandate was finally given to a President with a strong enough will to translate the nation's desires into reality. Since his election, President Reagan has cut both business and personal taxes, reduced government regulation and influence in the economy, and stabilized the value of the dollar within international markets.

Reagan has so far failed in his efforts to persuade Congress to cut government spending, especially in politically sensitive social programs. It seems that vested interests have been able to prevent even modest reductions in these areas. Kondratieff suggests that the solution to this problem is long overdue. We are already beginning to see the massive international problems a large and growing federal deficit can cause.

## LARGEST DEBT IN HISTORY

At present, the nation is faced with its largest deficit in history—over $180 billion. The primary results of this large national deficit are severe disruptions in the domestic and international financial markets. Interest rates are kept much higher than normal as a result of the need for the government to sell federal securities to pay for the deficit. This soaks up valuable funds from investors who might otherwise have used their capital for building production facilities and funding research and development projects that help the country remain competitive in the world markets. Because our interest rates are higher than normal, the dollar becomes proportionately more attractive than other currencies, causing its value to rise. This makes our exports more expensive in world trade. In 1984, our balance-of-trade deficit approached a record $150 billion.

Even more importantly, the federal debt seems to have taken on a life of its own as the cost of paying the $150 billion interest on the national debt is over 75 percent of the budget deficit itself. If deficits of this size continue for much longer, the value of the dollar could rapidly degenerate in a self-feeding spiral until all government securities are shunned by investors. In response to this immediate possibility, the government has begun to take some positive short-term steps. In July of 1984, Congress repealed the withholding tax paid by foreign investors for U.S. securities, thus greatly enhancing their attractiveness in the vast Eurobond markets.

The Treasury is also studying the feasibility of issuing a series of largely "untraceable" bearer bonds to overcome the reluctance of most foreign investors to buy our registered government securities.

To cater to the domestic investor, the government has reduced the maximum personal tax to 28 percent and reduced the maximum corporate rate to 34%. Unfortunately, these policies can only give minor support to the government debt problem. It is apparent that radical steps must soon be taken to bring government spending back into line with revenues before serious international problems begin to escalate. Presently, such conventional proposals as a significant reduction in all areas of government spending, an increase in taxes, and the sale of government assets to the public are being considered by both conservative and liberal power groups in Washington.

After the 1986 election, it was widely accepted that regardless of which party controls Congress some measure of fiscal reform would be the first order of business. A few alternative options being discussed in Congress are such relatively radical concepts as balanced-budget amendments, increased excise taxes, a national consumption or sales tax, and higher progressive tax rates in conjunction with a further decrease in tax deductions.

Although history suggests that the most efficient way to balance the budget is by simply reducing government expenditures, large spending reductions in many entrenched defense and social programs may not be possible during this cycle. The sheer size and scope of powerful special-interest groups may continue to make it politically unfeasible to rapidly reduce spending in these areas. Thus, probabilities favor one or more of the more radical approaches.

In any event, we expect a strong attempt to be made to bring government fiscal policy under control in the final years of President Reagan's second term. History indicates, however, that no matter how efficiently the deficit problem is resolved, it will make no material difference in the eventual outcome of the long-term cycle. The massive debts built up over the years of the growth and plateau phases must eventually be reduced to more realistic levels.

## RECORD BUSINESS DEBT

In addition to the government, most of the nation's business interests are rapidly approaching critical levels of illiquidity, which historically makes them vulnerable to financial shock. At the end of 1986, total business debts of nonfinancial corporations exceeded $2 trillion for the first time in history (Figure 29). In contrast, this same business debt level totaled only $80 billion in 1950, near the bottom of the cycle. More importantly, the critical ratio of liquid assets to short-term liabilities, which measures the ability of a corporation to absorb a rapid financial shock, is the historically low level of 25 percent.

By comparison, in 1950, the ratio stood at a healthy 80 percent. If the economy expands as expected, the projected upsurge in consumer spending should quickly translate into increased business profits. In all prior postwar plateau periods, this upsurge in long-term confidence

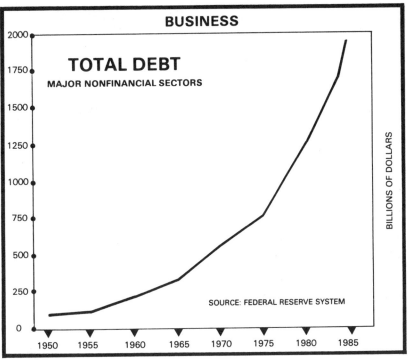

**BUSINESS**

**TOTAL DEBT**

**MAJOR NONFINANCIAL SECTORS**

SOURCE: FEDERAL RESERVE SYSTEM

BILLIONS OF DOLLARS

**Figure 29.**

backed by higher profits always lead to a significant increase in capital spending for new plants and equipment. This one final burst of corporate-debt accumulation on top of the already overburdened balance sheets of most major corporations should again set the stage for widespread business bankruptcies during the first year of the depression.

As expected, the most important sources of new loans to fuel this boom are coming from foreign sources. Over the past 12 years, direct foreign investments in U.S. factories, warehouses, mines, oil wells, land and other enterprises have grown by a staggering 700 percent to $130.0 billion. In 1986 alone, this capital inflow increased over $50 billion. More importantly, the capital is pouring into declining smokestack industries as well as those involved in high technology, natural resources, and consumer-oriented businesses. The Japanese, whose U.S. investments have been growing faster than those of any other industrialized country, are moving into a wide range of manufacturing industries, such as autos, steel, and food processing.

For both economic and political reasons, foreign investment in the United States is expected to continue rising strongly in coming years. This country's relative political stability is especially attractive at a time when political tensions are rising throughout the world, particularly in the developing countries. An additional motivating factor is the fear that the United States will become increasingly protectionist in the wake of record trade deficits that are costing thousands of jobs and billions of dollars in profits in domestic businesses.

## TRADE WAR LOOMS

Significant signs of the first stages of a trade war are already visible. Nations are beginning to impose trade barriers more aggressively in an attempt to stabilize unemployment and social unrest. Recently, President Reagan imposed 144 new quotas on textile imports from 36 countries, mostly in the Third World. In addition, political pressure in Congress is aimed at promoting other trade-restricting legislation. Protectionist amendments enacted in the Senate and pending in the House of Representatives have revived a long dormant bill to create a new trade department. In the steel industry, companies and labor unions have joined forces to push legislation that would limit foreign imports to a 15 percent share of U.S. steel consumption.

In addition, worldwide protectionist legislation is looming for copper, farm products, autos, and many other major products.

The European Economic Community (EEC) has recently placed restraints on the imports of steel, tape recorders, automobiles, and 10 other important manufactured products from Japan. In turn, Japan has retaliated by restricitng imports of textiles, apparel, autos, telecommunications equipment, footwear, leather, and pharmaceuticals from the EEC.

The increase in these new trade obstacles is accelerating. Listed below is a small sample of new international trade barriers implemented during the 1980 to 1986 period:

- Argentine:   Banned television commercials produced by foreign firms.
- Australia:   Slapped tarriffs on Japanese outboard motors, alleging that Japan is flooding the market.

- France:   Increased bureaucratic red tape on imports, increased restrictions on Japanese videocassette recorders; and stalled on imports of Swiss cheese.
- Great Britain:  Imposed new restrictions on foreign insurance firms (banks, firms); limits on Japanese cars.
- Hong Kong: Began boycotting French brandy to punish France for setting quotas on watches made in Hong Kong.
- Indonesia:  Required foreigners who sell parts for government oil refineries to spend an equal amount on Indonesian products.
- Japan:  Placed quotas on beans and citrus fruits; enacted red tape against cosmetics and tariffs on cigarettes.
- United States:  Set new quotas on sugar imports; voluntary limits on European steel; Japanese cars; "Buy American" rules for new bridges and roads.

If, as we expect, this represents only the initial stages of a 1930-style trade war in which retaliatory actions quickly follow one another, the final consequences will be a rapid collapse of world trade and severe economic dislocations.

The most obvious indication of a general unravelling of international trade will be a rapid rise in unemployment. This already seems to be occurring in Europe. In one study, it is estimated that since 1979, the number of jobless in the industrialized nations of Europe climbed from 16 million to 32 million. Much of this unemployment is presently being attributed to weaker countries dumping their products on stronger ones at below-production costs. It is estimated that over half of all world trade is restricted by quotas, tariffs, and bars in one form or another, as compared to 40 percent in the mid-1950s.

By the time the plateau period is completed, we estimate that this figure could approach 60 percent. This is pressuring industrialized countries to invest overseas to safeguard their foreign markets. The rush to insure access to U.S. markets is most clearly demonstrated by Japan. From 1980 to 1982, Japanese investments in the U.S. doubled to over $8.7 billion. They have since increased to $35 billion.

The immediate impact of such investment on the U.S. economy is the creation of jobs, not just for workers at plants purchased or built by foreigners, but also among suppliers of the new foreign-owned enterprises. Moreover, new technology, advanced production techniques, and improved management skills are being transplanted from abroad to the U.S., greatly boosting productivity in many hard-pressed industries. Even passive investments that do not involve technological transfers or management changes, such as the multi-billion dollar purchases of energy and resources companies made by foreign entities in 1981, have the effect of creating wealth, at least for the shareholders who were bought out.

Because of these factors, we expect the debt level of the average U.S. corporation to expand at least 25 percent from its present highly overextended levels as the plateau progresses. Unfortunately, in certain sectors of the U.S. economy, such as real estate, transportation, and farming, that are suffering from the combined effects of massive long-term debt loads, falling asset prices, and illiquid underlying assets, little new investment capital will be forthcoming.

A good case in point is the farming industry. As they have so often in the past, farm and farm-related industries are again apparently at the forefront of the deflationary momentum now sweeping the world. As alluded to in Chapter IV, agricultural and farmland prices tend to closely follow the commodity price cycle. In each of the three long-term agricultural cycles in the United States, farm income and farmland prices reached their highest levels at the peak of the commodity cycle and tended to trend steadily downward to its trough.

Within this cycle, farm debts for both land, equipment, and seed all tend to greatly expand during times of high crop prices at the top of the cycle. During the postwar recession and plateau, the repayment of this debt becomes an increasing burden on the farmer. Finally, with the onset of depression, this unsustainable debt load forces widespread bankruptcies and foreclosures, so that by the end of the depression, farmland and equipment have fallen to small fractions of their former values.

In our present cycle we are witnessing a classical replay of this basic scenario. At the height of the Vietnam War, most farm real estate was selling at its highest level in history. From 1967 to 1973 alone, the average farm more than quadrupled in price. During these years the prices of most grains more than doubled, allowing farmers to make record profits. This sharply increased profits allowed farmers to greatly add to their landholdings, buy new equipment, and add new employees. Most of the costs of this expansion were financed on credit.

In the ensuing postwar recession and plateau, crop prices have fallen to the point that the farm industry is barely profitable. During this period, total farm debt more than tripled from $67 billion to over $270 billion in 1986. In 1986 alone, it was estimated that the mortgage interest on this debt was well over $25 billion with farm income expected to only reach $10 billion. Consequently, the industry is expected to be in the red by $5 billion. Were it not for the $25 billion in annual direct government support payments now in effect, and another $40 billion in other support payments, there is no doubt that most farms would be bankrupt and on the auction block at greatly reduced prices.

Already the price of farmland is falling rapidly (Figure 30). In many sections of Nebraska and Iowa, the average farm price has declined between 50 and 60 percent. It is estimated that nearly 50 percent of all farmers are already in deep financial trouble. Many are unable to find buyers for their property at any price.

For the remainder of the plateau, we expect the government to steadily reduce its support to the farming industry. It simply has no choice if it is to make any headway on the budget deficit. Once this support is removed, both the prices paid for crops and the price of farm real estate should decline even further. By the end of the plateau, we expect farm debt to become a major problem equal to foreign debt as a major source of instability in the domestic credit markets.

Even more importantly, the financial problems of farmers are a worldwide phenomenon. Perhaps the most obvious international problem is reflected in the EEC, which consists of the 10 most powerful countries on the European continent. For the past 22 years, the EEC policy has been to guarantee farmers up to 50 percent above world prices in order to insure their profitability. In 1986, it was estimated that this program cost the EEC well over $18 billion to maintain. In an historic policy decision in March of 1984, the farm ministers governing the EEC agreed not to continue paying dairy farmers open-ended subsidies for providing unlimited quantities of milk. They also decided that both the amounts of farm production and crop price supports will also be significantly reduced for the next few years on sugar beets, cereal grains, oil seeds, tomatoes, wine, butter, livestock, fruits, and vegetables. The EEC is simply running out of cash to support these programs.

In order to soften the blow to the farmers, the EEC suggested significant quotas and tariffs be placed on imported farm products, especially those coming from the United States and South America. *We interpret this as being the first round of the agricultural protectionist trade war so characteristic of all predepression periods.* We expect such confrontations to rapidly escalate in the next few years as international financial tensions become increasingly acute. *The collapse of international farm debt is always at the forefront of a depression.*

## PERSONAL DEBT

Of even more importance to individuals is the tremendous amount of personal debt accumulated since the termination of the growth

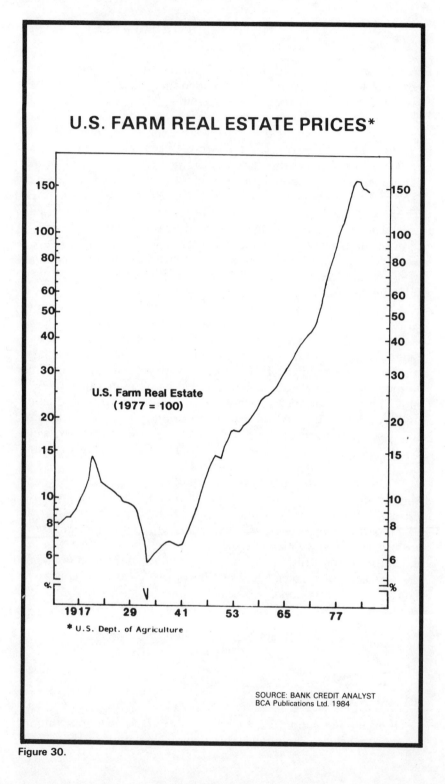

# U.S. FARM REAL ESTATE PRICES*

U.S. Farm Real Estate
(1977 = 100)

* U.S. Dept. of Agriculture

SOURCE: BANK CREDIT ANALYST
BCA Publications Ltd. 1984

Figure 30.

phase of this cycle in 1974 (Figure 31). During the growth phase, the
public based much of its spending patterns on the realization that jobs
were relatively secure and wage increases guaranteed. In addition,
virtually all investments, such as common stock and real estate, were
steadily progressing in value at rates much higher than the rate of inflation. When this real growth began to slow down in the late 1960s
and came to a virtual halt during the postwar recession in 1974, the
public quickly became disillusioned. This was expressed politically by
the election of public officials who promised a quick return to prosperity by the introduction of programs such as increased unemployment compensation, government guarantees to residential housing,
and incentives for commercial banks to loosen up on their lending
requirements.

At the same time, the public also took several significant steps to
compensate for this loss of real wealth. Perhaps the most obvious step

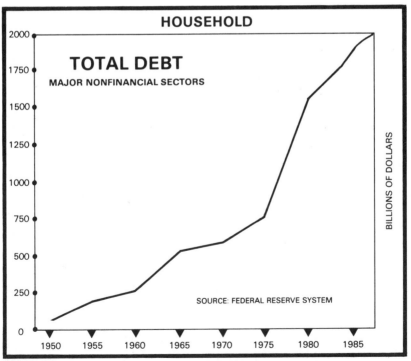

Figure 31.

was to allow a nonworking spouse to join the nation's labor pool. From 1974 to the present, it is estimated that the number of families utilizing both spouses in full-time jobs has more than tripled. This influx of wives into the labor force was greatly aided by government legislation that emphasized nondiscrimination in both salary and opportunity. The net effect was to greatly expand per capita family income, enabling most families to easily exceed the increase in the cost of living. At present, the average U.S. family enjoys its highest standard of living in history.

Perhaps the most obvious manifestation of American affluence is in the level of debt families have been willing to assume. The annual level of household borrowing grew from nearly $36 billion in 1974 to over $400 billion in late 1986. This increase is largely attributable to the sharp increase in installment credit, soaring from nearly $2 billion to over $120 billion, and mortgage debt, rising from $35 billion to almost $200 billion during this same period. At present, both mortgage debt and consumer installment debt, as a percentage of disposable personal income, are both at their highest levels in the history of the United States. Home mortgage payments alone exceed 50 percent of an average family's total disposable income as compared to 18 percent in 1950 near the bottom of the cycle. At the end of 1986, the country's total outstanding personal debt was well in excess of $2.2 trillion.

For the duration of the plateau, we expect the trend toward higher levels of personal debt to intensify. As the strength of the general economy and the stock market continues to rise, individual real wealth should explode upward. Historically, sharp increases in wealth and disposable .income generate enough added confidence to allow the public to participate in one last borrowing binge.

This feeling of confidence in the state of the economy usually spills over into the banking system. We are already starting to see the first signs of a general loosening in the levels of personal lending by the banks. Flush with cash from a generally accommodative Federal Reserve System and spurred by the virtual cessation of foreign loans, U.S.-based banks have been aggressively soliciting the public to borrow money. In many banks and retail stores, both credit terms and collateral requirements have been eased to induce the public to spend and borrow. The burgeoning use of various adjustable-rate mortgages, discounts, and extended loan maturities on new purchases have allowed these industries to thrive in the face of high real interest rates, low inflation, and a strong dollar.

*We expect the average consumer to expand his total outstanding debt by between 15 and 30 percent over the next two years.*

## CONCLUSION

*From an historical perspective, it is readily apparent that all sectors of the world economy have accumulated sufficient debt to make the international financial system highly vulnerable to a financial crisis. The only critical question that remains is where or when such a shock will occur, forcing the financial system into depression.*

This is difficult to determine. Historically, the initial financial shocks often come not from troubles at big banks but from smaller banks on the periphery. When trouble starts at a bank, deposits are withdrawn first. The tests of the viability of a bank are in its ability to both hold onto deposits and/or raise them from outside sources. In a banking crisis, the first thing that occurs is a contraction of the interbank market as all financial institutions attempt to raise cash to weather the storm. Those banks unable to raise sufficient cash to pay off their depositors are the first to fail.

As these banks begin to edge into default, the panic spreads to other more stable institutions until at the height of the panic even the strongest and most conservative ones, including eventually those of the federal government, become suspect.

In the first and second U.S. debt cycles, the initial plunge into depression originated in the undercapitalized state banks of the frontier regions. These banks were characteristically highly leveraged in real estate speculation and farm mortgages. When prices started to decline in the postwar period, they began to experience massive foreclosures and loan defaults. Eventually, the crisis spread and involved the powerful financial center banks in the East. At the depths of the depression, even the financial integrity of the government came into question.

In the third debt cycle of the United States, the point of vulnerability first began to manifest itself in the international arena. By this time, the banking system began to take on an international flavor as branch offices of U.S. banks were established in most of the major foreign money centers of Europe. In the post-World War I era, nations most vulnerable to economic shock were those that incurred excessive war-related debts and failed to achieve sufficient economic recovery to pay off their loans. The minor economic powers of Europe, such as Luxembourg, Belgium, Austria, and most of the present-day Warsaw Pact countries were in this category. By 1928, most were bankrupt. This eventually pulled the rest of Europe and finally the United States into the maelstrom.

*In our present cycle, it appears that the weak link in the debt chain could be the offshore money center banks, such as those that are located in the Bahamas, Panama, the Cayman Islands, and other so-called "tax havens" around the world.* These countries derive most of their activity from the largely unregulated Eurodollar market. Unlike most private banks, these offshore banks are not protected by the umbrella of a central bank that might be counted on to lend virtually unlimited funds in times of financial crisis. They have either weak or nonexistent central banks. If a bank run starts here and is not immediately checked by decisive moves, the snowball effect could be irreversible. With the size and scope of the Eurodollar market now exceeding $3 trillion and with many lenders not legally backed by any financial institution and having no reserve requirements, the withdrawal of deposits could be dramatic.

With the implementation of computerized currency trading, the scramble for liquidity and safety could reach a crisis stage in hours, while in previous cycles it took months and even years. At this speed, no consortium of central banks would react with sufficient speed to abate the panic. Even if financial cooperation were possible, the scope of the panic would undoubtedly overwhelm all attempts at stabilization. Under these conditions, most financial markets could be closed for an indefinite period. This measure would, of course, be used only as a last resort by governments, since there would undoubtedly be a swift and severe negative reaction to such overt interference in the free markets.

Since most banks are in an extremely illiquid financial condition, any outright defaults have immediate and grave consequences. Because most of their loans are syndicated through hundreds of banks around the world, the panic will immediately spread worldwide. In the worst case, all financial markets could potentially cease to function at a time when efforts toward stabilization are most critical. One only has to look at the recent overwhelming withdrawals of deposits from the Continental Illinois Bank to realize the sensitivity of the banking system at this late stage of the debt cycle.

*For the remainder of the cycle, stay on the conservative side in all involvements with the debt markets. Minimal exposure to long-term debt, such as mortgages and long-term bonds, is advisable for the forseeable future. All short-term deposits should be kept in only the strongest and most stable financial institutions. We prefer Treasury-oriented securities such as Treasury bills and Treasury bill-oriented mutual funds. Avoid commercial paper, certificates of deposit over $100,000 in denomination, and conventional money market mutual funds primarily dealing in less than the highest-quality debt instru-*

*ments. Especially avoid all debt issues of foreign banks and financial institutions. Above all, pay off all your personal debts whenever possible.*

If these guidelines are carefully followed, risk exposure to the upcoming debt crisis should be greatly reduced. In Chapter VIII, we will include these concepts to develop a much more detailed and comprehensive investment strategy for the next few years.

*"Markets are never the same, but they are similar.
It is the task of the successful investor to recognize this
similarity from historical research, and use it profitably
in the current market environment."*

—William H. Kirkland

# Chapter VIII
# Harnessing the Power of the Cycle

## IMPENDING DEPRESSION

The United States is rapidly approaching the end of the plateau period of its fourth Kondratieff Cycle. In the previous chapters, we have systematically analyzed a variety of critical signals that historically indicate the onset of a major depression. World debt levels have reached their highest values in modern financial history. Bankruptcies in all sectors of the world business community, especially in the critical areas of basic industry, farming, transportation, banking, and world trade, are beginning to approach levels not seen since the early days of the Great Depression.

Political leaders of most of the world's major powers have shifted to much more conservative viewpoints. Governments are no longer being allowed to create currency and credit at will to pay for programs that increase inflation and deficit spending.

The public has mandated that high levels of inflation are both socially and economically unacceptable. These mandates have been translated into laws where the excesses of the growth phase of the present Kondratieff Cycle are being unwound in favor of less expensive, more traditional approaches. The power of labor unions and the size of Affirmative Action programs, Social Security, and Medicare are being significantly downgraded in stature.

This transition can be seen even more clearly in the investment markets. During Kondratieff plateaus, the steady transition of society from an optimistic to a pessimistic outlook for future prosperity is always extremely traumatic. Many investments are beginning to broadly reflect this growing pessimism. This has been especially true in the last few years of the plateau as international tensions rapidly approach the breaking point and the instability of traditionally profitable investments has increased.

Perhaps the best indication of the rising fears of impending depression is the exceptionally high interest rate level now prevailing in world financial markets. Even in the United States, the primary beneficiary of the accelerating redistribution of international investment capital, real interest rates are approaching record levels not seen since the last plateau period of the 1920s (Figure 32).

Even more pervasive is the collapse of world commodity prices. Investors have only to look at the recent precipitous decline in oil revenues to project the future demise of OPEC. Other commodity-oriented industries such as farming, mining, and real estate are in similar predicaments. The Kondratieff Wave Theory predicts that the peaks of the long-term cycles for each of these investments are well behind us, indicating their increasingly negative investment potential.

*For investors not presently aware of these long-term economic and social cycles, the subtle transition the nation is undergoing will continue to be extremely difficult to understand.* Investors are becoming increasingly uncomfortable about the present state of the world economy, but they lack sufficient knowledge to make the hard decisions necessary to eliminate high-risk positions and assume a more defensive posture. Such seemingly logical arguments as "The government would never let another Great Depression occur," and "It always made money before" are the most frequent excuses used to maintain the status quo. Most people have been caught up in the inflation-induced frenzy of making money to the exclusion of all rational judgment. Their dreams of wealth and financial independence have completely clouded all concepts of over-valuation and risk. Typically, these are the same individuals who are saddled with highly leveraged investments at cycle peaks.

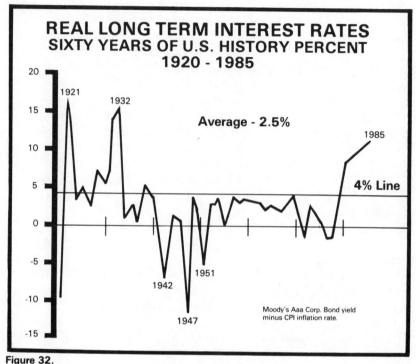

**Figure 32.**

As the depression unfolds, they continue to close their eyes to the danger of their predicament and steadfastly hold declining investments, hoping that a return to prosperity will bail them out. *Only when the bottom of the depression is reached will the "toughest" of them finally become desperate enough to sell their holdings, usually at a fraction of their previous values and at exactly the wrong time.*

For the few knowledgeable investors who have taken the time to understand the nature of long-term investment cycles (statistics suggest the figure is a small fraction of 1 percent of the population), the plateau and subsequent depression periods are looked upon optimistically. Rather than being fearful of the tremendous economic and social upheavals generated by depressions, these individuals look at the plateau as a once-in-a-lifetime opportunity to restructure their portfolios to take advantage of the transition from prosperity to depression. They understand that successful investors always achieve their most rapid advances in relative wealth during financial crises. *The more serious the panic, the greater the proportion of wealth that is transferred from the inefficient to the efficient.* They also understand that the leadership of the nation and the world will be held by those able to preserve capital during the depression phase of the cycle.

## PRESERVING YOUR INVESTMENT

For the duration of the plateau and well into the depression phase, there are three crucial investment guidelines that must be strictly followed: 1) the immediate restructuring of your portfolio, 2) a consideration of the safest investments, and 3) the proper apportioning of investment options.

The first guideline, and possibly the most important, is the immediate restructuring of your portfolio to a basically conservative posture. These last few years of the plateau present the long-term conservative investor with a higher degree of risk than any other point in the cycle. One major investment mistake at the top of the cycle can destroy a lifetime of accumulated wealth in a matter of days.

Now is not the time to hold investments that cannot be readily sold at the owner's discretion, or that have required an excessive amount of borrowed money in their acquisition. In this latter stage of the Kondratieff Cycle, virtually all investments are significantly overvalued and are either approaching or have reached the tops of their respective cycles. Although there may still be some potential for capital appreciation in the near term, in an extended time frame, their value will decline. Until they reach a more "normal" valuation, only their short-term speculative potential should be considered.

The name of the game for the foreseeable future is the preservation of one's wealth, not its expansion. Highly leveraged or exotic investment strategies, such as tax shelters, limited partnerships, corporate takeovers, and arbitrage should be strictly avoided. These investments are invariably under severe financial stress in bad economic times. Caution should also be exercised regarding highly volatile investment strategies employing the buying and selling short of common stocks, options, and commodity futures. There is no doubt that great personal fortunes will be made on the short side of the market by traders during the depression, but short selling in any form should be used only by professional traders.

The second guideline of our basic investment strategy concerns the structure of your investment portfolio. The primary consideration is that you will still be able to gracefully continue your present life-style should the worst possible financial crisis occur. During this period of the cycle, there are only a few investments that offer this level of safety. In all prior U.S. financial panics, the most sought after investments have been government-backed securities—U.S. Treasury bills, notes, and bonds. *Of the three, only Treasury bills have completely shielded the investor against capital erosion.*

Treasury bills are interest-bearing securities bought at a discount and redeemed for face value at maturity. The maximum maturity is one year. Historically, Treasury securities are considered a safe haven in times of national or international financial panic based on the assumption that if other forms of investments fail, the government will be able to maintain its integrity and stand by its debts. It is assumed that in the worst case, barring a complete collapse of all public respect for the government, currency will still be printed to pay off the debt. In addition to their low investment risk, Treasury bills have extremely high liquidity and are easily purchased.

At present, the daily market volume of Treasury bills is in the hundreds of billions of dollars per day. In this market, the owner of a Treasury bill can easily raise cash by buying or selling at extremely reduced commission costs through any national bank, brokerage house, or Federal Reserve bank. For these reasons, Treasury bills have always played a dominant role in the portfolios of conservative investors during past depressions. The upcoming depression should be no exception.

However, history is rife with examples of governments that were unable to withstand depressions and were replaced by foreign antagonists or internal revolution. Although the violent overthrow of our present government is highly unlikely in view of the overwhelming strength and stability of the United States, the conservative investor should implement an investment strategy to take this possibility into account.

*Historically, the only effective hedges against the complete destruction of a country's monetary system have been gold bullion and gold coins as a form of money, and commodities as a form of barter and trade.* Physical gold is usually preferred over gold-related investments, such as gold-oriented common stocks, mutual funds, commodity futures, and deposit receipts. In changes of government, private ownership of paper assets is often lost through nationalization or confiscation. Companies located in gold-producing regions such as South Africa and South America, will most probably be faced with a high degree of social and political unrest during the depression phase of this cycle.

Physical gold should be purchased in the form of coins and bullion and kept in a safe and accessible location. *Avoid any third-party control of your gold.* In bad times, embezzlement and theft are common. Because gold tends to decline in price throughout the plateau and during the initial years of the depression, the gold content of your portfolio should be kept at a minimum, in proportion to the degree of instability in the economy.

For the most conservative investors, a portfolio heavily weighted with Treasury securities and gold may be considered sufficient. These individuals will be content to wait for the collapse of the economy and attempt to pick up undervalued investments in its aftermath. They realize that, at the bottom of the depression, Treasury bills will probably yield less than 1 percent, and that their interest paid will be drastically reduced. However, they also understand that the deflationary aspects of the depression will greatly increase the buying power of the dollar in real terms and thus greatly augment their overall return.

To these investors, preservation of capital regardless of current income is of primary importance. More aggressive individuals may prefer to employ additional strategies to potentially enhance their financial positions during the depression. For these individuals, a thorough study of long-term investment cycles as presented in this book is especially useful.

As we have seen in previous chapters, many investments have reached the peak of their long-term cycles and should be avoided. These include commercial and residential properties and real assets, such as art, antiques, rare coins, commodities, and other inflation hedges. Of the remaining possibilities, we consider only common stocks and bonds to be of low enough risk to warrant some degree of speculative consideration.

As we have seen in Chapter VI, the peak of the long-term stock cycle usually occurs coincident with the end of the plateau period. This is especially true in nations of the world, such as the United States, that possess a high degree of political and financial stability. If we assume that we still have between two and four good years left in the stock market cycle, common stocks could be looked upon as a viable investment alternative for a portion of an investor's risk capital.

In order to successfully participate in the highly volatile stock market we envision for the remainder of the plateau, investors will be required to make correct stock selections. From our analysis of prior cycles, we have determined that the best group of stocks to purchase will be well-capitalized, blue-chip companies that pay steady dividends and show a long history of profitability and growth. As international economic and financial conditions continue to deteriorate, the public, foreign interests, and institutional money managers will prefer to seek the safety and security of these high-quality stocks. Just as they were selectively bid up to extraordinary heights in the late 1920s in response to rapid a increase in instability in the world economy, they should also be bid up in this cycle. In times of stress, the liquidity and financial stability of these stocks are attractive. It is assumed that they can be easily sold in a financial panic.

*Of these blue-chip stocks, issues that appear most attractive are the computer and electronics industries, drug manufacturers, domestic banking, and consumer goods. Industries to avoid are agriculture, transportation, international banking, and construction.*

The proper diversification of a common-stock portfolio is also a very important consideration. A portfolio should contain at least 20 individual common stocks and be properly balanced within a broad range of industry groups. For those investors not experienced in common stock portfolio management, the use of a blue-chip-oriented, no-load mutual fund might be a logical alternative. Use a fund that contains at least 50 different common stocks in a wide variety of industry groups. *The fund's minimum capitalization should exceed $150 million and allow instant redemption of assets by telephone or bank wire, or allow the assets to be immediately transferred to a Treasury bill-oriented money market fund by telephone.*

The final near-term investment consideration is long-term bonds. Contrary to most other investments, bonds are unique in that they tend to appreciate during periods of deflation. This is primarily due to the inverse relationship of the price of a bond to its market yield. Normally, bonds have a face value of $10,000 and are issued at a fixed interest rate determined by the market. If interest rates go up, investors are willing to pay less for the bond, and the price declines.

Conversely, if the interest rates go down, investors are willing to pay more for the bond, and the price advances. Because extended periods of deflation usually force borrowing activity to extremely low levels, most interest rates fall to their cyclical lows at the depth of the depression.

It is not unusual to find deep-discount, high-quality bonds appreciating 300 to 400 percent or more during a severe depression. In the environment we foresee, interest rates should trend upward for the duration of the plateau as the scramble for credit and liquidity intensifies. During this period, bond prices could be subjected to intense downward pressure and should be avoided (Figure 33). Note that Treasury bills reach their peak yields coincident with the onset of depression, whereas bond yields peak 2-3 years later. However, once the depression is well under way, bond investments may be considered as a viable addition to conservative portfolios. Selections should include only those issues fully backed by the U.S. government. This does not include government agency bonds, such as VA, FHA, FNMA, mortgage associations, or municipal bonds. In a serious depression, the quality of these issues could quickly become suspect. It must be assumed that our government would fail to support its direct long-term debts only in the worst imaginable crisis.

With the proper balance of common stocks, gold, and U.S. government bonds and bills, a versatile and highly liquid investment portfolio is created to defend against virtually any foreseeable economic possibility.

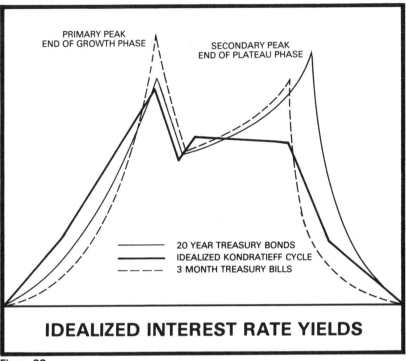

PRIMARY PEAK
END OF GROWTH PHASE

SECONDARY PEAK
END OF PLATEAU PHASE

| | |
|---|---|
| ———— | 20 YEAR TREASURY BONDS |
| ▬▬▬▬ | IDEALIZED KONDRATIEFF CYCLE |
| – – – – | 3 MONTH TREASURY BILLS |

**IDEALIZED INTEREST RATE YIELDS**

Figure 33.

Our third and final investment guideline involves the proper apportioning of these four investment options at each critical juncture of the remaining plateau and depression.

The purpose of any dynamic portfolio strategy is to continually maximize profits without exposure to undue risk. How this strategy is implemented is always largely determined by the ever-changing trend of the international economy. Attempts to predict the direction of the U.S. economy for the remainder of the plateau will be extremely difficult for e ʌen the most astute investors.

In the uncertain latter stages of the Kondratieff Cycle, a wide variety of spontaneous financial disruptions can easily invalidate the most carefully thought-out economic scenario. Such diverse situations as an outbreak of war in the Mideast, a debt default or repudiation in a major Third World country, such as Mexico or Brazil, or a run on the banks in Hong Kong could easily succeed in severely disrupting the international financial markets and plunging them into panic.

## USING THE KONDRATIEFF THEORY

These are risks the investor must evaluate when world debt levels reach their present heights. *It is during these highly fragile periods that the predictive power of historical precedent within the context of Kondratieff Wave Theory becomes most useful.*

In order to develop a logical economic scenario for the United States, three basic assumptions must be considered. *Our first assumption is that the upcoming depression will be deflationary in nature and should follow the same basic scenario as the three prior complete Kondratieff Waves. A quick review of the previous chapters of this book indicates that all the elements are in place for the emergence of a fourth period of long-term deflation.* We, of course, recognize that the upcoming depression will be unique, as both the markets and the financial entities backing them have become even more complex and sophisticated. We nevertheless expect the result to be the same as before: a deflationary depression with associated declining prices, lower interest rates, and reduced levels of debt.

*Our second basic assumption, based upon our analysis of the long-term cycles of debt presented in Chapter VII, is that the social and economic trauma of the upcoming depression should be much more violent and pervasive than any seen before, including the Great Depression of the 1930s.* This assumption is based on evidence that the depth and duration of a depression are directly proportional to the magnitude and composition of the nation's debt exposure at the termination of the plateau.

As we saw in Chapter VI, the U.S. has reached an historically unprecedented debt ratio of over 30:1. Our research indicates this level could reach 40:1 by the end of the plateau. In a comparative analysis of past depressions in the U.S., we have found that it is typical during the first few years that deflationary forces reduce the debt ratio to a more stable level of around 10:1. For example, during the Civil War depression, the ratio fell from 12:1 to 9:1 within two years. During World War I, the ratio fell from 15:1 to 10:1 within two years. Since the currency and coin levels, as well as the Treasury gold stocks, remained relatively constant in both cases, it must be assumed that the decline in the ratio was a direct result of the decline in demand deposits or loans in the banking system. If we assume that a debt ratio of at least 20:1 will persist until the onset of the depression and that it will decline to 10:1 within two years, we can further assume that the debt levels of the banking system will decline at least 66 percent during this same period.

Undoubtedly, a credit contraction of this magnitude within a very short period of time will be devastating to our financial system. History indicates that if the nation's money supply was reduced by 66 percent, the wholesale price level of most commodities would theoretically fall proportionally or even more. For example, during the Great Depression, the money supply declined only 30 percent, while the average price of commodities declined over 50 percent. Should the money supply fall 66 percent during this cycle, the corresponding decline in prices could approach 80 percent. A price drop of 80 percent in a matter of a few years is unprecedented in modern history and would be highly traumatic for the owners of real assets.

*Our third and final assumption is that the upcoming depression could prove to be much more prolonged than expected.* We base this assumption primarily on the overwhelming scope of the federal government's involvement in the economy. Historically, when the free markets are not subjected to excessive government regulation and interference during a financial panic, they tend to complete their natural cleansing process in a relatively rapid and efficient manner. This, in turn, enables the government and the currency to remain strong and stable even during the height of the panic.

*As we prepare to enter our next depression, we find an unprecedented level of government involvement in the economy.* As has been mentioned, it is estimated that the U.S. government generates more than 30 percent of the Gross National Product through an assortment of bureaucratic, regulatory, and social welfare agencies. Prior to the Great Depression, the level was always below 10 percent. It is easy to surmise that as the depression intensifies, the government will attempt to exert even greater influence on the economy. Already onerous tax burdens will no doubt be greatly increased to support the expanded social involvement of the government. As taxes and funding for these programs increase to more exorbitant levels, business will suffer. Government subsidies to bankrupt business interests will only heighten the distortions as assets transferred from strong and viable enterprises to weak and inefficient ones will prolong the natural cleansing function of the depression. This, of course, will be at the insistence of a public looking to the government for relief. After almost 40 years of ongoing prosperity, a return to a much lower standard of living is always difficult to accept.

If our basic assumptions are correct—that the upcoming depression will prove to be much more devastating and prolonged than at any other time in the history of the United States—we are now ready to proceed with the development of a hypothetical investment scenario that would have the best chance of exploiting the impending economic events.

For the remainder of the plateau, the U.S. economy will remain extremely robust, largely due to an accelerating influx of foreign capital, a sharply rising stock market, and a generally loose credit policy in the banking system. Supporting the rise in confidence of the public and the business community will be the significant progress being made toward balancing the federal budget. Reduced defense and welfare expenditures, coupled with increased revenues from the expanding economy, will be the primary causative factors.

President Reagan will continue to implement his long-term policies aimed at significantly reducing excessive government interference in the economy. The effect of these policies, in addition to the continuing worldwide glut of basic commodities and the moderate pace of world economic activity, will be the stabilization of the rate of inflation in the United States at the relatively low level of 0 to 5 percent. The continued decline in average wage rates of many highly unionized industries will also contribute greatly to the lower rate of inflation.

For the next year or so, we expect the international financial situation to stabilize in response to a gradual improvement in the world economy. Further indiscriminant extension of loans to all but the most financially and politically stable countries will cease. Rescheduling of both principal and interest payments will occur more frequently as international banks continue to stem the tide of widespread defaults, hoping for an eventual return to economic stability.

As we have noted in prior chapters, investment profits will be increasingly difficult to realize for the duration of the plateau. Virtually all investments, especially real assets such as real estate and gold, have already begun their long-term declines. Bond prices will continue to steadily decline as interest rates continue to rise in response to the credit demands of business and an increasing desire for liquidity. Common stocks and short-term money market instruments will continue to be the only viable investments. The relatively modest returns (5 to 10 percent) generated by short-term money market investments will be considered paltry when compared to common stocks advancing an average of 25 percent per year measured from the end of the midplateau recession in late 1983.

As the stock market surges, the public will become increasingly aware of the huge profits it has generated since the postwar recession ending in 1975, and will become caught up in a speculative euphoria. Credit used to buy stocks on margin will quickly increase to record levels. More aggressive investors will use even greater leverage (10 to 1 or more) to speculate with stock options and stock index futures. The average stock market investor's wealth will increase dramatically, allowing a rapid expansion in personal consumption. As a result, business confidence will soar, inducing large increases in production facilities.

With steadily falling budget deficits and widespread prosperity, the Reagan Administration will be convinced of the correctness of its policies.

Although interest rates will begin to rise in response to the increased credit demands of both businesses and investors, they will remain below levels that would negatively affect business growth. To most sectors of society, there will seem to be no apparent problems, causing a widespread feeling of comfort and complacency.

## THE COMING COLLAPSE

There may be an uneasy feeling among more sensitive individuals that something is not quite right in the world, but these feelings will be quickly dispelled by a host of economic experts who will "prove conclusively" that a new era of economic prosperity and social stability is at hand. Probably by 1987 or 1988, even though the boom continues unabated in the United States, the economic and financial structures of the weaker nations of the world will begin to show definite signs of approaching crisis.

As interest rates in the U.S. begin to accelerate upward from the rising credit demand in the financial markets, the resulting influx of foreign investment capital will begin to put intense upward pressure on the value of the dollar in international markets. This will cause high unemployment and inflation in many countries as the decline of the purchasing power of their currencies causes the price of consumer products to artificially inflate.

Debtor cartels will be created to protest this imbalance. Many of the weaker countries will begin to talk openly of repudiation and default, rationalizing that their debts are products of the powerful and imperialistic United States government and its financial arm, the international bankers. All pleas for assistance from the IMF and World Bank will be useless, since they will be rendered virtually powerless by the sharply reduced level of funding from the United States. As a result of their growing political and economic instability due to an inability to attract working capital, most lesser-developed countries will accelerate the implementation of trade barriers in an attempt to protect their domestic industries.

The loss of free trade will further stimulate the flight of capital from these countries. Currency controls will be implemented to contain this flight of capital, but will be largely ineffective. At some point, probably before the end of the decade, world financial markets will begin to anticipate the spread of these international financial and political problems to stronger countries and will begin to turn down. The stock markets of most of the more powerful European countries, including England, France, and West Germany, will begin to falter several years before the onset of world depression. The United States markets should begin to experience noticeable difficulties just prior to the actual fall.

As the peak of the stock market cycle approaches, most common stocks should become noticeably overvalued. As the price-earnings ratios of the broadly based market averages, such as the Dow average, advance to beyond the historically risky level of 20:1, the common-stock portion of a portfolio should be reduced by half. If the Dow average overextends to a price-earnings ratio of 22:1 or higher, all common stocks should be sold. In our present cycle, we consider it a high probability that the Dow average price-earnings ratio could exceed 23 to 25 before it finally begins to turn down. All proceeds of stock sales should be used to purchase U.S. government-backed securities, such as Treasury bills and bonds.

At least a 5 to 10 percent position in gold coins or bullion should continue to be held for safety. High-quality corporate bonds should be considered extremely risky and avoided completely. Most will be collateralized by assets that may appear financially solid on the surface but that may have hidden defects, which could prove disastrous during a financial crisis.

As the initial plunge into depression becomes more violent and pervasive, it will quickly become apparent that the economy is undergoing more than just a mild correction. Unemployment rates will soon exceed 15 percent and will show no sign of future improvement. Businesses will be forced to aggressively pare down their work forces and reduce levels of unsold inventory by sharply lowering prices. The average American's level of wealth and standard of living will decline over 25 percent the first year of the depression as money becomes scarce and investment prices collapse.

On the surface, the first year of the depression will appear as one of revaluation of prices to more historically average levels rather than an outright panic. Common stocks will decline and then stabilize at levels where the price-earnings valuations and dividend yields will be within historically normal ranges. The prices of industrial commodities, commercial and residential real estate, precious metals and gems will decline to prewar levels—approximately 30 to 40 percent below present prices. Lower-quality investments, such as over-the-counter common stocks, undeveloped real estate properties, and overseas investments, should decline further and faster.

## MISREADING THE SIGNS

Ironically, during the first year, businesses will experience sharply reduced earnings but not to the degree that there is widespread concern.

*Neither business leaders nor the general public will accurately perceive the nature and scope of the ongoing economic transition.* The depression will be viewed as a major recession, the kind so often experienced in the previous 45 years. Layoffs will continue to be widespread but will not be considered excessive. Most business managers will make valiant efforts to maintain the cohesion of their work forces, hoping for a reversal in the economy. Supporting the hopes of the business community and the public will be their conviction that, should the recession develop into a financial panic, the government and the Federal Reserve System will do whatever is necessary to prevent a depression.

By the start of the second year of the depression, the economic outlook should markedly improve. The Federal Reserve will have responded to the financial crisis by significantly stimulating the economy through the use of its currency and credit-creating powers. We estimate that a rise in money growth supply of approximately 60 percent per year would suffice to stabilize the decline of consumer and producer prices without generating undue inflationary expectations. The markets will continue to be in a state of mild shock, but will remain cautiously optimistic about the economy's ability to emerge from its prevailing low levels of activity. Through the encouragement of government officials, the public will readily accept the idea that the economic correction is a healthy response to the formerly overextended financial markets, and that the present revaluation of prices to "normal" levels is a healthy and necessary process. In order to further secure the financial system and restore public confidence, the Federal Reserve will greatly increase stock margin requirements and initiate additional brokerage firm regulations to insure that excessive stock market speculation will not recur.

Since the basically conservative Congress will have no major political trends to respond to, fiscal policies will continue to emphasize balancing the federal budget by further sharp reductions in government spending, especially in the areas of defense, farm supports, and education. Because the public has been psychologically conditioned to support the economic and social benefits of reduced government interference in the economy, further spending cuts will continue to be the President's highest priority. This will be especially timely, since government tax revenues will have been noticeably reduced by the subnormal levels of economic activity.

In summary, during the first 18 months of the depression, the economy will enjoy the benefits of sharply lower interest rates, a steadily declining inflation rate and a modest increase in industrial productivity. In the experience of most investors and businessmen, the combination of these positive fundamental economic indicators has always heralded the end of a recession and the emergence of the next period of recovery. This would normally be the case if it were not for the overwhelming economic and political chaos in the international markets.

Although the adverse effects of the depression will have engendered only a relatively moderate level of deterioration in the United States, an opposite scenario will exist for most of the rest of the world. For many countries, the slide into their long-term depression cycles will have already commenced while the United States lingered in the final years of its plateau period following the recession in 1982.

The main cause of these Third-World political and economic difficulties will be debt problems. Throughout the late 1980s, many bankers in the financial center nations will have expected both lower real interest rates and a world economic rebound to defuse this debt time bomb. Both of these hopes will fail to materialize.

As their depression phases unfold, most of these countries will begin to default on their international debts. This will start with such relatively insignificant entities as Chad, Buhari, Colombia, Chile, and Guatemala, and eventually extend into more important countries, such as Poland, Korea, Mexico, Brazil, Argentina, and the Philippines.

It will not be long before most major debtor nations will be at or near the point of declared bankruptcy. This will immediately cause loan activity in the financial capitals of the world to drop sharply. As virtually all foreign trade and cooperation are curtailed, the world economies will plunge into deep depression *en masse*.

Since the respective governments of these debtor nations will be largely blamed for the ongoing economic difficulties, serious episodes of political unrest will become increasingly common. This may take several forms. Religious zealots in the Middle East and Africa will increasingly attempt to purge all secular and democratic leadership. In South America, Africa, Southeast Asia, and southern Europe, Socialist and Communist elements will incite insurrections against their basically militaristic/democratic governments.

## HEADING OFF PANIC

As the crisis spreads to America, heated debates will occur concerning what measures should be taken to forestall the panic. Liberal factions will demand massive reliquification of the financial system through currency and credit injections by the Federal Reserve System. They will argue that both the economy's price structure and debt levels must be supported in order to avoid an even deeper financial panic.

Opposing factions, which will include the Federal Reserve as well as the Administration and most members of Congress, will suggest that excessive printing of paper currency might support prices temporarily, but in the long run would lead to anarchy and the rise of dictatorships. They will further suggest that such inflationary policies would immediately cause a rapid collapse of the dollar in the international currency markets that, in turn, would create more severe problems in the financial markets. They will conclude that the dollar must remain the key currency of the world, and that the loss of its integrity must be avoided.

After careful consideration, the government will tentatively embrace this conservative position and attempt to shift the bulk of its foreign debt responsibilities to existing international institutions. Unfortunately, these institutions, which include the IMF, the World Bank, the Bank of International Settlements, and to a lesser extent foreign banks, will be incapable of containing the rapidly expanding banking crisis. Their primary problem, both during the plateau and subsequent to the break into depression, will be an inability to either accumulate new deposits from member nations or collect the interest and principal on loans extended to creditor nations.

As a result, citizens of the major creditor nations, especially those of Europe, Japan, Saudi Arabia, and the United States, will become increasingly reluctant to extend more tax dollars through the IMF to support debtor nations. It will finally be accepted that these debtor nations will never be able to generate sufficient income to repay their outstanding debts and should be abandoned. International cooperation will rapidly diminish in favor of isolationism. *As a result, by the end of the second year of the depression, the debt collapse will have gained a momentum that no financial entity will be able to reverse, no matter how powerful.*

As this realization spreads to the international markets, it will become increasingly apparent that the world is in the midst of a serious financial panic. In the international arena, many nations will finally declare bankruptcy and repudiate all debts. Revolutions and political instability will be widespread even in previously stable countries. Both socialist and military dictatorships will increasingly replace moderate and centrist governments. Food shortages and unemployment riots will become worldwide phenomena.

International financial cooperation, as well as trade between nations and central banks, will virtually cease as a result of a rash of bilateral protectionist trade legislation. The U.S. will begin curtailing its foreign military commitments to save money and to retaliate for the lockout or nationalization of American business interests abroad. World unemployment will reach record levels, and tax revenues will be alarmingly reduced. Business bankruptcies will be widespread in all sectors of our economy, and federal budget deficits will reach extraordinary heights.

The problems of the ongoing depression and its resolution will now become the highest government priority. Conservative factions will still have tentative control, but will begin to be increasingly subdued by rising public dissatisfaction. Noted economists and financial experts will start to voice a variety of suggestions to alleviate the suffering. The idea of remonetizing gold to a much higher price to liquidify the banking system and promote financial stability as Franklin Roosevelt did in 1933 will be suggested and quickly rejected by the financial authorities as impossible under present conditions.

In 1933, the U.S. could get away with this inflationary technique because it controlled most of the world's monetary gold. Because it will control less than a quarter of its former total, it will be reasoned that any strong preferences for gold by either the public or by financially desperate nations could potentially reduce our gold reserves to the point where national stability would be seriously jeopardized. Other arguments, such as a massive injection of credit and currency into the economy to support failing businesses and financial institutions, will be rejected once again as potentially destabilizing, but it will be agreed that monetary growth should be increased.

As a result, the money supply will be sharply increased by as much as 40 percent a year, but the government will continue to shun massive direct intervention in the economy, other than by allowing the Federal Reserve to support distressed financial institutions by encouraging access to the "discount window," and by sharply reducing cash reserve requirements for banks. A drop in reserve requirements to 1 percent from its present 4 percent would be likely.

Although Congress will still remain basically conservative in its economic policies, it will become politically expedient to implement a series of welfare programs to convey to the public that it sympathizes with their plight. Of equally vital importance will be the stabilization of the rapidly growing federal budget deficits. In order to accomplish these two goals without significantly disrupting the fragile economy, defense spending will be cut as much as possible. Since the U.S.S.R. will also be suffering greatly from the depression, competitive military spending will be postponed indefinitely. The scope of expensive social programs, in terms of subsidies for education, scientific research, residential housing, and to a lesser extent medical care and Social Security, will also be sharply reduced. Moderate tax increases affecting affluent private individuals will be implemented to generate additional revenues, and tax-shelter benefits will be either reduced greatly or eliminated. Corporate tax increases will be kept moderate initially, based upon the belief that any hope of early economic recovery would depend largely upon the strength and stability of the capital base.

The third year of the depression will be remembered as the most traumatic in the economic history of the U.S. Virtually all markets, including stocks and bonds, real estate, and international commodities, will be in free-fall as the drive for liquidity intensifies. The inability of the economy to maintain its high levels of debt and prices will finally cause a financial panic not seen since the days of the Great Depression. Investors and businessmen will begin to indiscriminantly sell whatever they own to raise cash.

Since the markets for real estate, unprofitable businesses, and most consumer items will virtually dry up, many owners, unable to make interest payments, will file bankruptcy or simply walk away from their obligations. Financial institutions holding the paper will be increasingly saddled with these unmarketable assets. The unemployment rate will quickly reach the politically intolerable level of 20 percent as consumer demand dries up and businesses are forced to cease operations.

Service-oriented businesses will be the most seriously affected. The financial service industry will probably be the most threatened as client losses will immediately translate into lawsuits initiated on the advice of attorneys desperate for business.

## GOVERNMENT ACTIONS

During this phase of the depression, the political structure of the country may also become threatened. The public will increasingly clamor for government assistance to improve their desperate economic situation. The eventual response will be vigorous, including the implementation of a wide range of monetary and fiscal programs aimed at halting the decline. One of the President's first acts will be a complete restructuring of the tax codes in order to generate desperately needed revenues. Federal income taxes will be raised dramatically, especially for those individuals and corporations whose taxable earnings exceed $50,000. All remaining tax shelters, including those in equipment leasing, real estate properties, and oil and gas drilling programs, will be abolished.

A progressive wealth tax of at least 1 percent will be imposed on all individuals whose net worth exceeds $500,000. Anything remaining of the preferential capital gains tax will be rescinded, and capital investment losses will no longer be deductible unless matched by an equal gain. To support the government debt markets, all corporate pension and profit-sharing plans will be required to invest at least 50 percent of their assets in U.S. government obligations. ERISA will be modified to require percentage withdrawals to be raised substantially in the early years of retirement.

With respect to fiscal policy, the earliest age at which a retired person can receive Social Security benefits will be raised from 65 to 70, and benefits will be restricted to only those individuals whose net worth is below $200,000. Government job projects will be greatly increased, especially in the area of public works. To assist distressed middle-class renters and homeowners, rent controls and mortgage moratoriums will be imposed on all mortgage lending and financial institutions. To keep distressed financial institutions solvent, the President will invoke the Monetary Control Act of 1980 for the first time, which will immediately guarantee the solvency of banks and lending organizations.

The efficacy of this policy will be greatly aided by the Federal Reserve's action to increase the money supply at a minimum rate of 50 percent per year. To prevent large-scale cash withdrawals by foreign governments and institutions, a substantial portion of their assets held as deposits in U.S. commercial banks in the form of currency, gold, and Treasury securities will be frozen. This will be rationalized by the government as "in the national interest." Much of the substantial foreign deposits of gold held in the vaults of the Treasury may be confiscated at the same time to insure full payment on present and future international debt defaults. If these policies prove inadequate, nationalization of the banking system may prove necessary.

*Unfortunately, these drastic monetary and fiscal measures will still prove inadequate in stabilizing the financial markets. In fact, the policies of increased taxation and the added costs of adhering to additional bureaucratic regulations will serve only to exaggerate financial problems in the economy.* As is also typical in severe depressions once the public's confidence has been shattered, reassuring pronouncements by government officials will elicit a negative response by the markets. In fact, the expected massive government intervention in the economy will tend only to increase insecurity and further weaken the economy.

Although rallying intermittently, the stock market will continue to reflect these inefficiencies by steadily declining. Real estate prices will fall to a point where most homeowners' mortgage equity will be wiped out. Since the market for real estate will virtually dry up due to a lack of demand and the unavailability of mortgage money, it will become almost impossible to sell property. The few real estate transactions that do occur will be either for cash or with the seller holding the mortgage.

Because unemployment will now exceed 30 percent (even though the government will employ over 10 million citizens in various make-work projects), over half the nation will depend on food stamps to a substantial degree. As a result, political instability will become a major problem. Since the survivability of the government is at its highest level of risk at this stage, the prudent investor should begin to increase the percentage of gold in his portfolio to around 20 percent. Gold investments often become especially profitable at this time since they are typically hoarded, causing an artificially buoyed price. Treasury bills and bonds should constitute the remainder of the portfolio.

As the combination of massive government intervention and the natural countercyclical forces of the markets begin to succeed in stabilizing the panic, most asset-oriented investments will begin major reversals. At this point, most investments will be extremely undervalued, often selling for less than 20 percent of their former highs. Many lower-quality companies and syndications will have fallen into receivership and will be in the process of liquidation.

This will be an opportune time for investors and entrepreneurs fortunate enough to have ready cash to buy these assets at exceptionally good prices. As reduced risks are perceived, relatively large amounts of foreign investment capital will begin to flow into the United States to purchase these undervalued assets. The increased volume of gold coins and bullion coming into America from both foreign private owners and financial institutions will be especially strong. In addition, many foreign central banks will prefer to keep the bulk of their treasury gold on deposit in the United States, pending the return of civil stability. So much gold should eventually be transferred into the United States that our financial leaders will begin to favor its remonetization to promote stability and recovery.

Since there is always the possibility that the actual bottom of its first down-leg has not yet been fully completed at this tentative stage of the depression, it is imperative that asset-oriented investments be made in markets that have demonstrated a high degree of liquidity and stability. Possible choices might include high-quality common stocks, nonleveraged commodity futures, and select commercial properties. For a typical portfolio, we recommended that 40 percent remain in government-backed bills and bonds, 20 percent in gold coins or bullion, and the remainder limited to high-quality common stocks, such as those associated with the financial markets (banks and insurance companies) and well-capitalized, high-dividend-paying growth companies that have shown good relative strength during the more traumatic periods of the panic.

## THE POLITICAL AFTERMATH

*Politically, the stagnation period is the most dynamic and eventful part of the depression phase.* During the last Kondratieff stagnant period encompassing most of the 1930s, we saw the rise of military and socialist dictatorships in Europe, South America, the Middle East, and the Far East—all at the expense of previously democratic forms of governments. Regardless of their title or ideology, these newly instituted governments were usually totalitarian, with the final consequence to the public always the same: a loss of personal freedoms and extensive government control of the economy and financial markets. There is no reason to expect that the stagnation period of this cycle will be any different.

Specifically, during this cycle we expect most of Central and South America to change quickly from their present relatively democratic regimes to tightly controlled military dictatorships formed by the overthrow of existing governments. These revolutions will form in response to the need to officially default on their international debt obligations. As a result, international trade will virtually cease, causing commodity export-oriented economies to suffer greatly.

As unemployment rapidly exceeds the 50 to 75 percent level, and adequate supplies of food become of paramount importance, the public will violently rebel against existing governments. Under the guise of nationalism, most essential domestic and foreign-owned business interests will be confiscated. In addition, strict currency controls will be imposed to keep investment capital and gold from leaving the country. These policies will prove to be of no consequence as virtually all financial assets will find their way to safer havens.

Eventually, anarchy will reign, as all existing production facilities are forced to cease operations due to lack of spare parts and proper maintenance. From a long-term investment viewpoint, throughout the remainder of the depression and well into the next growth phase, all potential investments in Central and South America should be strictly avoided. Any presently existing investment capital should be removed as rapidly as possible.

In the Middle East, we expect even more radical political and social changes to take place. As the price of oil falls to substantially lower levels (the price of a barrel could fall below $7), we anticipate most of the existing monarchies to be replaced by fundamental religious forms of government similar to the one now ruling Iran. Unlike Central and South America, the populations of most Middle Eastern countries will seek leadership based upon religious rather than military might. But they will still be the same philosophically.

There will be no economic or financial compromises. All banks and financial institutions will be dissolved and their assets confiscated by the state, since it is against religious law to lend money for interest. Personal wealth will be confiscated, and foreign debts will be immediately absolved. Most probably, there will be little transportable wealth to confiscate, since most of it will have already been removed from the country. Again, as in Central and South America, all present and future investments should be completely avoided. We cannot foresee any long-term investment potential in these areas for the rest of this century and possibly well into the next.

For most of the countries of the Far East, the primary factor promoting political destabilization will be the unavailability of food. In mainland China, Korea, and Southeast Asia, the inability of governments to feed their populations during periods of depression has always been a serious problem. At present, the People's Republic of China greatly depends on its outlying crop-producing regions to feed its billion citizens.

In times of depression, cooperation between the farm-oriented provinces and the industrialized seacoast always breaks down, causing famine followed by violent regional wars and revolution. In the distant past, the principles of Hinduism and Buddhism were able to keep most of these revolutions from spreading to the national level. During this cycle, we expect the present Communist-atheistic government of China to prove a weak substitute. During the upcoming depression, we would not be surprised to see the present centralized government largely disintegrate into a feudal economic system so popular in China for the past several milennia. As a result, despite its vast land armies and huge pool of cheap labor, China will be unable to retain its present strength in the aftermath of the upcoming depression. Perhaps it will be well into the middle of the next Kondratieff growth stage before mainland China can attain sufficient stability to emerge as a world power.

Although we expect the Philippines and, to a much lesser extent, Japan to experience severe economic and social changes, the fundamental problem of large-scale unemployment rather than hunger will present the most serious threat to the stability of their governments. With a strong sense of nationalism, and the financial and industrial ingenuity to back it up, Japan should again emerge as the dominant economic and military force in eastern Asia.

Of all the "Western" powers, Japan has the lowest level of national debt, the highest savings rate per capita, and the most sophisticated government/industrial complex in the world. Its only obvious problem is a heavy dependence on exports. Although this dependence on world trade and foreign markets will prove extremely troublesome during the first phase of the depression, by the end of the stagnant phase of the cycle, the economy should relatively easily adapt to the newly emerging world economic order. Until this stability becomes more established, long-term foreign investments in Japan should be avoided for the remainder of the plateau and depression. Since the country's stock markets should remain relatively strong for the duration of the plateau, some short-term investments might be considered, but at the first signs of danger, they should be transferred to safer havens.

The social and political transformation of Europe and the U.S.S.R. during the depression should prove extremely complex to investors. In the initial years, unemployment should quickly reach record levels as the twin burdens of reduced demand and high debt play havoc with the price structure of European economies. Social and political unrest will accelerate in proportion to the level of economic disarray in each country. There is little doubt that a rapid movement toward more socialistic and centralized forms of governments will develop as the conservative leaders now in power are blamed for the depression. There is also little doubt that many of the financially and politically weaker countries of Europe, including most of southern Europe, Italy, France, Sweden, Belgium, and Denmark, will try to hold up their presently overextended welfare systems with printed money and competitive currency devaluations. The resulting flight of investment capital should quickly prove these policies counterproductive.

Most of the financially stronger countries, including Great Britain, Germany, and Switzerland, will strongly resist such measures, at least in the initial years of the depression. However, as the depression intensifies, most will also begin to resort to similar policies. We expect cooperation between the EEC, NATO, and the central banks to greatly diminish. Nationalism and isolationism should again become the foundations of most international and inter-European relations, just as they have in the previous Kondratieff depressions.

As the depression stagnates, the basic problem of providing food will be of prime importance to the stability of each country. Widespread hunger during depressions is always a measure of a country's ability to grow sufficient crops to feed itself and purchase food products in the world markets should its crop production prove inadequate. The latter consideration is by far more important during the stagnant period of the depression.

During the initial years of the depression, there is always a glut of farm products as farmers try to compensate for falling prices with higher production volume. History is replete with instances of farmers having to destroy animals and crops before they reach market as a result of low prices. The primary causes of falling prices are low consumer demand and a basic shift toward the use of cash purchases. Eventually, in the latter years of the depression, so many farmers are forced out of business that reduced food supplies become a primary cause of political instability.

Those European countries that are able to retain strong currencies and avoid excessive capital and currency controls should remain in a relatively good position to purchase food and retain their existing democratic forms of government. Conversely, those countries that destroy their currencies by excessive inflation or currency controls will suffer great political instability and become unable to finance external purchases. We expect Russia, eastern Europe, and the Scandinavian countries to fall into this category. Of these, the plight of Russia will be the most disruptive to international stability.

. During times of depression, the Russian populace has always suffered greatly from lack of food. Were it not for the availability of foreign credit purchases and the still viable market for its commodity-based export industries, Russia would presently be in serious trouble. As the depression progresses and its commodity export industry plunges to much lower levels of activity, an inability to buy on credit will cause massive food shortages.

As internal instability grows, the U.S.S.R. will be presented with two basic choices. It can either cut back on military spending and concentrate its capital resources on agricultural enterprises, or seek new sources of food by military exploitation of its more fertile neighbors. Unfortunately, it is impossible at this time to accurately predict the international economic and political environment within which this decision will be made. We are certain the decision will greatly affect the future course of both the depression and international harmony for many years. One thing is certain, the west Asian and European continents will be threatened, and investments there should be increasingly avoided.

On a relative basis, the prime beneficiary of this rise in international tension during the stagnant period will be the United States. Even in the worst conditions that we can imagine, the U.S. would easily be able to supply its citizens with the basic necessities of life, even if international trade and cooperation were greatly reduced. Even though we expect the depression to be extremely traumatic, the U.S. will appear exceptionally stable, with the survivability of the present political system in little doubt.

## THE WORLD'S WEALTH

As during the last depression, we expect the U.S. to again become the receptacle of the world's wealth. As before, we expect risk capital, including gold, to be rapidly transferred to our financial system at the expense of the rest of the world. The flight of capital to our country will be in proportion to the severity of international tensions. Initially, this transfer will do little to stabilize the deflationary aspects of the depression. Once the momentum of a deflationary depression is in force, little can be done to forestall panic until it has run its course and the economic inefficiencies have been washed out. However, as the stagnant period unfolds, the world's wealth will promote our economic and political stability.

As mentioned previously, we expect a rapid transition toward government control of the economy through widespread socialization of the industrial base, enhanced social welfare programs for the poor, and a correspondingly sharp drop in defense spending. The bulk of the federal deficits generated by these programs will be paid for by the onerous taxation of corporations and the wealthy, as well as foreign investments and monetary creation. In general, we expect this stagnant period to closely parallel that of the last depression, enhanced on the downside by the much higher level of debt that must be washed from the system, and supported by the much higher rate of overseas wealth transferred to the United States.

In the first years of the stagnant stage, bond prices should continue to appreciate sharply. Most other investments, including stocks, real estate, and commodities, should advance, but at a much slower pace, largely reflecting the return to a more normal price structure from their deeply oversold levels reached at the trough of the first down-leg of the depression. The common stocks of financial institutions, such as banks and insurance companies, whose portfolios contain large bond and security holdings, should be exceptionally strong and could even experience record prices. However, after an initial period of sharp recovery, most investments will languish for the remaining 10- to 15-year duration of the stagnant period.

By its end, a semblance of confidence will have been restored to the U.S., but deep economic and political turmoil will continue to plague the rest of the world.

The third and probably most traumatic phase of the depression will be initiated by a series of major overseas bank failures or large business bankruptcies. Since the U.S. financial system will still be fragile due to the enduring effects of the first stage of the depression, there will be a very short time lag before the U.S. is again caught up in the credit contraction.

In general, the prices of most investments will collapse at an even faster rate than during the first leg of the depression. Real estate, commodities, and most financial stocks will reach their cyclical lows at its conclusion. Corporate and personal bankruptcies will also reach their highest levels during this period.

Although government bonds and money market instruments should continue to form the bulk of portfolios, it will be prudent to begin shifting a portion of assets into gold in response to a trend toward increased international instability. In these final years of the depression, gold coins, gold bullion and gold-mining stocks will be in heavy demand by both governments and investors. Most of the available gold bullion and coins will be hoarded during the height of the panic, further reducing supply and strengthening demand. The black market price of gold could double the official price. This will be the period of highest market risk.

Most revolutions and violent overthrows of existing governments occur during the trough years of the depression. Prudence in investing here is of utmost importance during this phase. A conservative portfolio should consist entirely of government-backed securities and discreet ownership of gold coins and bullion. At this juncture, a return to gold in the world financial system could become imperative.

Once it is perceived that probabilities favor a monetization of gold, most governments should begin to accumulate as much gold bullion as possible on the assumption that those countries able to attract the largest hoard at the time of remonetization will emerge from the depression with the greatest economic power.

Historically, as we saw in Chapter V, the accumulation of gold by the government will be accomplished using several techniques: the purchase of gold from the public markets at a much higher than free-market price, forced confiscation of privately held gold coins and bullion, nationalization of gold and silver mines, government-backed incentives to enhance exploration, and the sequestering of foreign gold. When enough gold has been accumulated by the Treasury to comfortably back the dollar, it will again be remonetized. With the dollar again fully backed by gold and the nation's financial and political systems in a basically cautious posture, the U.S. should emerge from the next depression around the year 2000-2010 as the strongest nation in the world (Figure 34).

## BEWARE OF HISTORICAL VAGARIES

A prudent investor should be aware that history does not always precisely repeat itself. It must be considered that the world economy is significantly different in certain areas from past cycles. Government involvement in the economy and the financial markets is now much greater. Central banks have been given the power to create paper money and credit almost at their discretion. Furthermore, the central banks of the major financial powers have developed interlocking safety measures to support each other's interests in times of crises. Should a world credit and price collapse occur with unexpected breadth and force,

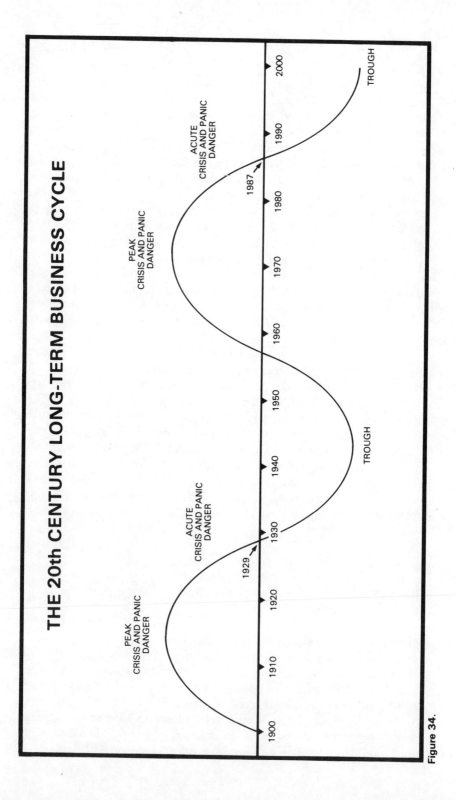

Figure 34.

these monetary authorities may decide that forestalling a full-scale depression by printing currency and credit in whatever amounts necessary would be worth the alternative risk of potentially hyperinflating the currency. If implemented improperly, these policies could quickly prove to be highly inflationary and politically destabilizing and could force a potentially drastic restructuring of the conservative portfolio suggested in the previous scenario. Since common stocks, gold coins, and bullion should perform well in an inflationary investment environment, a combination of them should constitute the bulk of an inflation-hedge portfolio. The weighting of each should be determined by the virulence of inflation as perceived by the investor.

In the event of an exceptionally rapid rise in inflation, a larger gold position relative to common stocks might be warranted. In financial panics, history indicates that gold has always risen in value at a much faster pace than alternative investments. This is primarily due to the perception that should the currency continue to depreciate, either a fully backed currency or an overthrow of the government would most probably occur. Should the latter happen, gold would be the only form of money. In our hypothetical hyperinflation portfolio, perhaps 70 percent of investments should be allocated to gold, 20 percent to common stocks, and 10 percent to U.S. Treasury bills. Treasury bonds should be avoided completely.

This position should be retained until financial order is completely restored and the currency stabilized. Potentially, the government could impose virtual dictatorial powers and might not hesitate to confiscate visible property, such as real estate or common stocks. No matter how attractive investments appear at the bottom, caution and prudence will be warranted for many years hence. Although we think hyperinflation of this nature is not likely, it must be considered as a possibility.

The final and perhaps most likely alternative scenario to a deflationary depression is an economy that oscillates in a relatively narrow sidewise manner for an extended period of time. In this scenario, the financial leadership of the world will prove marginally successful in holding up the fragile world financial system by a series of patchwork monetary and fiscal programs, to the degree that the massive forces of deflation will be successfully balanced by a wide range of banking and business bailouts by the central banks of the world. If successfully implemented, just enough currency and credit will be injected into the system to stabilize debt defaults and commodity prices without rekindling inflation. In this scenario, the economy would cease to grow and give the general appearance of stagnation. Some industries would prosper while others would continue to experience financial difficulties. Most investments would tend to be volatile, as the periodic rapid injections of money and credit into the financial system cause short-lived bursts of speculation in a basically trendless economy.

This is a perfect environment for trading in the markets. Individuals who elect to buy and hold investments will be disappointed. Gold and inflation-hedge investments, such as real estate and collectibles, will tend to languish in a broad trading range. In this environment, the emphasis will shift toward market speculation and timing and away from long-term investment. Most markets, especially stocks and bonds, could reach extreme degrees of volatility, similar to what we have experienced in the markets for the past 20 years. Should this scenario occur, the greatest emphasis in our portfolio would be concentrated in common stocks, bonds, and Treasury bills. At short-term market bottoms, the portfolio could contain up to 70 percent high-quality common stocks, 20 percent Treasury bills, and our standard 10 percent gold coin or bullion. At short-term market tops, the common-stock portion should be essentially sold in favor of Treasury bills and gold.

However, history suggests that an extended period of economic stagnation is quite rare. The public soon becomes restless and demands a return to prosperity. The most politically expedient answer is increased protectionism for our domestic industries in the area of world trade, and a sharp decline in our overseas military and economic commitments. Usually, these policies soon translate into international trade wars, competitive currency devaluations, and the unwinding of international cooperation. As before, the usual result is a deflationary depression, but of a much greater magnitude than if markets were allowed to orchestrate the correction on their own.

As you can see, each of the widely divergent economic scenarios we have envisioned eventually converges at the same point: the inevitability of a deflationary depression and resulting dissolution of the financial and economic excesses of the growth phase of the cycle. *Each suggests that government interference, no matter how well intentioned, only compounds the problem and always makes both the scope and duration of the resulting correction much more acute than it would have been had free markets been allowed to perform their basic functions.*

The free markets are not perfect. Left to themselves, they tend to overextend in an apparently irrational manner, never seeming to learn from past experience how to control the internal vices of fear and greed. Perhaps this seemingly irrational behavior is a characteristic acquired by mankind to achieve short-term levels of profit regardless of long-term consequences. If so, it must be assumed that the Kondratieff scenario will again emerge from the upcoming depression as the dominant economic force, just as it has in the last three complete cycles in the United States and throughout world history.

It must be further assumed that these cycles will continue to play a major role in the basic economic history of the world for the foreseeable future, so long as free markets continue to exist and humanity is allowed the freedom of choice. If this is so, then we would expect the basis of the Kondratieff Wave to be perpetuated almost indefinitely, each cycle being modified by changes in the relative power of the major players and the sophistication of the world financial system. In that sense, this book is more than just an investment strategy for the immediate future. It is a philosophical tool for understanding the nature of mass action from a long-term perspective. As in any mass hysteria, the key point to remember is: *do not buck the trend; it is too pervasive. Simply understand it and then flow with it to profitable investing.*

# Glossary

BALLOON PAYMENTS (mortgages) — A mortgage in which the majority of principal and interest is paid at the end of the contract.

BANK CREDIT — Money made available by a bank in the form of loans.

BANKRUPTCY — A person or entity legally declared unable to pay its debts.

BOURSE — A stock exchange located in Paris or certain other European countries.

CAPITAL SPENDING — The purchase by a business of new manufacturing facilities to increase production.

COMMERCIAL PAPER — Short term debt instrument issued by a corporation.

CREDIT CONTRACTION — An aggregate decrease in the level of borrowing in the economy.

CREDIT EXPANSION — An aggregate increase in the level of borrowing in the economy.

CURRENCY — Money usually in the form of coin and paper notes.

DEBT RATIO — The ratio of the amount of a nation's short term debt outstanding to its gold reserves.

DEBT MORATORIUM — A temporary postponement of principal and interest payments on an outstanding debt.

DEFLATION — A lessening of the amount of money in circulation resulting in a relatively sharp and sudden fall in prices.

DEFAULT — A failure to pay money due.

DEPRESSION — A period marked by slackening business activity and widespread unemployment.

DISCOUNT RATE — The rate of interest charged by the Federal Reserve to its member banks.

DISCOUNT WINDOW — Where the Federal Reserve lends money to its member banks.

DOWN LEG — A down phase in the movement of a price series.

DUMPING — Government subsidized selling of exports at below market prices to stimulate domestic employment.

ERISA — Employee Retirement Income Security, established IRS and labor department guidelines for pension plans.

FISCAL POLICY — The sum total of government economic policy during a fiscal year (e.g. taxation, spending).

FIXED INCOME SECURITITES — A debt security which has a fixed cash rate of return (e.g. bonds, mortgages).

FLOATING RATE LOAN — A loan in which the rate of interest fluctuates with market interest rates.

FORECLOSURE — To take away the right to redeem a mortgage when regular payments have not been kept up.

FREE TRADE — The unhindered flow of trade across international borders.

GROSS NATIONAL PRODUCT — The aggregate of all goods and services produced in an economy.

HYPERINFLATION — A highly accelerated inflation usually caused by the excess money creation policies of government.

INFLATION — An increase in the amount of money in circulation resulting in a rapid rise in prices.

INFLATION HEDGE — An asset which appreciates at least as rapidly as the decline in value of a currency during an inflationary period.

LAISSEZ-FAIRE CAPITALISM — The unrestricted interaction of capital markets in an economic system.

LEVERAGE — The use of borrowed money to increase purchasing power.

LIMITED PARTNERSHIP — Investment partnerships which usually limit the liability of the participant to the amount of money invested.

LIQUIDATION — The settling of accounts of a business during bankruptcy proceedings.

M1 — The sum total of currency and checking accounts (demand deposits) in the financial system.

MONEY SUPPLY — The total of currency and credit in the financial system.

MONETIZE — To legalize money.

MONETARY POLICY — Normally used by the Federal Reserve to manage the expansion or contraction of the economy by regulating the availability of credit at National Banks.

NO-LOAD MUTUAL FUNDS — Mutual funds which have no up front commission charges when they are purchased.

PENNY STOCK — A common stock that normally trades under one dollar per share.

PRICE EARNINGS RATIO — The ratio of the earnings per share of a common stock to its current price.

PRICE SUPPORT LEGISLATION — An attempt by government to maintain the price of a product by artificial means.

PUMP-PRIMING — Monetary and fiscal stimulus by government out of a recession.

PUT OPTION — A contract created by an exchange to sell a specified amount of stock at a certain price for a fixed amount of time.

RECEIVERSHIP — A process of bankruptcy which the assets of a company are administered by a receiver.

REIT — Real estate investment trust. A pool of diversified real estate investments usually sold to small investors.

REMONITIZATION — To reinstate as legal tender.

REPARATE — Compensation paid by a nation defeated in war for economic loss suffered by the victor.

RESERVE REQUIREMENTS. — Cash or cash equivalents held by banks to back the redemption of demand deposits.

RISK CAPITAL — That portion of an individuals assets used for speculative purposes.

SEQUESTER — To take possession of property or security for a debt or claim.

SHORT AGAINST THE BOX — Holding an identical short and purchase position in a security at the same time.

SHORT SALE — Selling securities in the anticipation of buying them back later at a lower price.

STATE CHARTERED BANK — Banks regulated by state government agencies.

STOCK INDEX FUTURES — A futures contract based upon the movement of popular stock indices such as the S & P 500, New York Stock Exchange Composite, or the Value Line index.

TARIFF — Taxes placed by a government to inhibit exports or imports from another country.

TAX HAVEN — A country where U.S. citizens and businesses transfer assets to reduce domestic tax rates.

TAX LOOPHOLE — A usually obscure means of completely avoiding taxes.

TAX SHELTER — An investment in which tax benefits are derived.

TRADE BARRIER — An impediment to the free flow of trade between nations such as bounty, tariff, and duty.

TRADE UP — The process of using the profits from a home sale to purchase a more expensive home.

TRADE WAR — The systematic implementation of trade restrictions between nations to inhibit imports.

WHOLESALE PRICE INDEX — A government index which reflects the cost of products at the wholesale level as opposed to the retail level. (Same as Producer Price Index)

# Index

**POWER CYCLES**

P.O. Box 7585
Phoenix, AZ 85011
(602) 274-2128

We wish to order and/or subscribe to the following:

1. POWER CYCLES (book), which covers the history and predictions based on the Kondratieff Wave — $19.95 _____

2. POWER CYCLES QUARTERLY REPORT, which will update topics covered in the book, as well as new information as fast as our computers can product it — $25.00 _____

3. Four POWER CYCLES cassettes in question and answer form, covering subjects of major interest to investors — $59.95 _____

4. CASSETTE-A-MONTH, a one year subscription, which will discuss pertinent trends as they tie in with the Kondratieff Wave, as well as other information regarding the stock and commodity markets — $150.00 _____

## COMBINATIONS

5. POWER CYCLES (book) and four POWER CYCLES cassettes — $75.00 _____

6. POWER CYCLES (book) and one year subscription to the CASSETTE-A-MONTH — $152.50 _____

7. POWER CYCLES (book) and one year subscription to the POWER CYCLES QUARTERLY REPORT — $39.95 _____

8. GRAND SLAM: POWER CYCLES (book), four POWER CYCLES cassettes, one year subscription to POWER CYCLES QUARTERLY REPORT, and one year subscription to the CASSETTE-A-MONTH — $247.50 _____

## SPEAKING ENGAGEMENTS

9. Bill Kirkland is available for keynote presentations, which include a 30-minute presentation on the Kondratieff Wave, and a 30-minute question and answer period. Please check if you are interested in a speaking engagement. _____

____Check enclosed in the amount of $ _____

____Please charge my _____ VISA _____ Mastercharge account in

the name of _____

with the _____ bank.

Account No. _____ Exp. Date _____

NAME: _____
　　　　(PLEASE TYPE OR PRINT)

ADDRESS: _____

CITY _____ STATE _____ ZIP_____

TELEPHONE NUMBER: _____